PEARSON CUSTOM LIBRARY

HOSPITALITY &
CULINARY ARTS

Introduction to Hospitality & Tourism Management
HTMS 2101
The Richard Stockton College of New Jersey

D1308634

Pearson Learning Solutions

New York   Boston   San Francisco
London   Toronto   Sydney   Tokyo   Singapore   Madrid
Mexico City   Munich   Paris   Cape Town   Hong Kong   Montreal

Senior Vice President, Editorial and Marketing: Patrick F. Boles
Senior Acquisition Editor: Debbie Coniglio
Development Editor: Christina Martin
Editorial Assistant: Jeanne Martin
Operations Manager: Eric M. Kenney
Production Manager: Jennifer Berry
Art Director: Renée Sartell
Cover Designer: Chrissy Kurpeski

Cover Art: "Pineapple," courtesy of Photodisc Photography/Veer Images; "Hotel Room Service Food," courtesy of Andersen Rodd/Getty Images.

Please visit our website at *www.pearsoncustom.com/custom-library/pearson-custom-hospitality-and-culinary-arts.*

Attention bookstores: For permission to return any unsold stock, contact us at *pe-uscustomreturns@pearson.com.*

Pearson Learning Solutions, 501 Boylston Street, Suite 900, Boston, MA 02116
A Pearson Education Company
www.pearsoned.com

ISBN 10: 0-558-53334-5
ISBN 13: 978-0-558-53334-2

Contents

Travel and Tourism and Hospitality
Services for Those Away from Home

Stephen Whitehorn © Dorling Kindersley

The journey of many travelers begins at the airport.

CHAPTER LEARNING OBJECTIVES

After studying this chapter you will be able to:

1. Distinguish between the travel and tourism and the hospitality industries.

2. Suggest how travel patterns have evolved.

3. List and briefly describe the types of organizations in the three segments that comprise the hospitality industry:
   - Accommodations (lodging)
   - Foodservices
   - Other hospitality operations

4. Explain the difference between commercial and noncommercial foodservice operations.

5. Discuss two basic ways that noncommercial foodservice programs can be operated.

6. Review critical issues that will confront the industry in, at least, the short-term future.

From Chapter 1 of *Discovering Hospitality and Tourism: The World's Greatest Industry*, Second Edition, Jack D. Ninemeier, Joe Perdue. Copyright © 2008 by Pearson Education, Inc. Published by Pearson Prentice Hall. All rights reserved.

FEEDBACK FROM THE REAL WORLD

In this chapter you will learn of the many professional opportunities within the diverse travel/tourism/hospitality industry. What can students do while still in school to learn as much as possible about the industry while keeping their options open about the segment in which they will begin their careers?

As you read this chapter, think about your answer to this question and then get feedback from the real world at the end of the chapter.

OBJECTIVE 1
Distinguish between the travel and tourism and the hospitality industries.

The industry that you are about to study is a challenge to define because it is large and complex. As you will learn, the numerous segments within the industry make it possible for almost anyone to enjoy a progressively responsible career within it. In this chapter we will focus our attention on this question: "What exactly is today's travel/tourism/hospitality industry?"

LET'S DEFINE TERMS

travel and tourism industry refers to all businesses that cater to the needs of the traveling public

hospitality industry refers primarily to organizations that provide lodging or accommodations and foodservices for people when they are away from their homes

Some people believe the terms **travel and tourism industry** and **hospitality industry** mean the same thing. For the purposes of this book, however, we will make an important distinction. The travel and tourism industry refers to all businesses that cater to the needs of the traveling public; the hospitality industry refers primarily to organizations that provide lodging or accommodations and foodservices for people when they are away from their homes. To clarify the distinction between the travel and tourism and the hospitality industries, look at Exhibit 1.

Note:

Although organizations offering some type of accommodations and/or foodservices represent the majority of those in the hospitality industry, the diversity

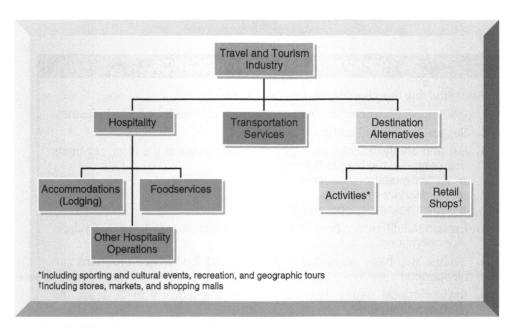

EXHIBIT 1
Components of the Travel and Tourism Industry

of the industry makes it difficult to develop a simple definition. For example, businesses offering conference center services and meeting, exposition (trade show), and entertainment management can also be considered part of the hospitality industry.

People traveling away from home need accommodations and transportation services that, obviously, nontravelers do not need. However, businesses that provide foodservices and destination activities offer products and services that can be shared by the traveling and nontraveling public. As well, lodging properties offer space for foodservices, meetings, and entertainment that are utilized by nontravelers. Also, other hospitality operations, such as private clubs, casinos, cruise ships, vending, and theme parks provide hospitality (lodging and/or foodservices) options for many travelers and nontravelers.

Our study does not address the entire travel and tourism industry as pictured in Exhibit 1. For example, many businesses enable tourists to enjoy activities on their vacations and holidays. These include tour bus operations and companies that offer biking, hiking, fishing, climbing, diving, and numerous other recreational activities.

Travel consultants (agents) assist their clients with travel, lodging, and related arrangements. Travel wholesalers arrange trips, including numerous excursions and other activities, and sell them to individuals and/or groups. Travel coordinators work for large business and governmental organizations and may make arrangements for employees who must travel as part of their work responsibilities.

Convention and Business Bureau (CVB) personnel market their communities to those considering meeting sites and to individual travelers. They also help coordinate the needs of groups that host meetings, conferences, and conventions in their areas.

Positions in the transportation services segment, as identified in Exhibit 1, also provide exciting opportunities. Examples include airport terminal managers and airline flight crew, gate agents, and reservations and passenger service positions. Rental car, railroad, ferry, and cruise ship lines businesses provide additional examples of the wide array of transportation-related positions in the travel and tourism industry.

We will look in-depth at two segments (accommodations and foodservices) that are an integral part of the hospitality industry. We will also study another segment (other hospitality operations), which includes segments such as theme parks, cruise lines, casinos, and recreation and leisure services that contain elements of both hospitality and travel and tourism. Finally, we will present an overview of the meetings business (meeting management, exhibition management, and special events management).

TRAVEL PATTERNS ARE EVOLVING

Traditionally, travelers could generally be divided into two types: those traveling for business and those traveling for pleasure. Today, however, there is often a blurring of this distinction.

Yesterday, persons frequently traveled on short business trips and relatively longer family vacations. Today, increasingly, business travelers take family members to conferences and conventions,

OBJECTIVE 2
Suggest how travel patterns have evolved.

Linda Whitwam © Dorling Kindersley

Many cruise ship passengers arrive in or near the port city by air and are bused to the ship.

3

EXHIBIT 2
Travel Patterns Have
Changed

	Traditional Travel Patterns		Modern Travel Patterns	
Traveler	Travel Goal	Travel Type	Travel Goal	Travel Type
Business	Business activities without family	Short trips	Business activities without family	Short trips
			Business meetings with family	Long trips
Pleasure	Family trips	Long vacations	Family holidays	Long weekends

cyberfares low-cost airfares (sometimes packaged with accommodations and rental cars) offered by airlines to increase business during slow travel periods such as weekends when there is minimal business travel

which extends the length of many business trips. The length of pleasure trips has decreased and, for many, involves several long weekends (often prompted by low-cost **cyberfares** offered by the airlines) throughout the year. These differences are reviewed in Exhibit 2.

The changes in travel patterns have not lessened the need for the products and services provided by organizations in the hospitality industry. Hotels and restaurants must still meet the needs of both those who travel and those who do not. However, it has become more of a challenge to do this as consumers have become more sophisticated and as competitive hospitality organizations increasingly find more creative ways to serve their guests.

SPOTLIGHT ON ORGANIZATIONS

Exhibit 3 suggests the wide range of organizations comprising the hospitality industry as we have defined it. It identifies many of the major categories of organizations within each segment of the industry. Let's look at these briefly now; the remainder of this book will consider more specifically the many types of organizations within each of the three segments.

ACCOMMODATIONS (LODGING)

amenities hotel products and services designed to appeal to guests

concierge the individual(s) within a full-service hotel responsible for providing guests with detailed information regarding local dining and attractions, as well as assisting with related guest needs

hotel a for-profit business that rents sleeping rooms and often provides other amenities such as food and beverage services, swimming pools and exercise rooms, meeting spaces, business centers, and concierge services; also referred to as motel, motor hotel, or motor inn

Where can people safely sleep when they are away from home? The answer to this question will, in part, suggest the array of opportunities that the traveling public has for rest at the end of a day. However, as you will learn later in this book, many of today's lodging properties remain competitive by offering much more than a safe night's sleep. **Amenities** can include food and beverage service alternatives, swimming pools and exercise rooms, meeting spaces, business centers, and **concierge** services to help travelers make many types of arrangements within the community. The term *amenities* can also refer to within-room giveaways such as soaps and shampoos.

Among the types of organizations in the accommodations (lodging) segment of the hospitality industry are the following:

Hotels

A **hotel** may be large or small, relatively inexpensive or more highly priced, and guests may drive up to the front door of their unit or take an elevator up many stories to their room. Hotels may or may not offer foodservices and other amenities, including those just noted. Lodging properties may be located

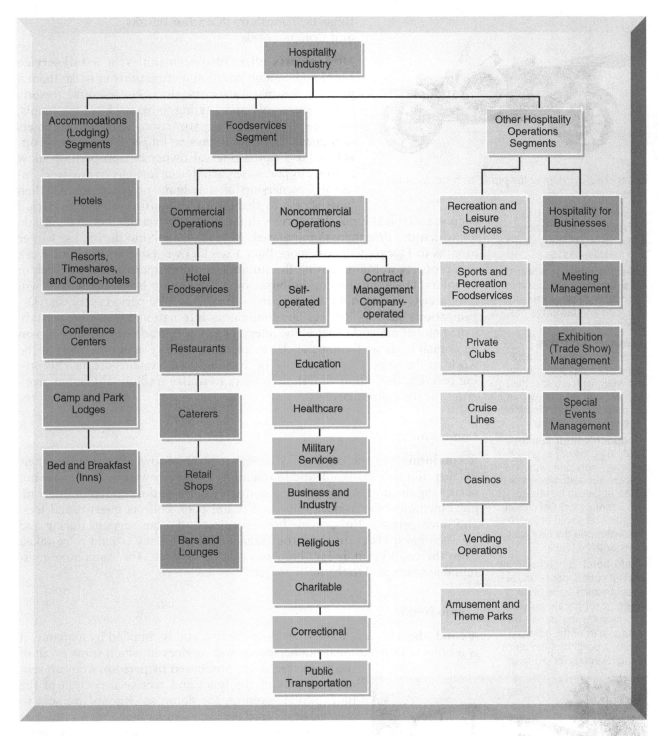

EXHIBIT 3
Close Look at the Hospitality Industry

along a highway, in a city or suburb, or at an airport location. They may be independently owned and operated or may be owned by an investor who has purchased a **franchise** for a popular brand and who has hired a hotel **management company** for daily operational responsibilities. While at least one type of hotel (extended-stay) markets to those desiring accommodations for several weeks or longer, most hotel properties generally rent rooms for one week or less.

franchise an arrangement whereby one party (the brand) allows another (the hotel owners) to use its logo, name, systems, and resources in exchange for a fee

management company an organization that operates a hotel for a fee; also sometimes called a contract company

Autos like this enabled the public to begin to travel extensively.

resorts full-service hotels with additional attractions to make them a primary destination for travelers

full-service hotel a hotel is considered full-service when it provides guests with extensive food and beverage products and services

timeshare properties lodging properties selling a part ownership (for example, one week within a specified time period) in a unit within the property; also called interval ownership

condominium (or condo) a lodging property in which units are individually owned; in some condominium properties, units can be placed into a rental pool with resulting guest fees split between the owner and the company managing the units

condo-hotel a hotel with traditional public spaces and services in which some or all of the guest rooms are provided by persons who can rent their units as part of the hotel and receive a portion of the unit's rental revenues for doing so

Resorts, Timeshares/Condominiums, and Condo–hotels

Most **resorts** offer all the amenities of a **full-service hotel** and enough additional attractions to make them a primary destination for travelers. For example, resorts may feature golf, spas, skiing, horseback riding, tennis, and oceanfront or other attractions sufficient to entertain guests for several days or longer. **Timeshare properties** (also called interval ownership properties) allow persons to purchase partial-year (usually in one-week intervals) ownership of a lodging property. Buyers then have access to that property for the same time period each year. Typically, purchase prices differ depending on the month or season for which the timeshare is purchased. A week's ownership during the winter months in Florida will cost more than a week's ownership in July; one week in a property in Maine during the summer is more expensive than a week in February. Once purchased, the buyer or others whom he or she desires will have access to a room in that property during that time period every year. Organizations such as Resorts Condominiums International (RCI) have established global networks that allow interval owners to trade their ownership on an annual basis with someone else in another property in another part of the world at the same or another time of the year. Point systems are also becoming popular; they allow timeshare owners to utilize traditional lodging properties for their timeshare.

Condominiums

A **condominium,** or condo is a complex in which owners can place their lodging unit on the organization's rental plan when they (the owners) are not occupying the unit. A management company markets the condominium complex, including the owner's unit on a rental plan, collects guest rental fees, and hires personnel to provide housekeeping and other services during and between guest visits. In turn, the management company is paid a fee taken from the condo rentals for these and related services. The remaining guest rental fees are paid to the unit's owner.

Condo-hotels

A **condo-hotel** is a relatively new lodging concept. As implied by its name, it is a hotel with traditional public spaces and services in which some or all of the guest rooms are purchased by persons who can rent units as part of the hotel and receive a portion of the unit's rental revenues for doing so. Rooms are sold to owners who can then use them as much (or as little) as they desire. Condo-hotels became popular in the early 2000s when traditional hotels suffered from excess capacity, and their owners and managers found a new source of revenue for the available rooms.

Conference Centers

Professionals in conference centers (also called professional development centers or executive education centers) assist organizations by planning meetings for their members. Many conference centers are operated by postsecondary institutions that work with associations

Do you think hotels have changed?

and large companies to develop and offer specialized programs. These centers may also offer programs to individuals desiring to learn about a more general topic. Large corporations may have in-house conference facilities in headquarters or other offices or retreats in rural or secluded areas. Foodservices range from those necessary for coffee breaks to full sit-down meal service.

Camp and Park Lodges

Many states and the federal government offer sleeping accommodations for visitors to parks and other nature conservatories that are much more formalized than just "a tent and a campfire." Sometimes operated by management companies, these facilities offer accommodations that are frequently as nice as those offered elsewhere in the area.

Bed and Breakfast (Inns)

These units, often called B&Bs, are generally very small (one-to-several guestroom) properties owned or managed by persons living on-site. Guests sleep in a room that is part of the owners' house and generally receive a breakfast meal, the cost of which is included in the guest room's rental price. These businesses are, in fact, the modern-day equivalent of the home owner of ancient times who opened his or her home to greet travelers who needed food and a night's rest before continuing on their journey.

FOODSERVICES

Travelers must eat while on their journey. They often do so in many of the same foodservice operations that are utilized by community residents who dine out for business and/or social purposes.

A wide variety of foodservice businesses exists to generate profits from the sale of their products and services to travelers and area residents. These are referred to as **commercial foodservice operations**. By contrast, another basic type of foodservice, **noncommercial foodservices**, is not in business primarily to produce, serve, and generate profits from food and beverage products. These two basic types of organizations make up the foodservices segment of the hospitality industry. With these definitions in mind, let's review the types of for-profit and not-for-profit foodservice operations.

Commercial Foodservices

Exhibit 3 identifies several types of commercial foodservice businesses.

Hotel Foodservices

Dining alternatives in hotels include those offered in coffee shops, dining rooms, and banquet operations and through room service. Hotel foodservice operations are classified as commercial because their goal is to make a profit that supplements that from the rental of sleeping and meeting accommodations.

Restaurants

A **restaurant** is a for-profit foodservice operation whose primary business involves the sale of food and beverage products to individuals and small groups of guests. Restaurants may have few or many seats; they may be freestanding or located within a hotel, resort, or shopping mall. They may or

---

conference centers organizations that assist associations, businesses, and individuals to meet desired continuing education needs

camp and park lodges sleeping accommodations in parks and other nature conservatories owned by governmental agencies and often operated by for-profit management companies

bed and breakfast (inns) very small (one-to-several guest room) properties owned or managed by persons living on-site; these businesses typically offer at least one meal daily; also called B&B

OBJECTIVE 4
Explain the difference between commercial and noncommercial foodservice operations.

commercial foodservice operations foodservices offered in hotels, restaurants, and other organizations whose primary financial goal involves generation of profits from the sale of food and beverage products

noncommercial foodservices foodservice operations whose financial goal does not involve generating profits from the sale of food and beverage products; also called institutional foodservices, on-site foodservices, and managed foodservices

OBJECTIVE 3
List and briefly describe the types of organizations in the three segments that comprise the hospitality industry.

restaurant a for-profit foodservice operation whose primary business involves the sale of food and beverage products to individuals and small groups of guests

RISING STAR PROFILE

Chuck Day
Revenue Management
Marriott International
Detroit Market

Using Technology to Help Guests

Chuck began working for Marriott Corporation in 1991 after receiving his university degree in hospitality business. He has held positions in sales, reservations, front office, and telecommunications and has worked at the downtown Chicago Residence Inn, the downtown Chicago Courtyard, and the O'Hare–Rosemont Residence Inn.

When he worked as a front-office manager in a 1298-room property, his typical workday (if there is one) was made up of voice mail, e-mail and meetings! E-mail was the primary method of communication, and he spent approximately 30 to 40 percent of his time reading and sending e-mail messages. Another 40 percent of his time was spent in the hotel lobby and in front-office areas, interacting with associates and guests. Most of the rest of his time in his workday was spent in meetings.

Chuck notes that his greatest operating challenge relates to finding and retaining great staff members. His priority guest-related challenge focuses on improving the hotel's ability to satisfy guests and to increasingly build guest loyalty to his organization.

Chuck was asked about his most unforgettable moment: "Being part of the opening management team for the O'Hare–Rosemont Residence Inn. Building a hotel from scratch is one of the most rewarding experiences I have had in my work life." When asked about a negative experience, Chuck responded, "I learned much on one occasion by realizing that I was not doing a specific job task as well as I could."

Chuck has some insight into how full-service hotels will be different in the future: "First, technology will play an increasingly greater role in all aspects of the business. It will improve staff productivity in tracking and reporting guest preferences and problem resolutions. I envision a traveler staying in one Marriott property on the West Coast who requests an amenity in his room. The guest will then travel to the East Coast in the same week and that amenity will be available in his or her new room.

"Hotel guests will be able to customize the environment of their sleeping rooms by providing profile information about desired room temperature, preferred television channels, and preordered room service, among many other services. Voice and data over Internet Protocol [communication services transmitted by the Internet, rather than a public-switched telephone network] will become the norm. Guests will be able to work from any hotel room in the world and will have phone calls and e-mails routed to them. They will have access to their information network. In effect, their office will travel with them! I also think that, in the future, activities designed to build and retain guest loyalties will be the driving force behind almost all industry initiatives."

When asked what, if anything, Chuck would do differently in his career he has a quick response: "Nothing! It has been a great ride so far, and I look forward to what is around the next bend."

Chuck's advice to young people considering a hospitality career is very helpful: "Make sure that you never lose touch with your personal happiness. People in the hospitality industry spend too much of their lives at work to not be happy while they are there! Your value as a human being is not measured by the job you do or by the position you hold or by the amount of money you make. It is measured by the person you are from the perspective of the people who are around you!"

may not serve alcoholic beverages in addition to food and may have extensive or limited menus. They may offer fine dining at high prices (gourmet food served by highly experienced service staff to guests seated at tables covered with tablecloths and set with the finest tableware), or they may be quick-service properties with lower prices (food served at a counter by a cashier). They may offer a theme such as a spaceship, Italian villa, or jungle setting to provide a complementary dining environment or, alternatively, they may only offer down-home cooking in a dining area with modest tables and chairs and/or booths and counters. Restaurants typically serve guests on-site; however, drive-through (in quick-service) and carryout (in many table-service) restaurants offer alternative service methods.

Caterers

Some foodservice operations produce food for off-site consumption. These can range from a takeout counter in the restaurant or a food pickup area in a restaurant's parking lot for food orders called in earlier,

Sunbathers in Acapulco near a high-rise hotel

Kenyatta Conference Center in Nairobi, Kenya

to drive-up windows in quick-service properties. These variations, however, differ from the more traditional catering businesses. **Caterers** typically produce food in their kitchen for transport off-site to a customer's location for service to hundreds (or more!) of guests. Some caterers also have dining space available for group service at the facility where the food is prepared.

Retail Shops

A wide variety of retail stores selling a wide variety of products may offer food and beverages to their shoppers. These range from large department stores offering sit-down meals, to grocery stores with significant square footage devoted to foodservice outlets, to convenience food stores and gasoline stations with counter space (or even larger areas) utilized to sell beverages, snacks, cold and hot sandwiches, and other items that were traditionally most frequently offered only by restaurants.

Bars and Lounges

Bars featuring the service of alcoholic beverages to guests seated at counters and **lounges** offering table-service alcoholic beverages generate more revenues from the sale of alcoholic beverages than they do from the sale of food products. However, some bars and lounges offer a limited menu of **short-order food items** requiring only limited production equipment, food ingredients, and cooking experience to produce.

Noncommercial Foodservices

You have learned that noncommercial foodservices are offered by organizations that, unlike their commercial foodservice counterparts, do not exist primarily to produce, serve, and generate profits from the sale of food and beverage products. Most noncommercial foodservice operations

caterers for-profit businesses that produce food for groups at off-site locations; some caterers have banquet space available for on-site use by groups desiring foodservices

bars for-profit businesses serving alcoholic beverages to guests seated at a counter (bar); limited table service may also be available

lounges for-profit businesses serving alcoholic beverages to guests seated at tables; a small counter (bar) may also be available

short-order food items food products that require only limited production equipment, food ingredients, and cooking experience to produce

Interior of a restaurant

Getty Images, Inc., Photodisc, Rob Melnychuk photographer

are not typically available to the traveling public; however, those available to travelers using public transportation such as airplanes and trains are an exception.

Noncommercial foodservices include those operated by educational institutions offering meals to, for example, primary, high school, and postsecondary students and healthcare facilities offering meals to hospital patients and those in nursing homes and retirement communities. Military services must feed their troops, business and industry organizations must provide meals to their employees while at work, and religious and charitable organizations feed their own members and those within the community who may be unable to buy food for themselves. Correctional facilities offer another example of an organization that must provide foodservices as part of their purpose, and airline and train passengers may receive meals while en route to their destinations.

There are two basic ways in which noncommercial foodservices can be operated:

OBJECTIVE 5
Discuss two basic ways that noncommercial foodservice programs can be operated.

noncommercial foodservices (self-operated) a type of noncommercial foodservice operation in which the program is managed and operated by the organization's employees

noncommercial foodservices (contract management company-operated) a type of noncommercial foodservice operation in which the program is managed and operated by a for-profit management company

- They may be **self-operated**; that is, the organization may employ a foodservice director and staff to manage and operate the program.
- They may be operated by a **contract management company**; that is, the organization may negotiate and contract with a for-profit management company to provide foodservices for the organization.

The use of contract management companies to operate noncommercial foodservices is becoming increasingly popular. Because contract management companies exist to make a profit, the distinction between commercial (for profit) and noncommercial (not for profit) foodservices is blurred.

OTHER HOSPITALITY OPERATIONS

To this point, we have discussed accommodations (lodging) and foodservice businesses. Other operations that we will also study in this book offer foodservices, so they are considered part of the traditional hospitality industry; but they also offer features that appeal to community residents and/or travelers, so they may be considered part of the travel and tourism industry.

OBJECTIVE 3
List and briefly describe the types of organizations in the three segments that comprise the hospitality industry.

The Store24 Companies Inc.

Convenience stores increasingly compete with traditional restaurants for foodservice purchases.

10

Sports and Recreation Foodservices

Food and beverages served at tableside in restaurants overlooking an athletic stadium's playing field, snack bars, and products transported to fans at their seats are examples of this segment of the industry.

Private Clubs

Private membership organizations **private clubs** of numer-

Fine dining at 30,000 feet

ous types exist for persons enjoying common interests. These include country (golf) clubs, city clubs, university clubs, yacht clubs, and military clubs. Clubs almost always offer some type of foodservices (ranging from very limited to very elaborate), and some also offer lodging accommodations for their members and invited guests.

Casinos

Casinos offering gaming opportunities are operated in the United States by commercial business corporations and Native American Indian organizations. Food and beverages and often lodging accommodations are part of the total entertainment package offered to casino visitors.

Cruise Lines

Cruise ships (very huge and very modern "cities on the seas") typically offer a wide range of food and beverage services, from fine dining to snack bars, fast-food outlets, and bars and lounges. Sleeping cabin accommodations are also an integral part of the experience being sold to passengers.

Vending Operations

Vending services offer food and beverage products at times when and/or in places where it is not convenient to offer **manual food and beverage services** to those being served.

Amusement and Theme Parks

Theme parks are generally very large recreational sites that are tourist destinations. Examples with which many people are familiar are Disneyland (in California) and Disney World, Epcot, and Universal Studios (in Florida). Many theme parks offer on-site hotels and numerous food and beverage outlets, ranging from sit-down restaurants with extensive menus, to quick-service outlets with limited menus, to food carts selling desserts and/or beverages and other items.

Meeting Management

Large associations and business organizations typically employ meeting planners to organize meetings, contact speakers, negotiate and select meeting sites, and attend to the seemingly endless number of details that occur as sessions are planned and conducted. Other professional

private clubs private membership organizations of numerous types that exist for persons enjoying common interests; examples include country (golf) clubs, city clubs, university clubs, yacht clubs, and military clubs

casinos a property that offers gaming opportunities for its guests; many casinos also offer food and beverage services and lodging accommodations for the convenience of their visitors

vending services food and beverage services that utilize equipment (vending machines) to dispense products

manual food and beverage services food and beverage operations in which food and beverages are served to consumers by foodservice employees

theme parks very large recreational sites that are tourist destinations

Getty Images-Photodisc, EyeWire Collection

Sports and recreational foodservices represent big business!

meeting planners provide specialized services for a number of external clients to assure that their meetings are successful.

Exhibitions (Trade Shows)

Many associations schedule meetings and conventions for their members and invite suppliers to their industry to exhibit products and services. A significant number of hours are frequently allocated for exhibits, and a large percentage of the budget of many associations is derived from suppliers renting display booths at these trade shows. Expositions are an integral part of the meeting business, which, itself, is an integral part of the hospitality industry.

Special Events Management

Large casinos and hotels are examples of organizations within the hospitality industry that utilize popular entertainers, theatrical performances, and other talent in an effort to attract guests to their business. Events such as sporting contests, weddings, anniversaries, and holidays create opportunities

---

THERE ARE JUST TOO MANY OPPORTUNITIES!

After reading this far, you might be overwhelmed at the wide variety of organizations and the positions within them that are available to one aspiring to a career in the tourism and hospitality industries. However, numerous other positions are available for those with special interests, and many will be explored throughout this book. Whatever your interests and wherever you might like to live, there are likely to be several (or more) professional alternatives for you to consider. Also, remember that many (most?) people change jobs and organizations as their career path evolves. It is probably the rule rather than the exception that tourism and hospitality professionals work in organizations in several (or more) hospitality segments during their career.

DID YOU KNOW?

Statistics that help to describe the industry become outdated very quickly, but you can keep up by searching the web.

- Want to know the dollars generated by the travel and tourism industry in the United States? Go to Travel Industry Association of America: www.tia.org and enter "tourism revenues" in the site's search box.
- Want to know current numbers about the restaurant industry? Go to National Restaurant Association: www.restaurant.org and enter "industry profile" in the site's search box.
- Want to know statistics for the lodging industry? Go to American Hotel & Lodging Association: www.ahla.com and enter "lodging industry profile" in the site's search box.
- Want to keep up with the ever-changing industry? If so, review these online resources that are published each business day:

  www.hotel-online.com
  www.smartbrief.com/nra
  www.smartbrief.com/ahla

for celebrations requiring hospitality services. The management of these activities provides exciting career possibilities.

CHALLENGES! CHALLENGES!*

OBJECTIVE 6
Review critical issues that will confront the industry in, at least, the short-term future.

You have learned that the travel and tourism industry, including the hospitality organizations within it, is broad, diverse, and complex. As such, it is difficult to generalize about challenges that confront the entire industry. However, some concerns can be noted that are likely to face owners and managers of these businesses and those who consume their products and services. As you will note from the following list, each challenge confronts numerous organizations in many other industries.

- *Changing labor conditions.* Concerns about a shrinking labor force, some growth in employee unionization, increasing benefits costs, and "front page" news about immigration issues will likely affect "how business is done" in the industry.
- *Escalating operating costs.* Expenses for energy, insurance, labor, and the impact of increasing franchise standards imposed on franchisees may affect the bottom line.
- *Rising energy costs.* As the cost of fuel increases, for example, hotel occupancy levels may be affected, and the cost of products that must be transported to properties will also increase.
- *Increased renovation and construction costs.* Costs associated with renovating existing and building new hospitality properties are on the rise.
- *Effects of and scares about natural disasters.* Tsunamis in the Indian Ocean, hurricanes in the southern United States, and the potential of avian flu around the world are examples of concerns that can affect the industry.
- *Ongoing concerns about safety and security.* Fueled by recurring news accounts about the "hot spots" throughout the world, persons in general and travelers more specifically are increasingly concerned about their safety.
- *Increased consumer expectations.* Those using the products of and services produced by the travel and tourism industry are becoming more sophisticated. They want "more for their money," and increasingly use technology to help them when making purchase decisions.
- *Accelerating change and merging of technologies.* Technology has changed much about how businesses are organized and how work is undertaken. It is difficult (but necessary) to keep up, and to assure that technology is used when and where it is best to do so.
- *Increasing consolidation of brands and companies.* Increasingly, there are fewer companies with an increased number of **brands** for consumer choices. "Who owns what," "What is the difference between brands," are among the questions that organizations must be able to effectively address for consumers.

brand name of a hotel chain; sometimes referred to as a flag

*Adapted from Top 10 global issues and challenges in the hospitality industry for 2006. Hotel-Online Special Report. Retrieved 12/30/2005 from www.hotel -online.com.

SUMMARY OF CHAPTER LEARNING OBJECTIVES

1. **Distinguish between the travel and tourism and the hospitality industries.**

   The travel and tourism industry refers to all businesses that cater to the needs of the traveling public; the hospitality industry refers primarily to organizations that provide lodging and meeting accommodations, foodservices and other hospitality services for people when they are away from their homes.

2. **Suggest how travel patterns have evolved.**

   Yesterday, business travelers took business trips without their family and long vacations with their family. Today, business travelers frequently take their families with them for extensions of business trips, and pleasure trips are increasingly long weekends.

3. **List and briefly describe the types of organizations in the three segments that comprise the hospitality industry: accommodations (lodging), foodservices, and other hospitality operations.**

   The accommodations segment includes hotels, resorts, timeshares and condominiums, conference centers, camp and park lodges, and bed and breakfast (inns). The foodservices segment consists of commercial foodservice operations—which include hotel foodservices, restaurants, caterers, retail shops, and bars and lounges—and organizations operating noncommercial foodservices. Examples include those in education, healthcare, military services, business and industry, religious, charitable, and correctional institutions, and public transportation. Other service organizations include private clubs, casinos, cruise ships, vending services, theme parks, meeting management, expositions (trade shows), and entertainment management.

4. **Explain the difference between commercial and noncommercial foodservice operations.**

   A commercial foodservice operation exists to generate profit from the sale of food and beverage products. By contrast, a noncommercial foodservice operation is utilized by an organization such as a school or healthcare facility. These organizations do not exist primarily to offer food and beverage products and services, but must do so as an integral part of conducting their business.

5. **Discuss two basic ways that noncommercial foodservice programs can be operated.**

   Some noncommercial foodservice programs are self-operated. These organizations employ their own management staff and others to operate foodservices. By contrast, other noncommercial foodservices programs are operated by a for-profit contract management company. It, in turn, employs the managers (and often the other employees) required to operate the foodservices program.

6. **Review critical issues that will confront the industry in, at least, the short-term future.**

   Nine challenges confront most, if not all, organizations within the industry:

   - Changing labor conditions
   - Escalating operating costs
   - Impact of rising energy costs
   - Increased renovation and construction costs
   - Results of natural disasters
   - Uncertainty about safety and security
   - Evolving consumer expectations
   - Accelerating change and merging of technologies
   - Consolidation of brands and companies

FEEDBACK FROM THE REAL WORLD

Our real-world advice comes from Authella Collins Hawks, Director of the Student Industry Resource Center (SIRC), *The* School of Hospitality Business at Michigan State University.

What can students do while still in school to learn as much as possible about the entire

industry while keeping their options open about the segment in which they will begin their hospitality career?

The field of hospitality is filled with limitless possibilities. It evokes images of faraway places, exotic locations, relaxation, and fun. Yet, while hospitality can encompass these settings, it is noteworthy that we can also find expressions of hospitality in providing lunches for school-children, nutritional diets in hospitals, and gourmet dinners in sky boxes at our favorite game.

So how does one choose from the myriad of options in the field of hospitality?

One begins by exploring! There are a number of entry-level or hourly jobs in all areas of hospitality. Pick a segment of the industry that attracts you and *go to work!* Exposure to the field in the form of an internship or part-time job helps you to understand yourself better in terms of what you like and what you value in a job. Finding out what you don't like is as helpful as identifying things that you do like, because it helps you in the process of eliminating choices.

Yet another way to help you to decide on what job is right for you is to *conduct a number of informational interviews* with those who are working in positions of interest. Have a prepared list of questions for these employees. Here are a few questions to ask: What do the employees do? How do they accomplish their tasks? What do they like about their jobs? How did they get started? This will add to the information you are collecting to analyze which job is right for you.

Another way to explore options for jobs that are of particular interest is to *shadow someone who works in a position that, one day, you would like to hold.* Observing a person as he or she goes about daily tasks will help you to better define the scope of responsibilities for the job. This will enable you to make choices. The advantage of shadowing someone is that, in a short time, you can get a feel for what she or he does. Employers are typically open to accommodating you since there is no pay involved.

Another key to keeping your options open is to *network.* Simply put, this means connecting with people in the field of hospitality in which you would eventually like to be employed. Those working in the field have friends, acquaintances, colleagues, and co-workers that you have yet to meet. One of these new acquaintances may be the very person who will open the door and help you to start your new job or career.

Another major factor in keeping your options open is to *continue your education* and to keep *developing your skills.* The hospitality field changes rapidly. There are new technology, enhanced training opportunities, and hundreds of articles in journals and trade magazines applicable to all areas of hospitality. Research and learn about your favorite concepts, new trends, hiring practices, and new products. Take classes to develop key skills, such as accounting, finance, and business management. Complete training in areas in which you would like to become stronger. Pursue a bachelor's or an associate college degree to make you a stronger management candidate for employment in the hospitality field. Employers also stress skills in leadership, written and verbal communication, computer basics, time management, organizational skills, and, most of all, a friendly and welcoming attitude.

If you are in an educational setting, be sure to *make the Career Service Office your second home.* It will help you to identify your strengths and gifts, to help you to determine the segment of the industry that is best for you. Career offices can also provide extensive information on employers in various hospitality segments, assist you in networking with those in the industry, and find internship and permanent job opportunities.

Last but not least, after you investigate and analyze all the information that you have collected, stop and pause to reflect, and ask yourself the following questions:

- Do I like what I am doing?
- Can I do this for more than eight hours a day and not resent it?
- Does what I do give me satisfaction in helping others?
- Do I smile often when I think about having a career in this field?

If most of your answers are yes, then perhaps you are on your way to selecting a career in hospitality.

MASTERING YOUR KNOWLEDGE

Discuss the following questions.

Part I: If you have already decided to study travel/tourism/hospitality management:

1. What factors most influenced you to learn about the industry?
2. To this point, what have you learned are among the most important ingredients for success in the industry?
3. What segment of the industry do you currently think offers you the most rewarding career? Why?
4. What are three things that you learned in this chapter that will benefit you when you become a hospitality manager?

Part II: If you are not certain about majoring in travel/tourism/hospitality management:

1. What are the pros and cons about a major in the industry?
2. What do you hope to learn from this book or course that will enable you to make an informed decision about a career in the industry?
3. In what type of organization do you think you could find a position that would be most compatible with your likes or dislikes?

Part III: For all students:

1. What is (are) your career goal(s), and what must happen for you to attain your goal(s)?
2. Have you made any decision(s) that you regret about your academic or professional career since you began your formal education? If so, what were the decision(s) and why do you regret it (them)?

LEARN FROM THE INTERNET

- Check out the following hotel and restaurant websites.

  Hotel Websites:
  - Hilton Hotels Corporation: www.hilton.com
  - Marriott Hotels, Resorts & Suites: www.marriott.com
  - Choice Hotels: www.choicehotels.com

  Restaurants
  - Houston's: www.houstons.com
  - Outback: www.outback.com
  - Ruth's Chris Steakhouse: www.ruthschris.com

  What points do these organizations make in efforts to differentiate themselves from the competition?

- Check out the following foodservice management company and hotel management company websites.

  Foodservice Management Companies Websites:
  - ARAMARK Corporation: www.aramark.com
  - Sodexho: www.sodexho.com
  - Canteen Food Service: www.canteen.com

  Hotel Management Companies
  - White Lodging Services Corporation: www.whitelodging.com
  - Tharaldson Lodging: www.tharaldson.com
  - Coakley & Williams Hotel Management Company: www.cwhotels.com

  What information would be of most interest to you if you were a business manager for a school or hospital or an independent hotel owner who was considering hiring a company to operate the foodservices and hotel?

- Check out the following Website addresses for organizations that are not in the lodging or foodservice segments.

  Non-Lodging/Foodservices Organizations:
  - Disneyland: www.disneyland.com
  - Bellagio Hotel & Casino: www.bellagio.com
  - Carnival Cruises: www.carnival.com

  What types of products and services do they offer that are similar to those offered by their hotel and foodservices counterparts? What types of products and services are different?

KEY HOSPITALITY TERMS

The following terms were explained in this chapter. Review the definitions of any words with which you are unfamiliar. Begin to utilize them as you expand your vocabulary as a hospitality professional.

travel and tourism industry

hospitality industry

cyberfares

amenities

concierge

hotel

franchise

management company

resorts

full-service hotel

timeshare properties

condominium (condo)

condo-hotel

conference centers

camp and park lodges

bed and breakfast (inns)

commercial foodservice operations

noncommercial foodservices

restaurant

caterers

bars

lounges

short-order food items

noncommercial foodservices (self-operated)

noncommercial foodservices (contract management company-operated)

private clubs

casinos

vending services

manual food and beverage services

theme parks

brand

The Secret
of Quality Service

From Chapter 2 of *Discovering Hospitality and Tourism: The World's Greatest Industry*, Second Edition, Jack D. Ninemeier, Joe Perdue. Copyright © 2008 by Pearson Education, Inc. Published by Pearson Prentice Hall. All rights reserved.

The Secret
of Quality Service

Fine dining is a great experience, and it is the service just as much as the food, beverages, and atmosphere that guests purchase with their "dining-out" dollars.

PhotoEdit, Jeff Greenberg photographer

CHAPTER LEARNING OBJECTIVES

After studying this chapter you will be able to:

1. Explain the concept of quality and review its impact on the level of service provided by a travel/tourism/hospitality operation.

2. Discuss the six ingredients in a recipe to develop a quality service system.

3. Describe the concept of moments of truth in guest service.

4. Recognize the important role of employees in consistently delivering quality service.

5. Defend the concept that guest service staff are professionals.

6. Review the components of the quality service philosophy utilized by the Ritz-Carlton Hotel Company.

7. State factors that will challenge the ability of organizations to deliver quality sevice in the future.

FEEDBACK FROM THE REAL WORLD

You are the new general manager in a travel/tourism/hospitality operation that is not doing well. Previously, it was very successful. There was very low employee turnover, and staff members gave a high priority to meeting (and, almost always, exceeding!) the expectations of the guests being served. Sharon (the manager who had been there for many years) emphasized guest service as a key to success, and she was proved correct each year as business volume (and profits) increased.

Today a different organization exists. Sharon retired, and several managers have been hired and have left over the past few years. Increasingly, the emphasis on cutting costs has replaced the philosophy of providing value for the guests. Staffing patterns have changed, so each employee now has much less time for the interactions needed to learn how guests' needs can best be met.

The Big Question: What should the new manager do to reestablish a culture that focuses on quality guest service?

As you read this chapter, think about your answer to this question and then get feedback from the real world at the end of the chapter.

You have learned that there are a wide range of organizations in the industry that we are studying. Some offer lodging accommodations; others offer food and beverage products and services; still others offer opportunities in recreation and leisure and meetings organizations. What must all these organizations do to be successful? The answer is simple and basic: they must provide quality guest service.

Some persons call the industry we are studying the *hospitality services* industry. A popular name for the segment offering food and beverage is *foodservices*. Persons paying for lodging, food, and beverages in the for-profit segment of the industry consider service to be a very important part of the experience that they are buying. Those utilizing foodservices in a not-for-profit facility are equally entitled to service that addresses their needs and meets their expectations. Consumers also appreciate the services provided by organizations in recreation and leisure and meetings business.

HOSPITALITY MANAGERS SERVE GUESTS

How would you treat a special friend or a relative whom you invite into your home for a meal? The answer to this question can help to define how visitors to a hospitality operation should be treated. The earliest travelers were offered meals and a safe night's rest by families living near trade routes and were invited into the family's home for today's equivalent of lodging and foodservices.

It is true that guests in your home would not be presented with a bill of fare covering the charges at the end of their visit. By contrast, those visiting the hospitality operation must pay their bill. However, the policies and procedures, service training activities, and basic philosophies of the organization can be developed with an emphasis on serving guests.

Do the terms *customer* and *guest* mean the same thing? Perhaps they do in a dictionary; however, in the real world of hospitality, the operator who treats the visitor as a guest will likely be more successful than competitors treating the visitor as a customer.

At its most basic level, then, every travel/tourism/hospitality organization must focus on service. It is typically the service, not the product (for example, food, beverage, or sleeping room), that most influences the guests' perceptions about their experience with an organization in the travel/tourism/hospitality industry.

THE CONCEPT OF QUALITY AND ITS IMPACT ON SERVICE

The concept of **quality** is widely discussed in the world of travel/tourism/hospitality management today. Unfortunately, it is much easier to talk about quality than it is to effectively implement it and keep it going within a hospitality operation.

quality the consistent delivery of products and services according to expected standards

For our purposes, we can define quality as *the consistent delivery of products and services according to expected standards*. Note that **service** (the topic of this chapter) is specifically noted in our definition of quality. This is important: the guest renting a room at a hotel, purchasing a meal at a restaurant, or paying dues at a private club is buying and desires to receive an expected standard of service as part of the payment. Increasingly, guests are willing to pay more as they visit hospitality properties offering service that meets (or, one hopes, exceeds) their service expectations. The perceived level of service quality is an important factor in the experience that guests receive during the visit to the hospitality operation.

service the process of helping guests by addressing their wants and needs with respect and dignity in a timely manner

INGREDIENTS IN A QUALITY SERVICE SYSTEM

The hospitality industry's emphasis on quality is not just a fad that will soon go away. In fact, it requires a dramatic change in attitude about the need to focus on the guests and to use what is learned to reconsider how the operation should work. Entire books have been written about quality in the hospitality industry.[1] There are six ingredients in a recipe that should be used to develop and implement a quality service system. These are reviewed in Exhibit 1.

Quick-service restaurants meet the needs of a very large consumer market and, as the name implies fast service is desired by many guests.

George Goodwin, Color-Pic, Inc.

---

[1]See, for example, John King and Ronald Cichy, *Managing for Quality in the Hospitality Industry*. Upper Saddle River, NJ: Pearson Prentice Hall. 2006.

► Ingredient 1:	Determine who are the guests being served.
► Ingredient 2:	Assess exactly what the guests desire.
Ingredient 3:	Develop practical ways that systems can be modified or developed to consistently deliver what the guests want.
Ingredient 4:	Train and empower service staff to please the guests.
Ingredient 5:	Implement revised procedures.
└ Ingredient 6:	Evaluate and modify service delivery systems as necessary.

EXHIBIT 1
Components of Quality in the Hospitality Industry

IS SERVICE IMPORTANT IN NONCOMMERCIAL OPERATIONS?

There is a popular myth that noncommercial foodservice operations, such as in hospitals, nursing homes, and military bases, have a captive market. The myth continues by reasoning that it is, therefore, unnecessary to focus on the consumers' needs because they have few, if any, alternatives.

In fact, the focus on service is just as great in the noncommercial segment of the industry as it is in commercial hospitality operations. Consider, for example, how you feel if the wait in your school's cafeteria line is lengthy. How do you think hospital patients feel if a follow-up to their dietary concerns is not made by the facility's foodservice staff within a reasonable amount of time? What do you think is among the most frequent topic of conversation between nursing home residents and their families? Answer: the food! The answers to each of these questions cause us to focus directly on the foodservice operation and the level (quality) of service that it provides. Service is important in noncommercial foodservice operations!

Let's take a look at the ingredients in the recipe for quality guest service.

Ingredient 1

Determine who are the guests being served. Some hospitality operations may serve a narrow range of guests. Consider, for example, a small rooms-only lodging property with a strategic location next to a busy interchange on an interstate highway. Most of its guests probably desire the same thing: a relatively inexpensive, safe, and clean sleeping room at a price representing a value to the travelers.

Other hospitality operations may serve a more diverse range of guests. Consider, for example, an upscale restaurant that, at the same time, is serving busy executives conducting business over dinner, a couple celebrating a wedding anniversary, a group of senior citizens enjoying their once monthly dining-out social event, and a young couple on a casual date. What exactly do these seemingly diverse groups of diners have in common? (While it is up to the restaurant manager to determine this, a possible answer is this: freshly produced food delivered by servers who are attentive to the diners' unique needs in a special environment at a price that represents a value for the products purchased and the services received.)

Let's consider two other examples of hospitality properties serving diverse guest groups. First, a downtown hotel may serve business guests during the week and other guests visiting the downtown area for shopping and social reasons during the weekend. Second, a busy restaurant in a tourist destination may serve numerous groups of guests depending on the convention and

AP/Wide World Photos

Registration should be hospitable and flawless because it is a first step in service for many hotel guests.

group meetings in the city at that specific time. It is important for hospitality managers to assure that they know as much as possible about all the guests being served.

Ingredient 2

Assess exactly what the guests desire. A questioning process can be used to determine guests' wants and needs. Questions such as "What did you like about your visit?" and "What would make your visit more enjoyable?" can help a manager to determine guests' needs. These and related questions can be posed to guests by managers as they "manage by walking around" and/or by a simple questionnaire (comment card) given to guests at the end of a meal or in the guest room. Focus groups (in educational and business and industry settings) and member surveys about a wide range of issues (in private clubs) suggest additional ways to collect information about guest preferences in specific types of hospitality operations.

Every hospitality manager has another way to collect information about the guests: ask employees. It is ironic but true that, many times, **line-level employees** know more about the likes and dislikes of guests than do their **supervisors** or even the unit **managers**. These staff members frequently have greater amounts of guest contact than do any other employees in the hospitality organization. Consider, for example, the guest complaining about long lines at the time of check-in to a front-desk clerk or a food server receiving compliments (or complaints!) about food in the dining room. Want to know what the guests desire: ask employees who provide the products and services to them.

Ingredient 3

Develop practical ways that systems can be modified or developed to consistently deliver what the guests want. Two of the best ways to make procedures more guest friendly are to **benchmark** and to utilize **cross-functional teams** of employees. Benchmarking is the process of understanding exactly how one's own organization does something and, additionally, determining how it is done by the competition. If, for example, guests desire fast check-in (and most guests do!), it is important to determine what the property currently does and what other properties do to minimize guest check-in times.

Wise hospitality managers know the benefit of asking employees for advice about ways to improve a work method. Cross-functional teams are

line-level employees those staff members whose jobs are considered entry-level or non-supervisory; these are typically positions for which the employee is paid an hourly (rather than salary) compensation; examples include positions such as guest service (front desk) agents, room attendants, and food and beverage servers

supervisor a staff member who directs the work of line-level employees

manager a staff member who directs the work of supervisors

benchmark the search for best practices and an understanding about how they are achieved in efforts to determine how well a hospitality organization is doing

cross-functional teams a group of employees from different departments within the hospitality operation that works together to resolve operating problems

comprised of staff members from several departments who meet, brainstorm, and consider ways to improve work methods. (Consider a more traditional alternative of utilizing employees from the same department to address a problem: dining room service staff addressing a slow service problem may well conclude that the problem doesn't rest with them; it is caused by the cook! Alternatively, if employees from the dining room, food production, and even housekeeping departments address the problem, creative ideas not limited to "how we have always done things" might be generated.)

Ingredient 4

Train and empower service staff to please the guests. New work methods require, at the least, changes in how work is done. New or additional tools or equipment may also be necessary. Staff members must be trained in revised work tasks, but they must also be empowered to make decisions about the unique needs, if any, of the guests being served. **Empowerment** is the act of granting authority to employees to make key decisions within the employees' areas of responsibility. For example, service employees have a primary responsibility to please the guests. Empowered staff members are allowed to make decisions about how this is to be done as they interact with guests with differing wants, needs, and expectations. Before staff members can be empowered, they must be trained and provided with the tools and other resources needed to do their jobs.

empowerment the act of granting authority to employees to make key decisions within the employees' areas of responsibility

Ingredient 5

Implement revised procedures. Implementation does not always need to be on an all or nothing basis. Perhaps, for example, employees working on specific floors in a hotel or within specific work stations in a dining room could utilize new work methods to test and further refine, if necessary, the more guest-friendly processes before they are "rolled out" to the entire property.

> **CHECK IT OUT!**
>
> Enter "hospitality service training" into your favorite search engine to review websites of organizations that offer service training.

Ingredient 6

Evaluate and modify service delivery systems as necessary. Over time, guest preferences may (and are likely to) change. Technologies will evolve, as will, perhaps, new or improved work methods. These can affect what guests desire and/or how products or services can be most effectively delivered. In effect, then, the process of quality guest service is cyclical. It is driven by changes in (1) the guests being served and/or (2) guest preferences and/or (3) the work methods implemented to yield the desired quality of product or service outputs.

Today's requirement for quality service has itself evolved from a past emphasis on commodities and products and is becoming incorporated into something that guests are increasingly expecting: an experience. Exhibit 2 illustrates this shift using a simple component of almost every meal: bread. Long ago, bread was a simple commodity made of wheat that was likely grown by the family or someone in the community. "Yesterday" bread became a product that was purchased at a grocery store. Today, bread is considered part of a meal experience; warm, sliced bread served tableside is a featured amenity in many restaurants. In the future, bread may become part of a

Getty Images Inc.-Image Bank, AJA Productions

A beverage operation at poolside. These guests want to have fun, and they cannot if the staff's service does not allow them to do so.

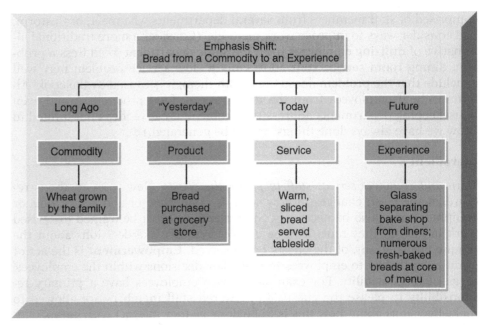

EXHIBIT 2
The History of Service: Bread as the Staff of Life

microbrewery a brewery that produces very small quantities of unique beers typically for consumption only on-site and/or for distribution within a small geographic area

diner's experience. Guests may consume a meal in a bakery (just as today food is served in many **microbreweries**). Diners might choose from numerous fresh-baked breads that are at the core of the menu. In fact, some specialty bakeries envision guests selecting bread for their meal in much the same way that they currently select wine to accompany their meal.

SERVICE AND MOMENTS OF TRUTH

OBJECTIVE 3
Describe the concept of moments of truth in guest service.

moments of truth any time that a guest has an opportunity to form an impression about the hospitality organization; moments of truth can be positive or negative

Moments of truth are opportunities that guests have to form an impression about a hospitality organization. While a moment of truth can involve an employee (for example, excellent or rude service), there does not need to be human interaction. (Consider, for example, negative impressions formed when guests walk through a garbage-cluttered parking lot that is downwind from a foul-smelling garbage dumpster or the positive first impression created by the

PhotoEdit, Frank Siteman photographer

All employees require training, and procedures to deliver service that meets the property's standards must be part of that training.

MANAGING THE MOMENTS OF TRUTH

Assume that a restaurant manager determines that there is a minimum of 42 times that a guest can form an opinion of the operation. (This includes when the guest enters the restaurant, receives the initial meeting and greeting by the receptionist, is escorted to the table, is seated, is given a menu, the lapsed time until the server's first visit to the table, and so on). Assume also that the restaurant is open for lunch (200 guests are typically served) and for dinner (250 guests are served on an average shift). The number of *planned* "moments of truth" is significant:

$$\left(\begin{array}{l}\text{Number of moments of}\\ \text{truth per lunch period}\end{array}\right) = \left(\begin{array}{l}200 \text{ guests} \times 42\\ \text{moments of truth}\end{array}\right) = 8,400$$

$$\left(\begin{array}{l}\text{Number of moments of}\\ \text{truth per dinner shift}\end{array}\right) = \left(\begin{array}{l}250 \text{ guests} \times 42\\ \text{moments of truth}\end{array}\right) = 10,500$$

$$\left(\begin{array}{l}\text{Number of moments of}\\ \text{truth per day}\end{array}\right) = 8,400 + 10,500 = 18,900$$

$$\left(\begin{array}{l}\text{Number of moments of}\\ \text{truth per week}\end{array}\right) = \left(\begin{array}{l}18,900 \text{ moments of}\\ \text{truth} \times 6 \text{ days of}\\ \text{weekly operation}\end{array}\right) = 113,400$$

$$\left(\begin{array}{l}\text{Number of moments of}\\ \text{truth per year}\end{array}\right) = \left(\begin{array}{l}113,400 \text{ moments of}\\ \text{truth per week} \times\\ 52 \text{ weeks per year}\end{array}\right) = 5,896,800$$

The manager in this example has 5,896,800 formal (planned) opportunities each year to make a good impression. Unfortunately, there are a seemingly infinite number of *informal* (unplanned) occasions when guest opinions can be formed. These include encounters with other employees, the perceived levels of cleanliness in the restaurant, and the guests' enjoyment of all food and beverage products served.

How can a manager effectively manage all moments of truth?

large vase of fresh, beautiful flowers on top of the receptionist's stand. Consider also the **"wow" factor** created when one of these fresh flower stems is given to lady guests as they are seated!)

Hospitality managers plan many aspects of a guest experience at their properties. For example, procedures are probably in place in a restaurant for guests to be seated, for orders to be taken, for food to be served, and for guest charges to be paid (among numerous others). Similarly, hotel managers, through an organized planning process (or by default!) have a system in place for guest registration, luggage transport to the room, guest security and safety while on-site, guest check-out, and other guest and property interactions. However, guests in these managers' restaurants and hotels will encounter (sometimes by chance alone) other moments of truth that can be favorable or unfavorable and, in the process, influence the guest's total perception of the visit.

Word-of-mouth advertising occurs when previous guests tell other persons about their experiences during a visit to the hospitality operation. Unfortunately, guests with negative impressions after a property visit are likely to tell more persons about their problems than their counterparts who have just

"wow" factor the feeling guests have when they receive or experience an unanticipated extra as they interact with the hospitality operation

word-of-mouth advertising favorable or unfavorable comments that are made as previous guests of a hospitality operation tell others about their experiences

Hotels market to persons traveling for pleasure. How are these guests' service expectations likely to differ from those of persons traveling for business?

Getty Images-Photodisc, EyeWire Collection

enjoyed a pleasing visit. Unfortunately as well, each time negative experiences are repeated, the extent of the problem is likely to be increased or exaggerated.

You can see, then, that our simple definition of quality at the beginning of this chapter (the consistent delivery of products and services according to expected standards) is, in fact, very difficult to attain. For example, if a hospitality operation serves 300 guests each day for several or more years, some guest-related problems will occur, regardless of the extent to which a service attitude exists and guest-friendly processes are in place. However, effective plans should be in place to minimize the number of service failures.

Managers may establish a goal of **zero defects** when quality service processes are implemented. In other words, it is their hope that there will be no guest-related complaints. However, doesn't a goal of zero defects create frustration since, even with the best intentions and most effective processes in place, mistakes (defects) will occur? Exhibit 3 illustrates how a decline in defects can be measured.

zero defects a goal of no guest-related complaints that is established when guest service processes are implemented

OBJECTIVE 4
Recognize the important role of employees in consistently delivering quality service.

Service Is Delivered by Employees

After viewing a video emphasizing quality dining service, one dining room manager was heard saying to another, "I'd give anything to have service staff like those shown in the video." What the dining room manager had seen was a series of situations in which a trained dining room server (1) provided a hospitable

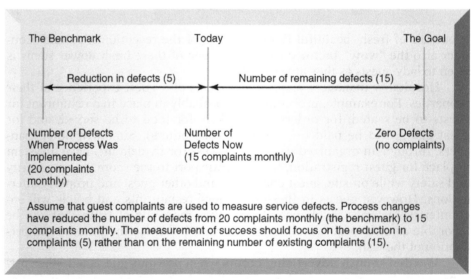

The Benchmark   Today   The Goal

Reduction in defects (5)   Number of remaining defects (15)

Number of Defects When Process Was Implemented (20 complaints monthly)

Number of Defects Now (15 complaints monthly)

Zero Defects (no complaints)

Assume that guest complaints are used to measure service defects. Process changes have reduced the number of defects from 20 complaints monthly (the benchmark) to 15 complaints monthly. The measurement of success should focus on the reduction in complaints (5) rather than on the remaining number of existing complaints (15).

EXHIBIT 3
The March Toward Zero Defects

Ali Faraj
Trainer
Marriott Call Center
Santa Ana, California

Providing Effective Guest Service Looks Easy!

Ali is quick to say that he has always been interested in the world of business because he "likes to make money." He was initially interested in the landscaping business and remembers attending a convention at a Hyatt hotel. The property really impressed him, as did the staff members and the service that they provided.

Shortly thereafter, he enrolled at a community college to major in general business. At the time, he did not even know that there were post-secondary schools that offered a formal hospitality education program. He did know, however, that he liked to be around people, that he enjoyed helping people, and that he really had an interest in making people happy.

While taking courses at the college, Ali met with a career services advisor who shared information about hospitality education programs in the state; the rest is "history," and Ali transferred into a program he knew "was meant for him."

Ali's college career was very impressive, even though he has a vision impairment that would make many people think that his accomplishments would not be possible.

While receiving his university education, he was:

- President of the Hospitality Business Consultants' Club
- A member of the board of directors of the school's Hospitality Association
- A member of the school's Student Hospitality Sales Organization
- A member of Eta Sigma Delta Honors Society
- An executive board member and a corporate ambassador for the school's Career Expo
- A reception server for a large school event (Les Gourmets)

Ali is very proficient in the use of technology. For example, screen-reading software (Jaws for Windows) is very helpful in allowing him to use technology that others, increasingly, take for granted.

Ali had no difficulty succeeding in his accomplishments: "I know I can do just about anything I set my mind to do. My challenge is to prove myself by showing others that I can do it. Some day, after working my way up the corporate ladder, I would like to be the general manager of a hotel in a reputable company, and someday I would like to own my own hotel!"

While in school, Ali completed a three-month internship at the Hyatt Regency Dearborn (Michigan). He spent 45 days as a front-desk clerk, and the remainder of the time he served as a reservations agent.

How, one might ask, can a person with limited vision serve as a front-desk clerk? "Just watch me!" says Ali. "Guests completed registration cards as usual, and I placed them in a stack to be filed by another desk clerk later. I checked guest identifications by standing next to another front-desk clerk who helped with details. Money readers that can scan bills and announce their amounts were available, and I used a one-sided headphone connected to a computer to handle other aspects of guest check-ins and check-outs in a very short amount of time."

Ali notes that his fellow employees at the Hyatt were very open-minded and willing to accept him because "it was no big deal!"

Ali spent a second summer at the same property and completed an internship in the accounting department. He worked with the hotel's assistant controller, credit manager, and income audit manager. In these capacities, he performed bank statement reconciliations and did postings to the income, general, and payroll journals. He also made 30-day accounts-receivable collection calls and other calls for credit references.

Ali's accounting work was made easier by the use of a "talking" calculator. He also scanned documents into Word/Excel programs and then used the Jaws software noted previously.

During his senior year of hospitality studies, Ali completed an accounting internship at the university's Hotel and Conference Center, and he worked 15 hours weekly while taking 13 credits and serving in a leadership capacity with three hospitality student groups.

(continued)

After graduation, Ali worked for a brief time as a manager for a valet parking company with responsibility for day-to-day operations, including marketing and hiring.

Then, in 2005, he was hired as a worldwide reservations agent for the Marriott Call Center. Soon after, he was promoted to a regional agent and then became an on-the-job trainer for new staff members. In recognition of his training abilities, Ali became an assistant trainer for new classes and, at the time of this writing, he was starting to revise the training department and its resource materials.

Ali has some great advice for hospitality students: "Have a goal; try your best to fulfill it. Never say 'I can't' unless you've tried it—over and over and over again!"

He also displays his emphasis on commitment and enthusiasm when he says, "I am continuing to move forward in my career, and I will work hard so I can be successful in the hotel industry. I love proving people wrong when they think that it is impossible for me to do something because of my visual impairment. Just give me the chance, and I will show you that it can be done!"

greeting, (2) practiced the "art and science" of suggestive selling, (3) utilized product knowledge, (4) answered all guest questions about "what's on the menu," (5) helped other servers when they became especially busy during the work shift, and (6) met or exceeded the guests' service expectations.

Why couldn't (didn't) that dining room manager employ servers who consistently did these relatively simple and commonsense things? What kind of service was the manager's staff providing to guests if they did not do what was emphasized in the training video? Unfortunately, many persons considering a recent experience in a foodservice operation might also ask, "What was wrong with the staff? What was wrong with their supervisor for allowing these things to happen? If I can realize the negative impact it has on their business, why can't the supervisor?"

The quality of service provided to guests in any type of hospitality operation is affected most by the staff members providing the service and by the processes that the employees use to provide the service. If this is true and the employee is a key element in service delivery, what role, then, does the manager play?

It has been said that the vast majority of all problems in a hospitality operation are caused by the manager! This observation runs contrary to the traditional manager who thinks, "If only I could find good employees, my operating problems would be solved." In fact, it is the manager who effectively (or ineffectively) recruits, orients, trains, motivates, and empowers staff members to serve the guests. It is the manager who does (or does not) serve as a role model to emphasize the importance of guest service in the hospitality organization. Managers cannot delegate the **accountability** that they receive from their own bosses to subordinates. Instead, managers are (and should be) held responsible for the extent to which the hospitality operation is successful. As emphasized throughout this chapter, service is an essential ingredient in the success of any hospitality organization. What can managers do to best assure that employees know and consistently practice effective guest-service skills? Some helpful tactics are listed in Exhibit 4. Let's briefly discuss them:

accountability an obligation created when a person is delegated duties or responsibilities from higher levels of management

employer of choice the concept that the hospitality operation is a preferred place of employment within the community by those who have alternative employment opportunities

- *Maintain a vision of service priority.* Managers must understand the critical importance of service. They must recognize that what they do (and don't do) and what they say (and don't say) are the biggest factors in determining the extent to which service is emphasized in their operation.
- *Recruit and select service-minded staff.* The hospitality operation should strive to be an **employer of choice** within the community; its **turnover rate** should be relatively low, and experienced staff members

EXHIBIT 4
Manager's Checklist
for Effective Guest Service

✓ Maintain a vision of service priority.

✓ Recruit and select service-minded staff.

✓ Provide effective orientation and training.

✓ Supervise with a service emphasis.

✓ Empower staff with decision-making authority for service.

✓ Emphasize continuous quality improvement.

EXHIBIT 4
Manager's Checklist
for Effective Guest Service

should understand and consistently apply quality service principles. However, applicants will still need to be recruited and selected. They should effectively answer open-ended questions such as "What would you do if a guest pushed his way to the front of the check-in line and demanded to be registered immediately?" or "What would you do if a guest indicates the desire for food to be served immediately, and there is a backup of several large food orders in the kitchen?"

- *Provide effective orientation and training.* The manager's emphasis on quality guest service continues at the time of new-employee orientation. Staff members should be introduced to the property's **mission statement**, which should emphasize the critical importance of guest service. They must be trained in guest-friendly procedures. (There should be adequate time for new employees to gain the required knowledge and skills before they have significant guest contact.)

- *Supervise with a service emphasis.* Employees, like all other people, will normally do what they are rewarded to do. If service is important, hospitality managers should emphasize this by thanking staff members when exceptional guest service is rendered, discussing service-related problems, and noting service factors during times of performance appraisal. Employee compensation decisions should be based, in part, on the consistency of quality service delivery.

turnover rate a measure of the proportion of a work force that is replaced during a designated time period (for example, month, quarter, year); it can be calculated as number of employees separated ÷ number of employees in the work force = turnover rate

mission statement a planning tool that broadly identifies what a hospitality operation would like to accomplish and what it plans to do to accomplish it

DID YOU KNOW?

More than 88,000,000 websites are generated when the term "hospitality service" is entered in the Google search engine.

Hotels market to persons traveling for business. How are these guests' service expectations likely to differ from those of families staying at the hotel?

Hoechst-Celanese Corp.

WHAT MAKES SERVICE SPECIAL?

Service is an attitude as much or more than it is a skill. Hospitality employees provide special service to their guests when they:

Acknowledge guests and thank them for visiting

Smile

Maintain eye contact

Reflect a genuine interest in providing quality service

Consider every guest to be unique

Create a warm environment of hospitality

Strive for excellence in guest service skills

Are courteous, polite, and attentive

Determine what guests *really* want and need and then provide the products and services that address these wants and needs

Pay more attention to guests than to machines and co-workers

Invite guests to return

Aren't these things easy to do? Why don't travel/tourism/hospitality employees consistently incorporate these tactics into the ways that they interact with guests?

---

continuous quality improvement (CQI) ongoing efforts within a hospitality operation to better meet (or exceed) guest expectations and to define ways to perform work with better, less costly, and faster methods

OBJECTIVE 5
Defend the concept that guest service staff are professionals.

professionals persons working in an occupation requiring extensive knowledge and skills

licensing formal authorization to practice a profession that has been granted by a governmental agency

registration acceptance for one to work within a profession that has been granted by (typically) a nongovernmental agency, such as an association

OBJECTIVE 6
Review the components of the quality service philosophy utilized by the Ritz-Carlton Hotel Company.

- *Empower staff with decision-making authority for service.* The importance of employee empowerment was noted earlier in this chapter. Hospitality managers should facilitate, not direct, the delivery of service. Staff members who are in contact with guests require the ability to make quick decisions that focus on guest needs as they arise.
- *Emphasize* **continuous quality improvement (CQI).** Guests and the hospitality operations that serve them constantly change. Hospitality operations, then, either become better or worse; they never stay the same. Today's emphasis on "better, faster, cheaper" is important. However, the first two factors just noted (better and faster) should be developed with the guests' needs in mind. The third factor (cheaper) is also a meaningful goal as long as it involves taking error out of the products and services, rather than reducing value from the guests' point of view.

Guest Service Staff Are Professionals

Professionals are persons working in an occupation requiring extensive knowledge and skills. One often thinks about occupations such as medicine, law, accounting, and teaching to satisfy this definition. Persons in these occupations have formal education in a specialized body of knowledge and membership in their profession is controlled by, for example, **licensing** or **registration**.

Hospitality service personnel should be thought of as professionals in their own vocation because specialized knowledge and skills are required to be effective. Also, certification by professional associations, including the American Hotel and Lodging Association (www.ahla.org) and the National Restaurant Association (www.restaurant.org), is available.

Ritz-Carlton: A Case Study in Quality Service

The Ritz-Carlton Hotel Company, L.L.C., is widely known for its emphasis on quality. It has won the prestigious **Malcolm Baldrige National Quality Award**, which is administered by the federal government (National Institute of

Gary Ombler © Dorling Kindersley

The hotel's management team must plan service processes.

Standards and Technology, Commerce Department). The Ritz-Carlton's Employee Promise, Credo, and Service Values establish a foundation for quality excellence that is an important part of the company's corporate culture.

While very few organizations receive the Malcolm–Baldrige Award, the philosophies emphasized in the Ritz-Carlton Hotel Company Standards are useful benchmarking concepts for all service organizations, including those within the hospitality industry.

Malcolm Baldrige National Quality Award an award granted to relatively few U.S. businesses that demonstrate successful quality-related strategies relating to leadership, information and analysis, strategic planning, human resource development and management, process management, business results, and customer focus and satisfaction

Benchmark Against the Best: Ritz-Carlton Hotels

The Employee Promise[2]

At the Ritz Carlton, our Ladies and Gentlemen are the most important resource in our service commitment to our guests.

By applying the principles of trust, honesty, respect, integrity, and commitment, we nurture and maximize talent to the benefit of each individual and the company.

The Ritz-Carlton fosters a work environment where diversity is valued, quality of life is enhanced, individual aspirations are fulfilled, and The Ritz-Carlton Mystique is strengthened.

The Ritz-Carlton Credo[3]

The Ritz-Carlton Hotel is a place where the genuine care and comfort of our guests is our highest mission.

We pledge to provide the finest personal service and facilities for our guests who will always enjoy a warm, relaxed yet refined ambiance.

The Ritz-Carlton experience enlivens the senses, instills well-being, and fulfills even the unexpressed wishes and needs of our guests.

Service Values: I Am Proud to be Ritz-Carlton

1. I build strong relationships and create Ritz-Carlton guests for life.
2. I am always responsive to the expressed and unexpressed wishes and needs of our guests.

---

[2]© 1992–2006. The Ritz-Carlton Hotel Company, L.L.C., all rights reserved. Reprinted with the permission of The Ritz-Carlton Hotel Company, L.L.C.®
[3]Ibid.

The essence of hospitality: "Welcome to your home away from home."

Getty Images Inc.-Image Bank, David de Lossy, Ghislain & Marie

3. I am empowered to create unique, memorable, and personal experiences for our guests.
4. I understand my role in achieving the Key Success Factors and creating The Ritz-Carlton Mystique.
5. I continuously seek opportunities to innovate and improve The Ritz-Carlton experience.
6. I own and immediately resolve guest problems.
7. I create a work environment of teamwork and lateral service so that the needs of our guests and each other are met.
8. I have the opportunity to continuously learn and grow.
9. I am involved in the planning of the work that affects me.
10. I am proud of my professional appearance, language, and behavior.
11. I protect the privacy and security of our guests, my fellow employees, and the company's confidential information and assets.
12. I am responsible for uncompromising levels of cleanliness and creating a safe and accident-free environment.

CHALLENGES! CHALLENGES!

OBJECTIVE 7
State factors that will challenge the ability of organizations to deliver quality service in the future.

The consumers' interest in service is likely to increase in the future and, as today, organizations that meet (or exceed) these guest service expectations have a competitive edge over their counterparts who do not. While the recipe for quality service discussed in this chapter is easy to read and understand, it is much more difficult to implement. Managers cannot, for example, simply determine standards, develop required procedures that address them, and train staff members to follow them.

Several factors that affect the ability of the organization to maintain its quality service standards include the following:

- **Service philosophy of top-level managers.** Contrast the manager who is a role model for effective service by constantly talking about it and helping to deliver it with another manager whose leadership style is "do what I say, not what I do."
- **Service attitude of staff members.** As suggested, line-level employees are more likely to practice the service component of their jobs when their managers do so.
- **Employee selection and training.** Staff members who have a genuine interest in providing service and who are trained to do so will more likely be successful than others who consider their employment to be "just a job."
- **Changing guest preferences.** Managers must keep current with their guests' expectations about service and the best way to provide it.

Managers must evaluate technology and consider guest service implications, along with numerous other service-related considerations. The need for "high tech" with "high touch" is important, because service in the travel/tourism and hospitality industry is delivered by people, not by machines.

SUMMARY OF CHAPTER LEARNING OBJECTIVES

1. **Explain the concept of quality and review its impact on the level of service provided by a travel/tourism/hospitality operation.**
Quality is the consistent delivery of products and services according to expected standards. Service is an important component of our definition of quality, and guests at all types of hospitality properties are influenced by service as they form an impression of the experience that they receive from employees of the hospitality organization.

2. **Discuss the six ingredients in a recipe to develop a quality service system.**
The six ingredients for quality guest service are the following:
   1. Determine who are the guests being served.
   2. Assess exactly what the guests desire.
   3. Develop practical ways that systems can be modified or developed to consistently deliver what the guests want.
   4. Train and empower service staff to please the guests.
   5. Implement revised procedures.
   6. Evaluate and modify service delivery systems as necessary.

3. **Describe the concept of moments of truth in guest service.**
Moments of truth are positive or negative opportunities when guests form an impression about a hospitality organization.

4. **Recognize the important role of employees in consistently delivering quality service.**

The majority of problems in a hospitality organization are caused by the manager, not by employees. When employees cannot consistently deliver quality service, it is most likely due to problems for which the manager has responsibility.

5. **Defend the concept that guest service staff are professionals.**
Guest service staff are professionals in their own vocation because specialized knowledge and skills are required to be effective.

6. **Review the components of the quality service philosophy utilized by the Ritz-Carlton Hotel Company.**
The Ritz-Carlton's Employee Promise indicates that its staff members (ladies and gentlemen) are the most important resource in its service commitment to its guests. The Ritz-Carlton's Credo pledges the finest personal service and facilities for guests.

7. **State factors that will challenge the ability of organizations to deliver quality service in the future.**
Factors that will affect the ability of an organization to maintain quality standards include the service philosophy of top-level managers, the service attitude of staff members, and employee selection and training practices. Guest preferences will also change, and managers must keep up with and adapt to these changes.

MASTERING YOUR KNOWLEDGE

Discuss the following questions.

1. What is the definition of excellent service in the following situations?
   a. During time of check-in at a motel, on the highway, and at a Ritz-Carlton hotel
   b. During the process of taking food orders at a quick-service restaurant and at a high-check-average, sit-down restaurant
   c. In a corporate dining room of a very large and successful company and at a primary school cafeteria

FEEDBACK FROM THE REAL WORLD

Our real-world advice comes from Nancy Bacyinski, Regional Director of Operations for HDS Services in the Cincinnati, Ohio, market.

What should a new general manager of the hospitality operation do to reestablish a culture that focuses on quality guest service?

I would begin my new management position realizing that my greatest asset is my staff; they are my team. I would set up a meeting with personnel in each department and obtain feedback about the operation: What do they like? Dislike? What do our guests like? Dislike? How do they respond to our guests' needs?

An educational process would then begin. Our company team would work together to formulate a mission statement that focused on our role in serving our guests. We would define who the guests are and what they want and commit, as a team, to consistently move toward the goals expressed in our mission.

I would train the staff and empower all of them to be our ambassadors to please the guests. They would be given the authority, or power, to respond to guests to meet their expectations if we do not provide an acceptable level of satisfaction in our initial efforts.

I would realize that these changes cannot occur overnight; some time will be required for the staff to begin to respect and trust me. As well, I will need time to obtain a "big picture" overview of the best way to use resources (which are always in limited supply) to best address our mission and goals. I would understand that employees who are satisfied and happy will provide quality products and services to our guests. In turn, employee turnover will be lower, and those whom we serve will be happy with us. These results will yield the financial performance that is anticipated in our well-planned budget.

I will know we have been successful in our efforts when our levels of guests and employee satisfaction have increased and, at the same time, when our expenses have decreased.

This process, while oversimplified, provides a basic recipe that will help to reestablish the culture in the foodservice operation that had once been there but which, over time, is no longer there.

Consider the market being served, the definition of acceptable service in each alternative, and the role of value from the consumer's perspective in your analysis.

2. How do you personally define and evaluate service when you are a guest at a hotel or restaurant? Do you think other guests have the same concerns about service as you do? Review the six ingredients necessary to develop a quality service system. Assume that you are the manager of a restaurant in which the table reservation system for dinner is not working; many guests arrive on time for their reservation, but still must wait an excessively long time for an available table. Work through a potential solution to this problem utilizing the six-step method.

3. Think about the last time you visited a hotel or restaurant as a guest. What moments of truth do you recall? What impact did they have on your overall impression of the hospitality operation?

4. Discuss the following statement: "The vast majority of all problems in a hospitality operation are caused by the manager, not by the employee." Do you agree? Disagree? If you currently hold a job in the hospitality industry, what would your supervisor say about this statement?

5. Do you believe that line-level staff members in hospitality positions such as front-desk clerk and food server are professionals? Why or why not?

6. Review the components of the Ritz-Carlton Hotel Company's quality service statement

(Employee Promise and Ritz-Carlton Credo). What impact might they have on you if you were an employee of the Ritz-Carlton? Which of the concepts described in these statements would be applicable to employees working in *any* other travel/tourism, food and beverage, or lodging operation?

7. What are three things that you learned in this chapter that will benefit you if you become a hospitality manager?

LEARN FROM THE INTERNET

1. Check out the website for the Ritz-Carlton Hotel Company: www.ritzcarlton.com. Carefully review it and note how it emphasizes guest service in its messages to guests.

2. Check out the websites of the following hotel and restaurant companies:

   Hotels
   - Red Roof Inns: www.redroof.com
   - Baymont Inns & Suites: www.baymontinns.com
   - Motel 6: www.motel6.com

   Restaurants
   - McDonald's: www.mcdonalds.com
   - Kentucky Fried Chicken: www.KFC.com
   - Taco Bell: www.tacobell.com

What emphasis do they place on guest service?

3. Check out the websites of the following hospitality organizations:
   - Caesar's Palace Casino: www.caesarspalace.com
   - Galapagos Cruises Inc.: www.galapagos-inc.com
   - Gordon Food Service Distributors: www.gfs.com
   - Canteen Vending Services: www.canteen.com
   - Busch Gardens: www.buschgardens.com

What services do they offer? To what extent do they emphasize service?

KEY HOSPITALITY TERMS

The following terms were explained in this chapter. Review the definitions of any words with which you are unfamiliar. Begin to utilize them as you expand your vocabulary as a hospitality professional.

quality
service
line-level employees
supervisor
manager
benchmark
cross-functional teams
empowerment
microbrewery
moments of truth
"wow" factor

word-of-mouth advertising
zero defects
accountability
employer of choice
turnover rate
mission statement
continuous quality improvement (CQI)
professionals
licensing
registration
Malcolm Baldrige National Quality Award

Overview: Hotels, Hotels, Hotels!

Ciadade de Goa Beach Resort, Goa, India

Fredrik and Laurence Arvidsson © Dorling Kindersley, Courtesy of Cidade de Goa Beach Resort

---

CHAPTER LEARNING OBJECTIVES

After studying this chapter you will be able to:

1. Review the range of lodging property alternatives available to travelers.
2. Discuss three common ways to classify lodging properties.
3. Describe basic characteristics that all lodging properties share.
4. Explain common hotel ownership and management alternatives.
5. Describe how basic hotel functions are organized and integrated.
6. List challenges (opportunities) confronting today's hotel industry.
7. Review the wide range of positions within which one may work in the lodging industry.

From Chapter 4 of *Discovering Hospitality and Tourism: The World's Greatest Industry*, Second Edition, Jack D. Ninemeier, Joe Perdue. Copyright © 2008 by Pearson Education, Inc. Published by Pearson Prentice Hall. All rights reserved.

When many people consider the hospitality industry, they think about hotels and restaurants. While this is not technically correct, it is true that hotels and restaurants are a very significant part of the industry. In this chapter you will learn basic background information about lodging properties. While there are many ways that the numerous types of hotels are different, there are also ways in which they are similar. These are the topics of this chapter.

RANGE OF LODGING PROPERTIES

OBJECTIVE 1
Review the range of lodging property alternatives available to travelers.

Today's hotels are vastly different from the private homes, hostels, and inns that were the first sanctuaries for weary travelers. Owners of lodging accommodations have likely differentiated travelers by their ability to pay since the industry's beginning: more affluent travelers are willing to pay more for the products, services, and amenities that they receive as long as they receive a value. The earliest innkeepers along travel routes likely offered their guest choices (for example, a single room or a room shared with others) based on their ability to pay.

Today's lodging industry is one of **niche marketing.** There are innumerable types of hotels appealing to widely different types of travelers. This

niche marketing the process of offering products or services that appeal to a very specific subsegment (niche) of the market; for example, hoteliers may focus on the needs of long-stay business travelers, rather than all business travelers, and may provide amenities in lodging accommodations that persons in this subsegment desire

DID YOU KNOW?

The niches (small segments) of the hotel marketplace are becoming smaller and smaller. For example, many hotels cater to female travelers. Some do so with women-only floors accessible with special key cards for security, special room-service menus, upgraded bathrooms and toiletries, extra lighting, larger closets, and makeup mirrors. Some hotels cater to tall people with oversized king-size beds, heightened shower heads, and oversized bathrobes, and many properties advertise that they are pet friendly. At least one hotel (The Doubletree Hotel Tucson) offers allergy-friendly rooms, and persons with medical concerns have increasing access to services offering physicians' house calls in guest rooms.

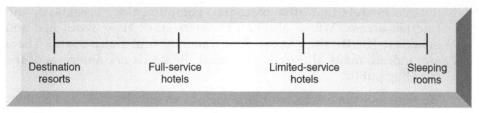

EXHIBIT 1
Range of Lodging Property Alternatives

WHO STAYS IN HOTELS?

Persons staying in hotels can be classified according to the purpose of their travel:

Business or corporate (individuals)   Long-stay guests
Business or corporate (groups)   Airline-related guests
Convention or association groups   Government or military guests
Leisure travelers   Regional "getaway" guests

diversity in lodging alternatives has emerged in efforts to meet the increasingly specific demands of increasingly narrow segments of the traveling public.

What is a **hotel?** In its most basic definition, a hotel is a building that offers sleeping rooms. This definition, however, is not very helpful because of the wide range of alternatives that we have already noted. Exhibit 1 illustrates one way to classify the range of properties that are considered hotels. Let's learn more about these basic types of lodging properties.

- Destination **resorts** typically offer lavish accommodations, several food and beverage outlets ranging from gourmet (high check average) to poolside snack bars, the highest possible service standards, and, typically, recreational alternatives, such as golf, spas, tennis, aquatic, and other activities, depending on the type of guests for whom the property is marketed. Destination resorts are frequently offered in locations with additional attractions, including snow skiing, ocean (beach) activities, and/or horseback riding.
- **Full-service hotels** have at least one thing in common (food and beverage services) and range from modest, small properties with a dining room along the nation's highways, to properties with meeting and banquet spaces near airports, to high-rise centers appealing to business travelers in the nation's cities.
- **Limited-service hotels** also have one thing in common (no or almost no food service; continental breakfasts are sometimes offered as an amenity included in the price). Most are typically found in suburban and highway locations. There are two basic types: traditional properties that rent sleeping rooms to guests for several (or fewer) days and **extended-stay** properties that market to guests desiring lodging accommodations for longer time periods (generally one week or longer).
- **Sleeping rooms** may offer barracks-style sleeping accommodations, such as youth hostels, or small, private rooms or even small sleeping compartments that serve travelers in some airport locations. These properties offer private or shared restroom facilities. There are also

hotel a for-profit business that rents sleeping rooms and often provides other amenities such as food and beverage services, swimming pools and exercise rooms, meeting spaces, business centers, and concierge services; also referred to as *motel, motor hotel,* or *motor inn*

resorts full-service hotels with additional attractions to make them a primary destination for travelers

full-service hotel a hotel that provides guests with extensive food and beverage products and services

limited-service hotel a lodging property that offers very limited food services or none at all; sometimes a complimentary breakfast is served, but there is no table-service restaurant

extended-stay hotel a mid-priced, limited-service hotel marketing to guests desiring accommodations for extended time periods (generally one week or longer)

sleeping room a lodging alternative of basic sleeping accommodations with or without private rest room facilities

hostel a lodging accommodation, typically available in a dormitory style, that is generally inexpensive and frequented by youthful travelers.

upscale **hostels** that offer balconies, complimentary breakfasts, and Internet access. Where else can travelers stay? How about bed and breakfast (B&B) sites, spas, dude ranches, and houseboats? There are, indeed, many alternatives to meet the needs and interests of the traveling public.

We have still not exhausted the range of lodging alternatives. Facilities not frequently thought of as hotels may also provide sleeping rooms. Examples include private clubs, cruise ships, casinos, and privately owned and timeshare condominiums. (All these and other not so frequently thought of components of the hospitality industry will be discussed. Facilities offering sleeping accommodations for people living away from their homes, such as schools, colleges, and universities with residential services, and healthcare facilities can also be considered part of the lodging industry and will be addressed.)

CLASSIFICATION OF HOTELS

OBJECTIVE 2
Discuss three common ways to classify lodging properties.

rack rate the price at which a hotel sells its rooms when no discounts of any kind are offered to the guest; often shortened to *rack*

Lodging properties can be classified in numerous ways. As shown in Exhibit 2, common classifications include location, rate, and size. In 2003, most U.S. hotels were in suburban and highway locations, were low to mid-priced ($30 to $59.99), and had less than 75 rooms.[1] This description of an average hotel should be of great interest to those aspiring to careers in the lodging industry. Numerous excellent positions are available in the industry. However, the number of very large properties with very high **rack rates** in large city centers and/or exotic locations is relatively small. As well, general manager positions with duties such as those glamorized in movies and television do not exist, although positions in hotels of all sizes, price ranges, and locations offer challenging and exciting professional opportunities.

Some industry observers classify properties within the lodging industry by guest-room rental charges. Resulting classifications fall along a range such as that suggested in Exhibit 3. These classifications do not correlate very easily with the rate structure suggested in Exhibit 2. It is difficult to classify hotels strictly by rack rates because room charges vary significantly among geographic regions. For example, the most expensive hotel available in a small northern Midwest town may be one-half (or less) of the rate charged for the least expensive, safe, and clean hotel room in a major East or West Coast city.

EXHIBIT 2
Common Ways to
Categorize Lodging
Properties

By Location	By Rate ($)	By Size (rooms)
Urban	Under 30	Under 75
Suburban	30–44.99	75–149
Highway	45–59.99	150–299
Airport	60–85	300–500
Resort	More than 85	Over 500

These classifications are used by the AHLA; check out current statistics applicable to each classification on AHLA's home page (www.ahla.com). Reproduced with permission from the American Hotel & Lodging Association, 1201 New York Avenue NW, Suite 600, Washington, D.C. 20005.

[1]www.ahla.com; check the website for current data.

42

DID YOU KNOW?

- The largest hotel in the world, Asia-Asia, is scheduled for completion in 2010. Located in Dubai, it will have 6,500 rooms. Of these, 5,100 will be four-star and 1,400 will be five-star rooms.*

  Source: Dubailand to double Dubai hotel rooms with $27bn project. Retrieved May 2, 2006, from www.ameinfo.com

- If "money were no object," how much could you spend for a one-night stay at some of the world's best hotels? Here's a sample:[†]

  The Mansion at the MGM Grand (Las Vegas): $5,000
  Fregate Island Private (Seychelles): $2,482
  Le Toiny (St. Barthelemy, French West Indies): $2,092
  Singita Private Game Reserve (Sabi Sand, South Africa): $2,200
  The Wakaya Club (Fiji): $1900

  [†] *Source:* World's Most Expensive Hotels 2005. Retrieved May 21, 2006, from www.msnbc.com.

LODGING INDUSTRY CHARACTERISTICS[2]

OBJECTIVE 3
Describe basic characteristics that all lodging properties share.

As seen previously, we can classify hotels by location, by rate, and/or by size. These factors suggest differences between lodging properties. However, all properties share several common characteristics:

- *Emphasis on safety, cleanliness, and service.* Few, if any, guests consider only the room and other physical attributes of the property when making a stay or no-stay decision. For example, safety and cleanliness are very important considerations. Friendliness (hospitality) of employees is also important and, along with the property's physical aspects (size, location, quality of maintenance, furnishings, and other factors), is part of the guests' evaluation mix. By contrast to their retail store counterparts, then, there are intangible (difficult to quantify) aspects of the purchase decision that potential hotel guests consider.
- *Inseparability of manufacture and sales.* It is not possible to separate the "manufacture" (production) of a guest room with its "sale." A room exists and is sold at the same site. (Contrast this with, for example, the

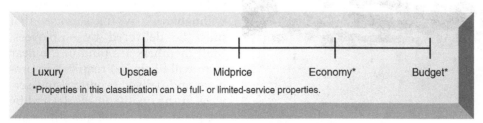

EXHIBIT 3
Range of Lodging Properties Classified by Guest-Room Rental Charges

---

[2]This and the next section are from David Hayes and Jack Ninemeier, *Hotel Operations Management,* 2nd ed. Upper Saddle River, NJ: Pearson Prentice Hall, 2007.

Getty Images, Inc.-Photodisc, Steve Mason photographer

Tropical hotel guest room. The location, view, and amenities are among the many factors that this couple considered when they selected this hotel.

manufacture and sale of an automobile, shirt, or television set. They are typically manufactured at one site and sold at another.) The hotel's general manager and his or her staff, then, must be experts at both manufacture and sales. Their counterparts in many other industries must normally be experts in only one phase of business: either manufacturing products or selling them to the consumer in the marketplace.

● *Perishability.* If a guest room is not rented on a specific date, the revenue is lost forever. By contrast, an automobile, shirt, or television can be sold tomorrow if it is not sold today.

● *Repetitiveness.* The steps involved in making guest rooms ready for sale or for preparing a specific meal or drink and then renting (selling) them are basically the same every time the guest room, meal, or drink is sold. These routines (operating procedures) allow for some standardization. At the same time, however, they create challenges. It is always important to focus on the individual needs of guests, and standardization can provide less opportunity for staff creativity in the decision-making processes used to perform required work.

labor intensive the need for people rather than for equipment (machinery or technology) to perform required work tasks

● **Labor intensive.** In many industries, including the automotive and electronics segments, technology and equipment have replaced people in some work activities. By contrast, in the lodging industry this has occurred only to a lesser degree. For example, technology is being used in the front office, sales, and accounting departments, where many tasks are highly automated. However, technology could be utilized even more

Getty Images, Inc.-Photodisc Javier Pierini photographer

Beach resort in Buzios, Brazil

in the industry: automated check-in and check-out systems are available, and convenience foods can be used to reduce on-site labor, which is otherwise needed for food production. However, the traveling public increasingly desires and is willingly to pay for services that must be delivered by employees. Staff members are (and in the near term will likely be) required to produce and deliver products and services at the quality levels desired by the guests and to the quantity standards required by the property.

It is ironic that the two hotel departments that typically require the most employees (food and beverage and housekeeping) represent the areas in the typical hotel where technology has been least able to replace employees.

POPULAR RATING SYSTEMS ALSO CLASSIFY HOTELS

Many travelers utilize the rating system of the American Automobile Association (AAA) and the Mobil Corporation when making hotel selection decisions.* Both organizations utilize detailed and objective factors to rate hotels. The Mobil rating system utilizes stars:

A one-star hotel should be clean, comfortable, and well maintained.

A two-star hotel offers the basic quality of a one-star property plus additional features, including a restaurant, swimming pool, and room service.

A three-star hotel is one offering a truly excellent lodging experience.

A four-star hotel is luxurious and characterized by attention to detail and the feeling that guest comfort and convenience are the priority concern.

A five-star property is an elite property that is ranked superior in every area of the rating system.

The AAA rating system is similar, but utilizes diamonds:

A one-diamond property offers good but modest accommodations.

A two-diamond property has room decor and furnishing enhancements superior to its one-diamond counterpart.

A three-diamond property offers a marked upgrade in amenities, service, and facilities.

A four-diamond property displays a high level of service and hospitality.

A five-diamond property offers an exceptionally high degree of service, and the facility's operations set standards in hospitality and service for the industry.

*For more information, see Mobil Corporation at www.exxonmobiltravel.com and American Automobile Association at www.aaa.com.

HOTEL OWNERSHIP AND MANAGEMENT

OBJECTIVE 4
Explain common hotel ownership and management alternatives.

A motorist is driving along the highway and sees the **flag** of a popular hotel chain. The name is easily recognizable (made so, in part, by an extensive nationwide advertising campaign). A typical reaction is, "I guess that hotel company purchased some land and built another hotel to operate in this location." In fact, this is not likely to be the case. It is very possible (and most likely) that an investor has built the property on owned (or leased) land, hired a contract management company to operate the property, and signed an agreement with a franchiser to operate the hotel **brand.**

Hotels are owned and managed in numerous ways. Here are two:

- *Single-unit property not affiliated with any chain.* Some single-unit properties have been in business for many years, are extremely successful, and may be the most preferred hotel in a community or area. This, however, is the exception. These properties (sometimes referred to as **mom and pop hotels**) are generating a smaller market share in today's lodging industry nationwide.
- *Multiunit properties.* Properties that are part of a hotel chain are the most prevalent. The brand affiliation, whether international, nationwide, regional, or located within an even smaller area, is successful because of name recognition and economy of scale in operations and

flag the specific brand with which a hotel may affiliate; examples of currently popular flags include brands such as Comfort Inns, Holiday Inn Express, Ramada Inns, Hampton Inns, Residence Inns, Best Western, and Hawthorn Suites; hotels affiliated with a specific flag are sometimes referred to as *chain*

brand name of a hotel chain; sometimes referred to as a *flag*

mom and pop hotels a slang term sometimes used to refer to an independent property (one not affiliated with a brand) that is owned and operated by a single person or family

The limited-service hotel market is growing because many guests do not require extensive food and beverage service.

PhotoEdit, Jeff Greenberg photographer

because it is often easier to receive financing for business (unit or chain) growth.

Let's look at multiunit (chain) properties more closely:

franchise an arrangement whereby one party (the brand) allows another (the hotel owners) to use its logo, name, systems, and resources in exchange for a fee

franchiser one who manages the brand and sells the right to use the brand name

franchisee those who own the hotel and buy the right to use the brand name for a fixed period of time at an agreed-upon price

entrepreneur a person who assumes the risk of owning and operating a business in exchange for the financial rewards that the business may produce

investor an individual or organization that provides money for a business such as a hospitality operation with the goal of receiving a profitable return

management company an organization that operates a hotel(s) for a fee; also sometimes called a *contract company* or *contract management company*

- **Franchise** *hotels or nonfranchise hotels.* Franchise hotels are typically the chains with the greatest name recognition. The **franchiser,** such as Hilton Hotels, Sheraton, Hyatt, and Marriott, sells certain rights to a **franchisee,** such as to use the name (to "fly the flag"), to connect to the national reservation system, and to utilize proven operating procedures in return for numerous fees. An **entrepreneur** owning one or more hotels that are not affiliated with a franchise has the advantage of not paying numerous fees, but loses advantages such as name recognition and access to the franchiser's reservation systems.
- *Independently owned hotel or company-owned hotel.* Sometimes an **investor** (an individual or an organization) owns (or leases) land and builds the hotel. This is an example of an independently owned hotel. By contrast, a franchiser may buy land or build buildings for a company-owned hotel. (In fact, many franchisers own some properties outright, have partial ownership in others, and have no ownership in still other properties.)
- *Independent, company- or* **management company-***operated.* Day to day operations of a hotel might be the responsibility of an independent owner, the franchiser (in a company-operated property), or a management company. When the management company is used, the owner hires a professional hotel management company for the day to day operational responsibilities for the property. Many management companies operate hotels of numerous brands that are owned by many separate owners.

Exhibit 4 reviews the many types of hotel ownership and management alternatives that we have discussed. When reviewing the figure, you will note that a specific hotel property can be franchise or nonfranchise affiliated. If it is a franchise operation, it can be owned by an independent investor or by a franchise company (the franchiser). Also, you will note that a franchise can be operated independently, by the franchiser, or by a management company. Exhibit 4 also indicates that a nonfranchise property is one that is owned by an independent investor who may operate it himself or herself or, alternatively, hire a management company for operational responsibilities.

HOSPITALITY LEADER PROFILE

Daniel Pirrallo
General Manager
Millennium Harvest
House, Boulder

A Hotel with Tennis Courts or Tennis Courts with a Hotel?

Conveniently located on 16 acres of land adjacent to the University of Colorado, the Millennium Harvest House–Boulder is a prestigious 269-room property with 18,000 square feet of function space. It is the only facility in the region with on-property tennis courts. There are 15 in total, 5 of which are contained within an all-weather "bubble." The property generates about $1 million annually in revenue from its 500 Sporting Association members who join to use the indoor and outdoor pools and the workout and tennis facilities. The Millennium Harvest House–Boulder, in effect, is the closest thing to a tennis resort in the entire region.

Dan began his hospitality career by earning an undergraduate degree in hospitality management and spent almost 20 years with ITT Sheraton Corporation. He completed management training in Minnesota and then held food and beverage positions in Atlanta, Washington, D.C., and New Orleans. After serving as resident manager at the Sheraton in Dallas, Dan moved to the ITT Sheraton World Headquarters in Boston. There he served as the director of rooms and reservations for the eastern region. He then returned to operations as the hotel manager (the number two position) for the 1200-room Sheraton Boston Hotel. He served as the general manager of the Sheraton Suites in Wilmington, Delaware, and then returned to the Sheraton Boston as its general manager.

After ITT Sheraton was purchased by Starwood, Dan chose to join Anderson Consulting in Philadelphia. However, after a short while he missed the hotel industry and returned to it by managing the Millennium Knickerbocker in Chicago. He recently moved to his present position in Boulder, Colorado.

Dan's most significant current professional challenge is the economy. Since Boulder is a regional technical center, the economic downturn that began in early 2001 hurt the corporate transient market. The leisure market is less affected, but it is also now different: "We have had to shift our marketing efforts to the weekend drive market. Guests drive in for the weekend, rather than fly in for the week."

Recruiting employees for his business is also difficult, and it is especially challenging to screen applicants to assure that only qualified candidates with valid working permits or papers are hired. Dan says it is easy to summarize a hotelier's greatest challenge: "Find new business and take care of it!"

Marketing concerns also present opportunities. "Everyone is going after the same business. There is simply more supply [rooms] than demand [guests to occupy them]." Dan also notes that it is easy to lose control of rate integrity in specific market segments due to the increasing number of reservations made over Internet booking channels.

Dan's greatest service concerns involve his employees. With high staff turnover created by seasonal employment, it is difficult to quickly train employees to meet and exceed his guests' expectations. The problem is heightened because the downturn in the economy has created the need to keep management staff to a minimum. Training, therefore, must be very focused on quickly developing the employee's skills to deliver quality service.

Dan is optimistic about the short-term future of the corporate market. "You cannot replace face to face meetings with alternatives such as teleconferencing," he reasons. "The Millennium Harvest House provides an 'oasis to escape' for business travelers looking for a secluded place to hold productive meetings and to reduce the stress created by increased business demands."

Dan begins his day between 6:30 and 7:00 A.M. by answering e-mails and voice messages and by doing administrative paper work. He then holds a daily management-briefing meeting with his management team to discuss significant events of the previous and current day. By 8:45 A.M. Dan is off to the races as he meets with department heads to address the best ways to manage the business. Every day is different.

(continued)

"Some days you just run flat out." For example, when the University of Colorado football team plays at home, the hotel staff installs a 16-foot television so that the 3,000 to 4,000 fans can view the Colorado Buffaloes taking on their latest Big 12 challenger. These events generate as much as $80,000 in beverage sales in just one afternoon!

Dan knows that to be successful a hotelier must be involved in the community. He is active with the Boulder Convention and Visitors Bureau, Boulder's cultural and arts community, and the state and local area's hotel and lodging association.

Dan offers the following advice for those considering a hospitality career: "If you think of this type of work as just a job, then this may not be the right career for you. Hotel managers are always on the job 365 days a year. You must also keep in mind that you work when everyone else plays, and vice versa. You and your family must learn to accept this. Work hours are likely to be long early in your career, and they may be long later in your career as well." Dan, for example, now works 50 to 60 hours per week, but admits that he works some of the hours simply because he likes to be there.

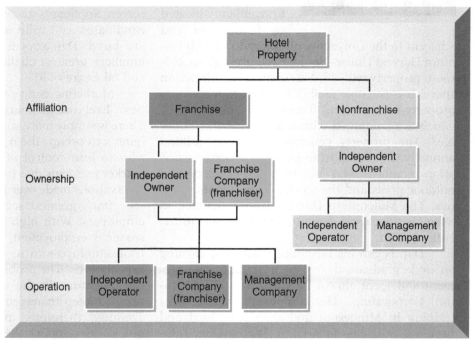

EXHIBIT 4
Hotel Ownership and Management Alternatives

MORE ABOUT FRANCHISE AND MANAGEMENT AGREEMENTS

Franchising is a network of business relationships that allows people to share brand identification, a successful method of doing business, and a strong marketing and distribution system.* The franchisee incurs less risk because proven operational methods developed by the franchisor are used to manage the business. However, the franchisee gives up the freedom of being completely independent and becomes part of the group committed to building a brand and increasing the groups' market share. The franchisee must also pay fees for the operating license and must comply with brand standards that have been established by the franchisor.

Today's hotel owners increasingly affiliate their hotels with other hotels under a common brand name. Most franchise companies do not own the hotels operating under their brand name. Instead, they sell the right to the brand name and determine the standards that must be followed. This arrangement can create conflict between hotel owners and franchisors. General managers of these hotels have an obvious responsibility to their employer (owner), but they also must abide by the franchise agreement signed by the property's owners.

With so many franchisors available, how is the best one for a specific hotel selected? Factors may include the quality and expertise of the brand managers, the perceived quality and service level of the brand, the amount of fees paid, and the percentage of revenue that will contributed by the brand's reservation system.

Many hotel owners do not want to manage properties. Instead, they may hire a management company to do so. Management companies often receive a predetermined monthly fee from the hotel owner in exchange for operating the property. The owner then assumes a passive position about operating decisions while, at the same time, assuming responsibility for all working capital, operating expenses, and debt-service fees, regardless of the hotel's profitability (if any).

Advantages to hotel owners may include: improved management quality may be realized, targeted expertise can be obtained, documented managerial effectiveness is available, the payment for services can be tied to performance, and partnership opportunities are enhanced. Potential disadvantages include that the owner has little or no control over the selection of the on-site general manager and other high-level managers, talented managers leave frequently, the interest of hotel owners and the management company may conflict, the cost of management company errors is borne by the owner, and transfer of ownership may be complicated.

*This discussion is loosely based on David Hayes and Jack Ninemeier. *Hotel Operations Management*, 2nd ed. Upper Saddle River, New Jersey, Pearson Prentice Hall, 2007. For a detailed discussion about franchise agreements and management contracts, see Chapter 13.

HOW HOTELS ARE ORGANIZED

OBJECTIVE 5
Describe how basic hotel functions are organized and integrated.

As you have learned, hotels are labor intensive. People, not machines, produce products and deliver service and, as consistently noted throughout this book, guests desire and are willing to pay for these "handmade" products and services when they rent a hotel room and/or purchase other accommodations at a lodging property.

Upscale hotels offer luxury guest-room accommodations.

Rob Reichenfeld © Dorling Kindersley

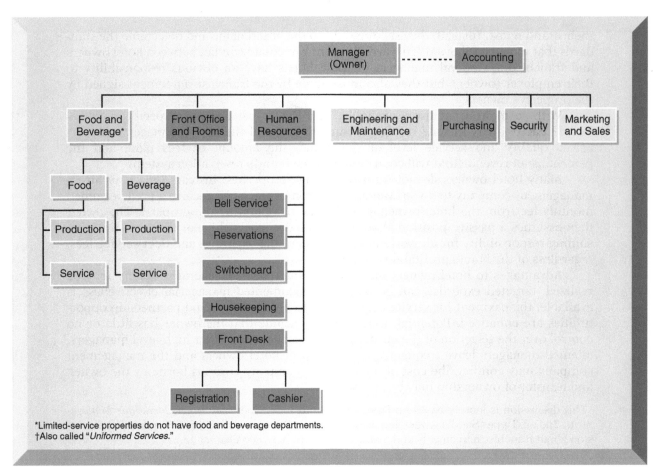

EXHIBIT 5
Organization of Hotel Functions

Guest rooms in limited-service hotels are comfortable.

Exhibit 5 identifies the minimum functions required in a lodging property of any size. (Note that some limited-service properties offer no or minimal food and beverage services.) In a very small (less than 75 rooms) limited-service property, the manager (owner) may personally perform all functions except those relating to housekeeping and engineering and maintenance. An external accountant and bookkeeper may be retained to compile operating data and for tax-reporting purposes.

By contrast, a larger (350 room) full-service property will likely have department heads who report to the manager, are responsible for each function,

NOT ALL HOTEL GROUPS ARE CHAINS

Many people think that all hotel groups belong to chains with the same company name, such as Hilton, Hyatt, and Marriott, or that all hotel groups represent a brand, such as Hilton's Doubletree, Embassy Suites, Hampton Inn, and Hilton Hotels.

While hotels that are part of the same company and brand do belong to a hotel group, there are other hotel groups that are not part of company or brand chains. These groups provide reservations and other marketing or sales services to independent hotels.

To check out some of these groups and the properties they represent, go to:

- Preferred Hotels: www.preferredhotels.com
- Leading Hotels of the World: www.lhw.com
- Relais & Chateau: www.relais&chateau.com
- Small Luxury Hotels of the World: www.slh.com

and supervise others with more specific responsibilities within that function, For example, an executive housekeeper may supervise inspectors, room attendants, public space cleaners, and laundry staff; a front-desk office manager may supervise front-desk reservation agents, bell staff, and van drivers. In a still larger (3,000 room) hotel there may be an accountant and controller who supervises the assistant controller who, in turn, supervises credit managers, payroll supervisors, and head cashiers, who then manage the work of entry-level staff within that specialty. As the size of the property increases, so do the number of positions and the more narrowly focused are the tasks within each position.

CHALLENGES CONFRONTING THE HOTEL INDUSTRY

Numerous challenges confront today's hotel industry. Most observers see these as long-term issues that will not "go away tomorrow." Persons entering the lodging industry in the near term, such as you and other students, will therefore be involved in the process leading to the way that the industry adapts to these challenges.

OBJECTIVE 6
List challenges (opportunities) confronting today's hotel industry.

REVENUE AND COST CENTERS

Hotel departments can be divided into revenue centers (if they generate revenue) and cost centers (if they exist to help revenue centers to generate sales).

Revenue Departments*	Cost Centers†
Rooms	Marketing
Food and beverage	Engineering
Telephone	Accounting
Fitness and recreation facilities	Human resources
	Security

*Hotels may also receive revenues from space rental (such as leasing a gift shop) and from sources such as parking garage fees, vending machines, and business center services. A relatively recent trend: hotels now sell guest-room furnishings, such as bedding (including the bed!), robes, and even desk lamps. See, for example, www.shopMarriott.com.

†Cost centers might be considered staff departments: hotel divisions that provide technical and supportive assistance to revenue departments.

Bed and breakfast in the Rocky Mountains

Exhibit 6 reviews some of the operating, marketing, technological, and economic challenges confronting today's lodging industry. Let's look at these challenges more closely.

Operating Issues

- *Labor shortages.* Labor shortages and their impact on the industry in almost every geographic location are consistently among the most difficult challenges noted by hoteliers (and by managers in all other segments of the hospitality industry as well). In many communities, hotel expansion is limited not by capital (money), but rather by human resources.
- *Cost containment.* Hoteliers are increasingly challenged to find ways to reduce costs without sacrificing the quality standards imposed to consistently meet guest expectations. The idea of "doing more with less" requires managers to think about ways to operate more effectively (in other words, to "do the right things in the right way") and to examine possibilities for cost savings that will not affect the guest's perception of value.
- *Increased competition.* Hoteliers everywhere indicate that their community is **overbuilt;** there are too many available hotel rooms relative to the guests desiring to rent them. The resulting competition, which often involves price cutting in efforts to provide greater value to guests, reduces still further the profits generated.

overbuilt the condition that exists when too many hotel guest rooms are available for the number of travelers wanting to rent them

Marketing Issues

- **Market segmentation** *and overlapping brands.* Market segmentation is increasing as lodging chains focus on a specific niche of travelers. Additionally, brands overlap. Some industry observers are concerned that franchisers may expand their number of brands to the point that investors who purchase from the same franchiser will be in direct competition with themselves! Also, as the number of brands increases, the ability of consumers to differentiate among them decreases.

market segmentation efforts to focus on a highly defined (smaller) group of travelers

EXHIBIT 6
Lodging Industry Challenges

Type of Issue	Challenges
Operating	Labor shortages
	Cost containment
	Increased competition
Marketing	Market segmentation and overlapping brands
	Increased guest sophistication and amenities
Technological	Interactive reservation systems
	Guest-room innovations
	Data mining
	Yield management
Economic	Dependence on the nation's economy
	Globalization
	Terrorism and safety

- *Increased guest sophistication.* Consumers have become more sophisticated and, as a result, so have the types of products and services that they desire. Amenities, including business centers, exercise and recreational facilities, and guest-room innovations, increase costs but, if not carefully selected, may not appeal to many guests being served by a specific property.

Technological Issues

The challenge of keeping up with the fast pace of technology is difficult and expensive.

- *Interactive reservation systems.* Increasingly, guests use the Internet's interactive reservation systems, and hotel companies are sometimes criticized for the (alleged) large number of keyboard clicks required to make a reservation.
- *Guest-room innovations.* Multiple telephone lines, interactive opportunities for ordering room service, and guest-room check-out are examples of amenities that guests increasingly desire, but that are very expensive to install and implement.
- **Data mining.** This technology allows marketing and sales personnel to find new ways to use guest-related data.
- **Yield management.** This computerized process allows managers to match guest demand with room rates (high demand means higher rates because of lessened discounts; low demand results in higher discounts).

data mining using technology to analyze guest- (and other) related data to make better marketing decisions

yield management demand forecasting systems designed to maximize revenue by holding rates high during times of high guest-room demand and by decreasing room rates during times of lower guest-room demand

Economic Issues

- *Dependence on the nation's economy.* When the nation's economy is good, business travel generally increases. **Hotel occupancy rates** and rack rates increase, which results in higher profit levels. The reverse is also true: business travel slows when the economy slows. Then occupancy and rack rates decrease. Discounts to increase occupancy are offered, which yield lower revenues and profit decreases.
- **Globalization.** Globalization affects the lodging industry dramatically because it influences the extent to which people travel both within the country and around the world. Therefore, it is not only the economy of the nation, but also the economies of individual countries, that play an increasingly larger role in the financial success of lodging properties.
- **Terrorism** *and safety.* Fear of travel after the World Trade Center and Pentagon attacks of September 11, 2001, and

hotel occupancy rate the ratio of guest rooms sold (including comps) to guest rooms available for sale in a given time period; always expressed as a percentage, the formula for occupancy rate is: Number of guest rooms sold ÷ number of guest rooms available

globalization the process by which countries and communities within them throughout the world are becoming increasingly interrelated

An elegant lobby in a luxury Manhattan (New York City) hotel.

Michael Moran © Dorling Kindersley

terrorism the threat of danger created and harm caused by persons for political or religious reasons

PhotoEdit, Deborah Davis photographer

A concierge provides information to guests in upscale hotels.

worldwide concerns about terrorism have brought safety issues to the forefront of every segment of the hospitality industry, including hotels. This issue, while beyond the hoteliers' control, will be of significant concern for the foreseeable future.

RISING STAR PROFILE

Anastasia Callahan
Senior Manager
Owner and Franchise Services
Marriott International

Diversify Your Experience!

Anastasia received her bachelor of science degree in food, hotel, and tourism in 1990. She learned innkeeping while in college by rotating through numerous positions at the Sherwood in Skaneateles, New York (in the state's Finger Lakes region). While there, she worked in front desk, housekeeping, bookkeeping, hostessing, and food serving (coordinating service staff).

After graduating from college, she began working for Marriott and, over the next 13 years, she worked with properties representing all its brands. She began her career in operations by working at the front desk. Then, for the next 8 years, she worked in positions related to inside and outside multiproperty sales, generating mostly transient and extended-stay business. Her responsibilities in these sales positions included assisting potential guests who contacted the hotel

for information about group meetings. She booked the business, handled details, and communicated the guests' needs to the operations staff that delivered the services. Her outside sales responsibilities involved identifying strategic ways to find business that fit available times within the hotel. Direct sales calls, prospecting, and maintaining decision-maker relationships were her main functions.

Her next position involved revenue management. These responsibilities included yielding and managing room inventory to maximize revenue-based demand. Analysis of historical trends, current knowledge of market conditions, and awareness of competitive pricing were critical parts of her position as revenue manager.

Most recently, she has served in sales and marketing positions with Marriott's Owner and Franchise Services Division. In this position, she has done three openings for Marriott's select-service and extended-stay brands (Courtyard, Fairfield Inn, Residence Inn, SpringHill Suites, and Towneplace Suites). She has helped with preopening sales and marketing in domestic hotels across the country in major and smaller markets. For example, in 2001 she assisted with 32 hotel openings; in 2002, her work involved 23 property openings. Each opening involves two days of preopening and one day of postopening assistance for a follow-up visit. She also assists with planning and research conference calls between the pre- and postopening visits.

In Anastasia's present position, she consults with owners and franchisees about preopening sales and marketing efforts, helps them to gain access to Marriott resources, and helps with pricing and monitoring the properties' opening business from a revpar index perspective. She uses the Smith Travel Report to measure the success of a new hotel from a market share perspective in addition to topline sales. This provides a benchmark for salespersons to gauge their results against their competition.

When asked about an unforgettable moment in her career, her response is unusual: "One time we visited clients and potential customers dressed up as squirrels. We passed out bags of peanuts that said, 'We'd go nuts for your business!' I know this is silly, but people still talk about it today, 5 years after we made the site visits" (and, most importantly, we secured business as a result of our persistence, humor, and good nature).

Anastasia becomes more serious when she discusses the most significant challenges facing her segment of the industry: "The most significant challenge in hotel sales is increased competition in overbuilt markets that challenge properties to compete for business and their fair share of room nights. These issues are being addressed through an increased focus on each property's direct sales (everybody at the property sells!), shifting share away from the competition, and gaining a much sharper sense of revenue and rooms inventory management."

Anastasia was asked about what, if anything, she would do differently in her career: "I would have spent more time in operations and gained the experience of being a general manager for a property at a younger age. Successful experience in that position increases one's later credibility in the industry."

Anastasia has some great advice for young people considering a career in hospitality: "Diversify your experience! My best advice to persons considering a career in hotel sales, marketing, and revenue management is to obtain a solid understanding of the entire organization for which they work. Persons must understand their role thoroughly, be great team players, and be open to learning and experiencing areas of the hospitality industry outside of their own segment."

LODGING INDUSTRY POSITIONS

An increasingly wide variety of all types of positions is available in the lodging industry. Exhibit 7 identifies many of these positions on a by-function basis. Some require highly specialized and technical skills, for

OBJECTIVE 7
Review the wide range of positions within which one may work in the lodging industry.

Hotels in airport locations are popular with business travelers.

Getty Images, Inc.-Photodisc, Jack Hollingsworth photographer

Accounting and Financial Management
Accounting Supervisor
Accounts Payable Clerk
Accounts Payable Supervisor
Accounts Receivable Clerk
Accounts Receivable Supervisor
Assistant Controller
Corporate Controller
Credit Manager
Director of Finance and Administration
Director, Purchasing Department
Hotel Controller
Night Auditor
Payroll Accountant
Payroll Assistant
Payroll Clerk
Payroll Supervisor
Purchasing Manager
Vice-president, Chief Financial Officer

Rooms Division and Facilities
Assistant Houseperson
Assistant Parking Facilities Manager
Assistant Reservations Manager
Automobile Valet
Bell Captain
Bell Staff
Cashier
Chauffeur
Coat Check Attendant
Concierge
Customer Service Representative
Electrician
Engineering Supervisor
Executive Housekeeper
Front-office Cashier
Front-office Manager
Groundskeeper
Guest Service Manager
Hotel Assistant Housekeeping Director
Hotel Front-desk Agent
Hotel Front-office Manager
Hotel General Cashier
Hotel Reservations Operator
Hotel Switchboard Operator
Inspector
Landscapers
Laundry Attendant
Laundry Manager
Linen and Uniform Attendant
Linen Distribution Attendant
Linen Room Supervisor

Lobby Attendant
Mail Information Clerk
Night Clerks
Night Manager
Night Supervisor
Package Room Personnel
Parking Facilities Attendant
Parking Facilities Manager
Receptionist
Reservations Clerk
Reservations Manager
Room Attendant
Rooms Division Manager
Seamstress
Security Director
Security Guard
Security Technician
Security and Loss Prevention Manager
Supply Clerks
Storeroom Person
Valet Parking Attendant
Vice-president, Operations

Food and Beverage
Assistant Baker
Assistant Banquet Chef
Assistant Banquet Manager
Assistant Beverage Director
Assistant Broiler and Grill Cook
Assistant Executive Steward
Assistant Food and Beverage Director
Assistant Fry Cook
Assistant Pantry Person
Assistant Pastry Chef
Assistant Restaurant Manager
Assistant Service Cook
Assistant Soup and Vegetable Cook
Baker
Banquet Assistant Cook
Banquet Bartender
Banquet Beverage Runner
Banquet Beverage Server
Banquet Busperson
Banquet Captain
Banquet Chef
Banquet Cook
Banquet Houseperson
Banquet Runner
Banquet Server
Banquet Steward
Bartenders
Beverage Manager
Beverage Runner
Broiler Cook

Busperson
Cashier
Catering Director
Catering Manager
Counter Person
Counter Server
Counter Supervisor
Dietary Aide
Dietitian
Dining Manager
Dining Room Manager
Director, Dietary Department
Dishwasher
Executive Chef
Executive Steward
Food and Beverage Controller
Food and Beverage Director
Fry and Sauté Cook
Head Broiler and Grill Cook
Head Cashier
Head Dishwasher
Head Fry Cook
Head Houseperson, Banquets
Head Pantry Person
Head Room Service Cook
Head Soup and Vegetable Cook
Head Steward
Hotel Food and Beverage Controller
Kitchen Attendant
Kitchen Manager
Kitchen Supervisor
Lounge and Bar Manager
Mâitre d'
Night Steward
Pantry Cook
Pantry Preparation Person
Pastry Chef
Pastry Cook
Receiving Clerk
Restaurant Manager
Room Service Attendant
Room Service Busperson
Room Service Manager
Service Bartender
Serving Line Attendant
Sommelier
Soup and Sauce Cook
Sous Chef
Steward
Steward's Runner
Vice-president, Food and Beverage
Waiter or Waitress

Human Resources
Manager, Equal Employment Opportunity

EXHIBIT 7
Lodging Industry Positions
Courtesy of the American Hotel & Lodging Association. www.ahla.com.

Personnel Assistant	National Sales Manager	Vice-president, Hotel Development
Personnel and Human Resources Manager	Promotion and Public Relations Specialist	**Activities**
Personnel Specialist	Regional Director of Sales and Marketing	Assistant Golf Professional
Quality Assurance Manager	Research and Statistical Manager	Assistant Tennis Professional
Training Manager	Sales Manager	Caddie
Vice-president, Human Resources	Vice-president, Sales and Marketing	Entertainer
		Golf Professional
Sales and Marketing		Golf Shop Salesperson
Assistant Vice-president, Sales and Marketing	**Information Technology**	Lifeguard
Catering Sales Representative	Manager, Information Technology	Recreation Specialist
Clerical Staff	Programmer and Analyst	Ski Instructor
Communications Manager	System Programmer	Social Activities Manager
Conference Coordinator	Systems Analyst	Spa Director
Convention Services Coordinator		Swimming Instructor
Convention Services Manager	**Leadership**	Swimming Pool Manager
Director of Communications	Assistant General Manager	Tennis Professional
Director of Convention Sales	Division President	Tour Escort
Director, Public Relations	Innkeeper Manager, Bed and Breakfast	
Director, Sales and Marketing	Hotel General Manager	**Other Positions**
Editor	Owner and Operator	Administrative Secretary
Graphics Manager	President, CEO	Association Manager
Group Sales Manager	Vice-president, Administration	Audiovisual Specialist
Group Sales Representative ·	Vice-president, Business Development	Translator
Market Researcher	Vice-president, Franchising	
Meeting and Conference Planner		

EXHIBIT 7
continued

example, many of the positions within the accounting and financial management areas and those within information technology. Others, such as those involving activities, require significant physical skills. Numerous positions require basic management knowledge and experience; for example, note the many management positions within food and beverage. Still other positions are entry-level (nonmanagement) positions that could represent one's first position in a career ladder "up the organization" to more responsible positions.

Russell MacMasters © Dorling Kindersley, Courtesy of the Bellagio Hotel, Las Vegas

Lobby of Bellagio Hotel in Las Vegas, Nevada

What are your interests? The wide range of positions noted in Exhibit 7 suggests that there are probably many ways to match your interests with challenging and rewarding positions within the lodging industry.

SUMMARY OF CHAPTER LEARNING OBJECTIVES

1. **Review the range of lodging property alternatives available to travelers.**
   Travelers can choose from destination resorts, full-service hotels, limited-service hotels, and sleeping rooms, along with seemingly innumerable other variations within this range.

2. **Discuss three common ways to classify lodging properties.**
   Lodging properties can be classified by location, rate, and size.

3. **Describe basic characteristics that all lodging properties share.**
   Common characteristics of all lodging properties include the following:
   - Emphasis on safety, cleanliness, and service
   - Inseparability of manufacture and sales
   - Perishability
   - Repetitiveness
   - Labor intensivity

4. **Explain common hotel ownership and management alternatives.**
   A hotel property can be franchised or non-franchised. If it is affiliated with a franchise, it can be owned by an independent investor or by the franchise company (franchiser). Regardless of ownership, a franchised property can be operated by an independent owner or operator, by the franchise company (franchiser), or by a management company. If a hotel is not franchised, it will have independent ownership and can be operated by the independent owner or by a management company.

5. **Describe how basic hotel functions are organized and integrated.**
   With the exception of limited-service properties (which do not have food and beverage departments), someone in the property must be responsible for front office and rooms (including bell service, reservations, switchboard, housekeeping, and front desk), human resources, engineering and maintenance, purchasing, security, and marketing and sales. Additionally, an accounting specialist is needed. As the size of the property increases, persons in specialized positions are hired to assume responsibility for increasingly more specific tasks within each function.

6. **List challenges (opportunities) confronting today's hotel industry.**
   Hotels are confronted with four basic types of challenges:
   - *Operating.* Labor shortages, cost containment, and increased competition
   - *Marketing.* Market segmentation and overlapping brands, increased guest sophistication, and the need for increased amenities
   - *Technological.* Interactive reservation systems, guest-room innovations, data mining, and yield management
   - *Economic.* Dependence on the nation's economy, globalization, and terrorism and safety

7. **Review the wide range of positions within which one may work in the lodging industry.**
   The chapter lists more than 200 positions that are applicable to the widely diverse lodging industry.

MASTERING YOUR KNOWLEDGE

Discuss the following questions.

1. What is your definition of the term *hotel*? (Provide a general definition that will apply to each type of hotel property discussed in this chapter.)
2. Provide a basic description for each type of traveler who would select a hotel in the location and rate categories noted in Exhibit 2.
3. What, if any, importance does a traveler place on the number of rooms (size) in a hotel when he or she makes a selection decision?
4. What are the five most important factors that you consider when you are selecting a hotel for an overnight stay? What factors would be important to the wealthiest of travelers? To those business travelers on a modest expense account? To families traveling with small children on a visit to see relatives?
5. If you work or have worked at a hotel, describe its affiliation, ownership, and operation according to the factors described in Exhibit 4.

FEEDBACK FROM THE REAL WORLD

Our real-world advice comes from Liana Clark, Director of Sales and Marketing for the Comfort Inns and Suites Downtown, in Chicago, Illinois.

Liana brings many years of hands-on experience to the task of answering the following questions. She began her hotel management career as a reservations sales agent. She then held progressively more responsible positions during her 9 years of experience in the positions of sales manager, director of new hotel sales support and, currently, director of sales and marketing.

We asked Liana to respond to the questions posed at the beginning of this chapter:

What exactly do the average travelers looking for a hotel room for a business or pleasure trip know about the hotel brands that they see and read about?

They do not know which brands are operated by which companies, nor do they know how different brands operated by the same company have been segmented. To help counter this, organizations such as Marriott and Choice are increasingly advertising their brand or organization affiliation: Fairfield Inns by Marriott, Sleep Inn by Choice, and Hampton Inns by Hilton are examples. What travelers do know is whether they prefer a specific brand based on their experience with that brand. They also know that they have an incredible amount of choice as they make lodging decisions.

How exactly do they decide where to stay on their next trip requiring overnight accommodation?

Previously, a decision was often based on "location, location, location." Today it is "rate, rate, rate." Of course, safety and cleanliness are absolutely critical, and no professional hotelier will compromise standards applicable to these concerns as a tactic to reduce rates. A traveler's definition of a fair rate considers the perception of value: Is what I receive worth what I must pay for it? Increasingly, business travelers are interested in perks such as airline miles, room upgrades, and other amenities offered to frequent guests as part of their organization's frequent-traveler program.

How do the guests' experiences at a specific property influence their interest in staying at the property again when they return to that location or in another hotel with the same brand when they travel to another location?

If guests have an enjoyable stay, they are very likely to return if they are in the area and more likely to utilize the same brand when they travel to another location. (By the way, there is no such thing as a "bad hotel stay"; visits are either enjoyable or horrible!) Therefore, all staff in a hotel must be involved in the business of relationship building. All employees influence the guests and decisions about where they will stay on their next trip. Lodging organizations and the individual units that comprise them need repeat business. To do this, guests must know that they will receive the same enjoyable experience with each visit. To best assure this long-term relationship, hotel managers must do several things:

- Find out about any problems and resolve them while the guests are there; guests are very forgiving when they know that you care and will address their concerns.
- Empower staff to take care of problems. The old saying "Sales personnel get the business; everyone else keeps it!" is very correct.
- Recognize that guests want service; hiring the right employees, providing effective training, and allowing staff to utilize guest-friendly procedures are great tactics to help to ensure high-quality service.
- Recognize that a guest's perception of one unit within a brand affects his or her attitude about all units in the brand: "As the brand goes, so goes the individual property."

6. What are some of the tasks that must be performed by persons with the responsibility for the functions noted in Exhibit 5?

7. How do cost centers (marketing, engineering, accounting, human resources, and security) assist the hotel's revenue departments (rooms, food and beverage, telephone, and fitness and recreation facilities)?

8. What do you think the general manager and his or her staff in a well-managed property in your community can do to address the following challenges (opportunities) noted in this chapter?

- Operating
- Marketing
- Technological
- Economic

9. If possible, ask management staff in local properties about other challenges (opportunities) that confront them and their property?

10. Think about your personal interests. Consider how they might be addressed in the positions listed in Exhibit 7. What are some positions that might potentially be of interest to you because the tasks that they require might be among those that you enjoy doing?

LEARN FROM THE INTERNET

1. Check out the following websites:
   - Hilton Hotels Corporation: www.hilton.com
   - Marriott Hotels, Resorts & Suites: www.marriott.com
   - Choice Hotels: www.choicehotels.com

   How do these organizations differentiate the numerous brands of properties that they franchise or operate? What, if any, emphasis (information) do these organizations place on a la carte dining and conventions and banquet food-services?

2. Check out the website for the American Hotel & Lodging Association (www.ahla.com). Review current data that describe the breadth of the U.S. lodging industry.

3. Review the following websites and learn what's happening in the lodging industry today.
   - Hotel Online: www.hotel.on-line.com
   - Hotel Business: www.hotelbusiness.com
   - AH&LA Smart Brief: www.smartbrief.com/ahla
   - Hotel News Resource: www.hotelnewsresource.com

KEY HOSPITALITY TERMS

The following terms were explained in this chapter. Review the definitions of any words with which you are unfamiliar. Begin to utilize them as you expand your vocabulary as a hospitality professional.

niche marketing
hotel
resorts
full-service hotel
limited-service hotel
extended-stay hotel
sleeping room
hostel
rack rate
labor intensive
flag
brand
mom and pop hotels

franchise
franchiser
franchisee
entrepreneur
investor
management company
overbuilt
market segmentation
data mining
yield management
hotel occupancy rate
globalization
terrorism

Overview: Profit-Making (Commercial) Foodservices

PhotoLibrary.com, Roel Loopers photographer

A common dining area in a shopping mall

CHAPTER LEARNING OBJECTIVES

After studying this chapter you will be able to:

1. Describe the basic types of commercial foodservices.

2. Discuss the marketing- and operations-related concerns that must be addressed as a menu is planned.

3. Review each process that must be managed in a comprehensive foodservices system after the menu has been planned: procurement, receiving, storing, issuing, production (preparing, cooking, holding), and delivery to guest (serving, service).

4. List traits of professional food and beverage servers.

5. Explain challenges (opportunities) that must be addressed by commercial foodservice operations.

From Chapter 10 of *Discovering Hospitality and Tourism: The World's Greatest Industry*, Second Edition, Jack D. Ninemeier, Joe Perdue. Copyright © 2008 by Pearson Education, Inc. Published by Pearson Prentice Hall. All rights reserved.

FEEDBACK FROM THE REAL WORLD

There is a saying that "It all starts with the menu!" Many experts in all segments of the foodservices industry believe this to be true.

- Why do some experts say that the financial success of a foodservice operation begins with the menu?
- What are some tactics of effective menu planning that can be most helpful?
- Who should be part of a restaurant's menu planning team? What role does each member play?

- What are the most difficult challenges confronting menu planners as they implement changes in an existing menu?

  As you read this chapter, think about the answers to these questions and then get some feedback from the real world at the end of the chapter.

OBJECTIVE 1
Describe the basic types of commercial foodservices.

commercial foodservices foodservices offered in hotels, restaurants, and other organizations whose primary purpose for existence involves generation of profits from the sale of food and beverage products

noncommercial foodservices (contract management company-operated) a type of noncommercial foodservice operation in which the program is managed and operated by a for-profit management company

restaurant a foodservice business that generates all (or most) of its revenues from the sale of food and beverage products

freestanding (restaurant) a restaurant that is the sole occupant of a building; freestanding restaurants typically have dedicated parking spaces for their guests

upscale (high check average) restaurants foodservice operations that offer the highest quality of food and beverage products and services; also called *luxury* or *gourmet restaurants*

You have learned that there are two basic types of foodservice operations. One type, **commercial foodservices,** is offered by those who wish to generate a profit from the sale of food and/or beverage items. The second type, **noncommercial foodservices,** is provided by organizations that exist for another reason (such as education or healthcare) but, as part of what they do, must provide foodservices to their constituencies and/or employees. In this chapter we will examine commercial foodservice operations.

OVERVIEW OF COMMERCIAL FOODSERVICES

Exhibit 1 shows the four basic types of foodservice operations in the commercial foodservices segment of the hospitality industry.

Restaurants

Restaurants are individual foodservice businesses that generate all or most of their revenues from the sale of food and beverage products. Some restaurants are **freestanding;** others occupy (share) space with other businesses.

There are four basic types of restaurants:

- **Upscale (high check average) restaurants.** Also called luxury or, sometimes, gourmet, these restaurants offer the highest quality of food and beverage products and service. Most serve alcoholic beverages and many offer extensive wine lists. They are typically relatively small and frequently are owned or managed by entrepreneurs. The number of **guests per labor hour** is typically lower than for other types of restaurants.
- **Casual-service (midscale) restaurants.** These moderately priced properties generally offer a fuller (wide range) but less formal menu than do their upscale counterparts. These properties also offer a less formal atmosphere and, often, an ethnic or theme environment. Many restaurants in this category serve alcoholic beverages. The number of guests per labor hour is typically more than in upscale (high check average) properties, but much less than for quick-service properties.

GOOD NEWS! GOOD NEWS! GOOD NEWS!

At their most basic levels, the principles of managing commercial and noncommercial foodservices operations are much more similar than they are dissimilar. While language may differ (for example, managers are responsible for commercial operations, and administrators are in charge of their noncommercial counterparts), the basic principles of managing the resources of the food and beverage operation are almost identical. For example, employees must be managed. Principles of recruitment, selection, orientation, and training, along with ongoing supervisory tactics involving motivation, performance appraisal, facilitating teams, and the consistent reinforcement of quality standards, are the same. As a second example, managers in operations of all types must, first, plan menus that focus on those being served. Then products that are required by the menu must be purchased, received, stored, issued, produced, and served and, as well, principles involving sanitation, safety, and cleanup are the same.

Why is the similarity between the two basic types of foodservice operations good news? Students studying the basics of foodservices may not know the industry segment in which they will be initially employed. However, this is not a problem, because the knowledge they learn and skills they acquire can be applied in any segment. Second, foodservice managers have increased freedom to move between industry segments as their careers evolve. As they do so, they will bring with them the knowledge and experience learned in earlier positions, regardless of whether previous work was in the commercial or noncommercial sector.

It is, indeed, good news that there are universal practices of management that apply throughout the world of foodservices. These are among the topics discussed in this chapter.

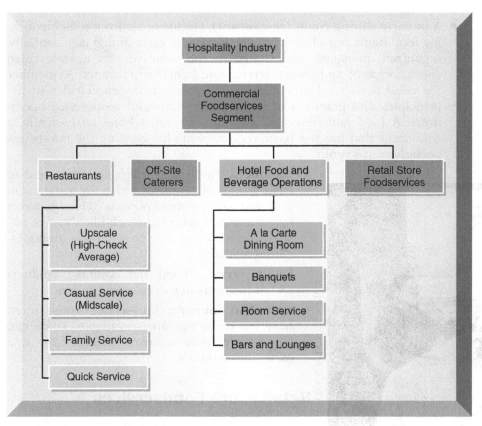

guests per labor hour the number of guests served per each hour of labor incurred by the property; if 10 hours of labor are incurred on a day when 50 guests are served, there are 5 guests per labor hour (50 guests ÷ 10 hours)

casual-service (midscale) restaurant a moderately priced restaurant offering a full, informal menu often with an ethnic theme or environment; alcoholic beverages are frequently served

EXHIBIT 1
Types of Commercial Foodservices

family-service restaurant a restaurant featuring table (and frequently counter) service and offering a wide range of value-priced menu items that generally does not offer alcoholic beverages

comfort foods familiar menu item prepared in a way that is reminiscent of how it was served during the customer's childhood or how the customer would prepare it at home; also called *homestyle*

California-style menu a menu featuring items traditionally available for breakfast, lunch, and dinner that are offered throughout the time the property is open for business

quick-service restaurant an operation that provides a limited menu and limited service (generally self-serve at counters or through vehicle drive-throughs) with low prices; also called *limited menu* or *fast-food restaurant*

off-site caterer a foodservice business that produces food items at a commissary (central kitchen) for transport to remote locations for service; some caterers also offer on-site banquet (dining) areas

commissary a kitchen that produces food for at least some off-site consumption; also called *central kitchen*

a la carte dining room (restaurant) a foodservice operation in which guests order from a menu featuring individually priced items

- **Family-service restaurants.** These restaurants appeal to families and others desiring familiar or **comfort foods.** Many feature a **California-style menu** in which items traditionally offered for breakfast, lunch, and dinner are available throughout the time the property is open for business. Most family-service restaurants do not serve alcoholic beverages.
- **Quick-service restaurants.** Often called limited-menu or fast-food operations, these operations typically provide a limited menu and service (often self-service at counters or drive through without entering the building) with low check averages. The number of guests per labor hour is typically much higher than in upscale, casual-service, or family-service restaurant properties.

Off-Site Caterers

Off-site caterers are businesses that produce food items at a **commissary** (central kitchen) for transport to remote locations for service. In practice, this description is less clear. Some caterers also offer on-site banquet (dining) areas. A distinguishing characteristic is that the majority of an off-site caterer's business comes from the sale of a preselected menu to relatively large groups of people in a banquet-type setting.

Hotel Food and Beverage Operations

You have learned that hotels offering food and beverage services are called full-service properties. The following are the four basic types of foodservices offered by these properties.

- **A la carte dining room (restaurant).** Guests order from a menu offering food items priced individually. Hotel a la carte dining is, essentially, organized, managed, and staffed in the same way as upscale (high check average) and casual-service (midscale) restaurants. Remember the good news we learned earlier: there are many similarities in the principles and practices of managing commercial foodservice operations. A food and beverage operation within a hotel is, basically, a restaurant that has the basic requirements for meeting the guests' expectations at a profit.
- **Banquets.** These are meal functions served to large groups of people in which the same menu is served to all or most persons. (Hotel banquet operations are managed much like those of off-site caterers when they have on-site dining facilities available.)
- **Room service.** Food and beverage products served to guests in their sleeping rooms.
- **Bars and lounges.** Full-service hotels often have bar or lounge areas available. These can be adjacent to or in areas different from a la carte dining rooms.

Retail Store Foodservices

Businesses such as convenience stores, grocery and food markets, and gasoline stations sometimes generate some (a relatively small percentage) of

Tourists spend a significant amount of money on food and beverage purchases.

Shaen Adey © Dorling Kindersley

KNOW COMMON MENU TERMS

The word *menu* is French and means a *detailed list*. The menu, then, provides readers with a list of available food items. There are several common types of menus:

A la carte menu. The phrase *a la carte* implies individually priced; an a la carte menu lists food items that are separately priced. The charge is then based on the prices of the items that the guest orders.

Table d'hôte menu. This term basically implies *all at one price*. The guest charge does not vary based on what is selected. Some hotels and restaurants offer, for example, a Sunday or holiday buffet for a specified (fixed) price. The items offered on this buffet are a table d'hôte menu because the guest is charged a fixed price that is unrelated to the specific buffet items selected.

Cyclical menu. The word *cyclical* refers to a cycle; the foodservice operation may, for example, plan a 28-day menu, which is then repeated. (Cycle menus are most typically offered by noncommercial foodservices, but may also be used by commercial buffets.)

Du jour menu. Also called *daily specials*, the phrase *du jour* means *of the day*. Many foodservice operations offer daily specials (du jour items) in addition to their regular menu items.

their revenues from the sale of food and beverage products intended for immediate consumption.

Note: While technically not considered retail stores, licensed street vendors and persons operating unlicensed store-front or street-corner businesses also sell food and beverage products to the public with the hope of making a profit.

CHECK IT OUT

A central theme of this book is that the travel and tourism industry and the numerous segments of hospitality that are part of it are changing at an increasingly fast pace. Here's another example: Entrepreneurs in an ever-increasing number of locations around the country have introduced a new concept in which customers electronically order a specified number of different meals. They then visit a *food assembly center* (commercial kitchen) and follow recipes at work stations that have been supplied with the ingredients needed for the meals they have ordered. For example, frozen chicken breasts, chopped onions, and seasonings may be required for a chicken entrée they have prechosen. The customers can assemble these ingredients to prepare a meal that will just need to be transported home for the oven or freezer. All applicable ingredients will have been peeled and chopped, so the customer does not need to have a knife, cook an item, or wash dishes or pots and pans.

Want to learn more? Go to www.supersuppers.com.

MENU PLANNING: A CRITICAL FOODSERVICE PROCESS

We noted at the beginning of this chapter that the management of any type of foodservice operation involves similar processes. These are reviewed in Exhibit 2. Each process is important, and basic management principles must consistently be utilized to assure that the foodservices operation is successful.

We will begin our study of foodservice processes where they begin: with the menu. Industry experts agree that "it all starts with the menu!" Menus must offer items desired by those being served (*guests* in commercial

banquet a food and beverage event in which all or most guests are served items on a preselected menu

room service food and beverage products served to guests in their sleeping rooms

retail store foodservices businesses such as convenience stores, grocery and food markets, and gasoline stations that generate some (a relatively small percentage) of their revenues from the sale of food and beverage products intended for immediate consumption

a la carte menu a menu in which food items making up the entire meal are sold at a fixed price

table d'hôte (menu selections) a menu in which food items are sold at a fixed price

cyclical menu a menu in which food items rotate according to a planned schedule

du jour menu a menu in which some or all food items are changed daily

This person is enjoying his breakfast at a family service restaurant before beginning work.

PhotoEdit Inc., Robert Brenner photographer

OBJECTIVE 2
Discuss the marketing and operations-related concerns that must be addressed as a menu is planned.

marketing the business from the perspectives of those who consume the products or services provided by the operation

competitor any business attempting to attract the same guests as one's own business

foodservices). Foodservice managers must use **marketing** principles to learn what guests will buy and at what price to effectively differentiate their business from that of their **competitors.**

Menu Planning

Our study of commercial foodservice management begins with the menu. While being planned, it must focus on the guests and address operating concerns.

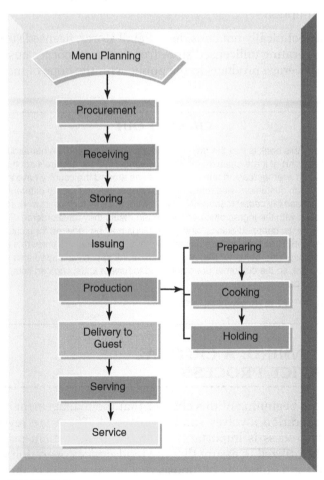

EXHIBIT 2
Overview of Foodservice Processes

66

Entire books have been written on the topic of **menu planning.**[1] However, two of the most important considerations relate to the guests (what they want and will pay for) and to the resources available to the foodservices manager to provide menu items that meet the operation's required quality standards.

Menu Planning: Focus on the Guests

The guests are the most important consideration when planning the menu. It is critical to determine, first, the menu items that will be of interest to guests. What guest-related factors should be considered as the menu is planned? Exhibit 3 helps to answer this question. You will note that there are many factors, including these:

Getty Images, Inc.-Photodisc, Steve Mason photographer

Businesspersons check out their menu in the a la carte dining room of a hotel.

menu planning the process of determining the food and beverage items to be offered by the foodservice operation that will most please the guests while generating acceptable revenue and/or cost objectives

- *Purpose of visit.* Guests dining in a commercial foodservice operation are there for a reason. They want an experience that is in concert with the purpose of their visit. They may just be hungry (for example, when travelers on an interstate highway stop at a roadside family-service restaurant), or they may be celebrating a special occasion (such as hotel guests who have successfully negotiated business arrangements), or a

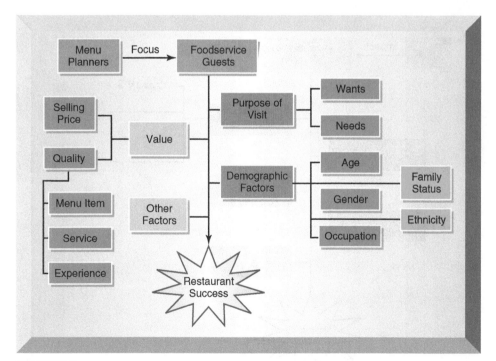

EXHIBIT 3
Menu Planning: Focus on the Guests

---

[1]See, for example, Jack Ninemeier and David Hayes. *Menu Planning, Design, and Evaluation.* Richmond, CA: McCutchan Publishing Corporation, 2003.

couple or a family may visit an upscale restaurant for a birthday event. Some commercial menu planners also consider their guests' nutritional needs (although these are more likely a concern of noncommercial menu planners, who must consider nutritional requirements for those receiving all or most meals from the foodservice operation).

value (menu item) the guest's perception of the selling price of a menu item relative to the quality of the menu item, service, and dining experience

- **Value** is the concept that relates to a guest's perception of the selling price of an item relative to the quality of the menu item, service, and dining experience. Guests desire to "receive what they pay for"; they do not want to feel cheated and, increasingly, many guests will pay more for a higher perceived quality of dining experience.

demographic factors factors such as age, marital status, gender, ethnicity, and occupation that can help to describe a person

- **Demographic factors** are concerns, such as the potential guests' age, marital status, gender, ethnicity, and occupation, that are likely to influence menu item preferences. Efforts to answer the question "Who will be visiting the restaurant?" will be of significant help in the menu planning task.
- *Other factors.* Social factors such as income, education, and wealth may influence what a potential guest desires in a commercial foodservices experience. Other factors such as life-style and even personality (for example, the extent to which one desires to try new foods) can also be relevant to restaurant selection decisions.

repeat business revenues generated from guests returning to a commercial hospitality operation as a result of positive experiences on previous visits

The goal of every menu planner is to offer items that please the guests. When this is done, guests are more likely to provide **repeat business.** At the same time, they will tell their friends, and **word-of-mouth advertising** helps the restaurant to remain successful.

word-of-mouth advertising informal conversations between persons as they discuss their positive or negative experiences when visiting a hospitality operation

Menu Planning: Focus on Operational Concerns

Exhibit 4 highlights some of the ways that the menu, once planned, affects the foodservice operation. Let's review these operational aspects of menu planning more closely.

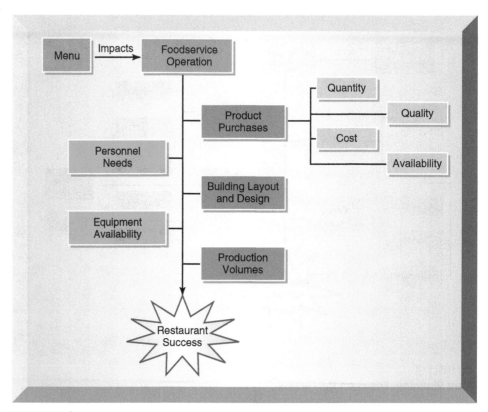

EXHIBIT 4
Operational Aspects of Menu Planning

- *Product purchases.* All ingredients required to produce all menu items must be consistently available in the required quantity and quality and at the right cost. If this does not occur, guests may be disappointed because desired items are not available. There will also likely be significant operational disruptions as alternative menu items will need to be produced.
- *Personnel needs.* Staff members must be available to produce and serve the items required by the menu. Consider differences in the experience and skill levels necessary, for example, for an effective order taker at a quick-service counter and a server performing tableside flaming activities in an upscale (high check average) restaurant.
- *Building layout and design.* If, for example, the menu specifies a help-yourself salad bar, the space must be available for the serving counters and to accommodate guest **traffic** in the salad bar area. As a second example, a menu featuring fresh-baked breads requires the property to have the allowable square feet necessary for an on-site bake shop (or, at least, bake ovens).
- *Equipment availability.* If the menu requires fried foods and grilled items, for example, the proper number of deep-fat fryers and grills will be necessary based on anticipated business volume. The space needed to place the equipment and obtain adequate ventilation as dictated by local or other fire safety codes must also be considered.
- *Production volumes.* A properly planned menu anticipates business volume. For example, it is difficult (impossible?) for a kitchen to have one oven and to produce baked appetizers, entrées, desserts, and breads in any significant volume. The menu planner in this operation must be careful about the potential to **overload** the oven.

traffic guests and/or employees who occupy or move within a specified area

overload (equipment) the act of requiring equipment to produce more than it is reasonably capable of producing

DID YOU KNOW?

Traditionally, nutritional concerns have been considered to be most important in the noncommercial segment of the food service industry. Today, however, nutrition is becoming more of a concern for the dining-out public.

There is evidence that oversized portions contribute to obesity. Simply stated, when many persons are offered larger-sized portions than they might desire, they will consume them. Unfortunately, when larger-than-necessary meals are routinely consumed, weight gain can be significant.

A study directed by ARAMARK Corporation of approximately 5,300 adults found that:

- Americans eat away from home an average of 5.6 times weekly.
- More than 50 percent of restaurant guests desire half-portion entrées, and they would be more likely to order healthy items if they were part of a value-priced combo meal.
- More than 80 percent of restaurant guests believe restaurants should make nutrition information available for menu items, and they would like to have healthy items highlighted separately on the menu.

It appears, than, that commercial operators are likely to become more concerned about nutrition as their guests become more interested in it.

Source: Nanci Hellmich. "Bigger Portions Will Be Eaten" and "Diners Want More Info and Smaller Entrées." *USA Today*, October 20, 2005.

OTHER FOODSERVICE PROCESSES

After the menu is planned, other processes must be effectively managed to assure that the foodservice operation will be successful. Exhibit 2 indicates, in sequence, the processes that must occur after the menu is planned. We will review these here.

Product Procurement

food (menu) items the food selections that the menu specifies will be available for sale to guests

ingredients the individual components of a food (menu) item; for example, flour and sugar are two ingredients in bread

procurement the process of determining the right quality and quantity of all food products and ingredients that should be purchased and of selecting the supplier who can provide these items at the right price and at the right time

quality (of a food item) suitability for intended use; the closer an item comes to being suitable for its intended use, the more appropriate the product's quality

theft to steal all of something at one time

pilferage to steal small quantities of some item over a period of time

stockout the condition that arises when a food or beverage item needed for production is not available on-site because it is not in inventory

value (procurement) the relationship between price paid to a supplier and the quality of product, supplier information, and service received

After the menu is planned, the **food items** and **ingredients** needed to produce it will be known. These, then, are the items that must be purchased. Exhibit 5 identifies five special concerns in **procurement.**

Quality is, perhaps, the single most important concern when purchasing food and beverage items. The term *quality* requires the purchaser to consider the intended use of the items; the closer an item comes to being suitable for the intended use, the more appropriate the product's quality. Consider, for example, maraschino cherries, which might be required both at the bar for a drink garnish and in the kitchen as an ingredient in a fruit gelatin salad. A whole cherry with stem (at a relatively higher cost) might be required at the bar because it is most attractive; chopped cherry pieces (at a relatively lower cost) might be used in a fruit gelatin salad. It is not possible to think about quality without, first, considering how the product will be used.

A second very important procurement factor relates to the quantity of items needed. If too much product is available, money that could be utilized for other purposes is tied up in inventory. Also, the quality of some products can deteriorate in storage, space must be available to house excess inventory, and there is increased chance of **theft** and **pilferage.** By contrast, when an inadequate quantity of product is available, **stockouts** occur. Guests can be disappointed because a desired item is not available, and production (operating) concerns can arise if substitute items must be produced.

The *right* price refers to the cost of a food item or ingredient that provides a good **value** for the foodservice operation. Wise purchasers realize that more than just a product is purchased from a supplier. They also receive product information and service from the supplier. It is the perceived value of these three factors (product quality, information, and service) that should most influence the purchase decision.

The right time for product delivery must also be considered. The supplier offering a good deal on an item needed for tomorrow's banquet that is not delivered until next week is obviously not providing value to the

This happy couple is celebrating a special occasion in a restaurant.

Getty Images, Inc.-Photodisc, Robert Koene photographer

MENU PLANNING: FOCUS ON MENU DESIGN

After the menu is planned, it must be designed. In a quick-service restaurant, a menu board or other signage may announce available items. In a banquet provided by a restaurant, hotel, or commercial caterer, there may be a simple menu card at the guest table (if the meal is served to seated guests) or, alternatively, name cards identifying items may be available by each help-yourself serving dish on a buffet line.

In most upscale and casual-service restaurants and in hotel room-service operations, a menu is made available to guests. Traditionally, the purpose of providing a menu was to simply inform guests about available items. Today, however, menus are seen as powerful in-house selling tools. They are designed to influence and encourage guests to select items that are popular (the guests like them) and profitable (the foodservice operation desires to sell them). A process called **menu engineering** can be utilized with almost any type of menu, including menu boards and even those utilized by non-commercial foodservices without selling prices, to take advantage of the selling opportunities that an effectively designed menu can provide.

purchaser. Purchasers who must frequently **expedite** orders should look first at their operation to determine if there is a problem with the flow of information between production, storeroom, and purchasing personnel. In the absence of these problems, they may be wise to select suppliers who can consistently deliver required products on a timely basis.

As noted in Exhibit 5, the right supplier is, then, the one who can consistently deliver the right quality and quantities of product at the right price and at the right time. Some foodservice operations desire to have as few suppliers as possible to eliminate paperwork and to enhance their relationship with suppliers. Other foodservice managers, by contrast, are concerned about making product selection decisions on a by-supplier basis. Whichever of these (or intermediate) approaches is used, the importance of procurement to food-service success cannot be overlooked.

menu engineering the process of menu evaluation that allows menu planners to determine items that are most popular and profitable and to use this information to design menus that emphasize selected items to be sold

expedite (purchasing) the act of facilitating a delivery of food and beverage products previously ordered from suppliers

Receiving, Storing, and Issuing

After products are purchased, they must be received, stored, and issued to production areas. **Receiving** involves the transfer of ownership from the supplier

OBJECTIVE 3
Review each process that must be managed in a comprehensive foodservices system after the menu has been planned: receiving, storing, and issuing.

receiving the transfer of ownership from a supplier to the foodservice operation that occurs when products are delivered to the operation

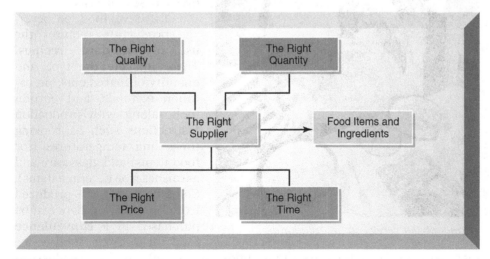

EXHIBIT 5
Five Special Concerns in Procurement

storing the process of holding products under optimal storage conditions until they are needed for production

issuing the process of moving products from storage areas to the point of use (place of production)

production the process of readying products for consumption

standard recipes a written explanation specifying exactly how a food or beverage item should be prepared; a standard recipe lists the quantity of each required ingredient, preparation techniques, portion size and portion tools, and other information required to assure that the item is always prepared the same way

"scratch" (food preparation) the use of individual ingredients to make items available for sale; for example, a stew may be made on-site with vegetables, meat, and other ingredients, and a Bloody Mary mix can be made on-site with tomato juice and seasonings

convenience food food or beverage products that have some labor built into them that otherwise would need to be added on-site; for example, beef stew can be purchased in a ready-to-serve form (just heat it), and a Bloody Mary mix can be purchased ready to pour

make or buy analysis the process of considering quality, costs, and other factors in "scratch" and convenience food alternatives to determine how products should be purchased for the operation

Foodservice operations purchase many items, such as this dishwasher and the dishes being washed, in addition to food and beverage products.

Formal platter service in an outdoor dining area

to the foodservice operation. It occurs when the products are physically delivered. **Storing** is the process of holding products in optimal storage conditions (in a secure space with proper temperature, humidity, and product rotation, for example) until they are needed for production. **Issuing** involves moving products from the storage area to the point of use (the place of production). Basic receiving, storing, and issuing procedures are similar for food products and their beverage counterparts. An overriding concern is that purchased products obviously cost money. These products must be protected until the time of production so that they can be utilized in menu items that are produced at the lowest possible cost.

Production

Production is the process of readying products for consumption. Many people think first about cooks working in the kitchen when they think about production. However, it is also important for systems to be in place for bartenders in bars (beverage production units) as drinks are prepared. In fact, concerns about beverage product and revenue theft at the bar provide great incentives for management staff to implement control procedures that address these concerns.

Effective food or beverage production requires the use of **standard recipes.** These indicate the type and quantity of ingredients, preparation methods, and portion tools, along with production instructions such as cooking times and temperatures (for food items) and glassware and garnishes (for beverage items). Some items may be produced from **"scratch"**; others can be purchased in a **convenience food** form. Chefs, foodservice managers, and/or purchasers should undertake a **make or buy analysis** to determine which items should be made from scratch and/or purchased as a convenience food.

Conversation at a busy restaurant bar

chained recipe a recipe for an item (such as a sauce) that is, itself, an ingredient in another recipe (such as a casserole)

The production of food items generally requires more elaborate and more extensive preparation skills than those for beverages. On a typical menu, the range of food items may require different levels of preparation skills. For example:

- Hamburger patties that must only be grilled or oven baked
- Casserole-type dishes that require cleaning, prepreparing (cutting and chopping), and cooking of numerous ingredients
- Elaborate sauces that may require experience in stock reduction and preparation for a sauce that is itself an ingredient (**chained recipe**) in another menu item

per portion a single serving of food; for example, a portioned hamburger patty

batch cooking the process of preparing smaller quantities of food several times during a serving period, rather than the total number of portions required at the same time

The items produced can be made individually (**per portion**) or in batches. The term *per portion* relates to preparing one portion of a menu item for service. By contrast, **batch cooking** refers to preparing a number of portions of a menu item at the same time. Some ingredients require **preparing** as a first step in production to get them ready for **cooking** (the application of heat). For example, fresh celery will need to be cleaned and chopped if it is an ingredient in a stew. When food items are batch cooked, a final step, **holding,** may be necessary until menu items are served.

preparing steps involved in getting an ingredient ready for cooking or serving; for example, celery must be cleaned and chopped before being cooked in a stew or cleaned and sliced before use on an appetizer tray

cooking applying heat to a food item

holding the task of maintaining food items at proper serving temperature after they are prepared; holding involves keeping hot foods hot and cold foods cold

Guests at a casual-dining restaurant

Product Delivery to Guests

In a table-service operation, food items that have been prepared by cooks are transferred to foodservice personnel, who then serve them to the guests. Bartenders

OBJECTIVE 3
Review each process that must be managed in a comprehensive foodservices system after the menu has been planned: delivery to guest.

COMMON TYPES OF RESTAURANT SERVICE

Prepared food can be presented to guests in several ways:

American (plated) service. Food is preportioned onto plates or other serviceware in the kitchen and is served to guests seated at the table.

Traditional French service. Foods, such as a classic Caesar salad or a flaming steak Diane are, respectively, prepared and cooked in front of the guests at their table.

Russian (platter) service. Food is placed on serviceware in the kitchen and is brought to the guests' table by the server. Individual portions are then placed by the server onto the guests' plates.

English (family) service. Food is placed in serving dishes, brought to the table by the server, and placed on the table so that guests can pass the food items around the table.

Buffet (self-service). Guests help themselves to a variety of food that has been placed on a serving counter.

Counter service. Guests indicate orders to service personnel stationed behind an order counter, who then retrieve food for the guests.

Service styles can be combined in the same meal. For example, a Caesar salad may be prepared tableside (French service), and the entrée may be preplated in the kitchen (American service).

---

service bar a bar in which drinks prepared by bartenders are given to personnel who serve them to guests

serving the process of moving the food or beverage items that have been prepared from production staff to service personnel

service the process of transferring food and beverage products from service staff to guests

preparing drinks in a **service bar** also produce items for transfer to personnel who serve them to guests. The process of moving products from production to service personnel is called **serving.** Service personnel then deliver food and beverage products to guests in a process called **service.**

Systems for food and beverage serving must be effectively designed to minimize bottlenecks in service that can cause lowered food quality (such as cold food) and longer guest waits (for example, when a large volume of slow-to-prepare ice cream drinks hinders the production of other drinks). The speed and manner in which products are delivered to guests is very important: the perceived quality of service is an important factor considered by guests as they evaluate their foodservice experience.

OBJECTIVE 4
List traits of professional food and beverage servers.

TRAITS OF PROFESSIONAL FOOD AND BEVERAGE SERVERS

Professional food and beverage servers must be knowledgeable (for example, about the available food or beverage products and about work tasks required to serve their guests). They must also be skilled (to deliver service meeting the foodservice operation's quality standards). As importantly, professional servers must have an attitude that emphasizes pleasing the guests.

Exhibit 6 describes some of the traits required for professional food and beverage servers. These are important for servers in all operations, including sit-down (table service), cafeteria and buffet operations, walk-up counters and drive-up windows, or any other venue in which food and beverage products can be delivered to guests.

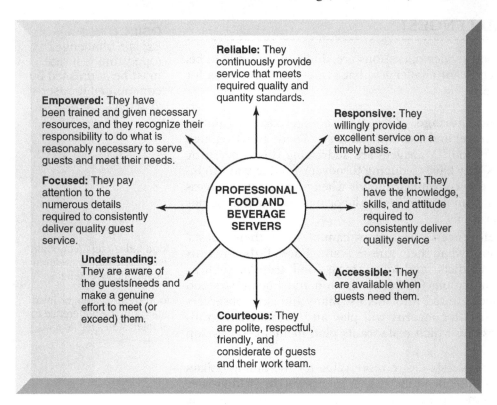

EXHIBIT 6
Traits of Professional Food and Beverage Servers

When reviewing the traits of professional food and beverage servers, you should begin to see that service is more than just taking an order and physically delivering it. Guests in all types of food and beverage operations want service that meets or exceeds their expectations. The proper attitude that precedes one's ability to deliver this service is absolutely critical to the success of the food server and his or her employer (the foodservice operation).

Francesca Yorke © Dorling Kindersley. Courtesy of the Coyote Cafe, Santa Fe

Open kitchen of Coyote Cafe, Santa Fe, New Mexico

CHALLENGES! CHALLENGES!

Managers in commercial food service operations are, and will continue to be, confronted with several significant challenges that present opportunities for creativity as they are resolved:

- **Addressing the labor shortage.** Like their counterparts in almost every segment of the travel and tourism industry, "There aren't enough staff members to go around." Managers are addressing this concern by keeping the employees they have (reducing turnover), finding ways to increase productivity (use of convenience foods when appropriate is an example), and recruiting from nontraditional labor markets such as senior citizens for selected positions.

- **Changing guest preferences.** Managers cannot meet their guests' needs unless they know what their guests want. **Food fads,** such as low-carbohydrate (carb) diets, and longer-term **food trends,** such as evolving concerns for nutritious food consumption, must be understood and, if applicable, incorporated into menus. Many industry observers believe that diet and health concerns will play an increasingly significant role in the process by which restaurants plan menus and develop recipes.

  food fad   a relatively short-lived interest in or preference for specific food items

  food trend   a longer-lived change in the preference for or interest in specific food items

- **Financial concerns.** As guests desire more value for the dining dollars they spend, it becomes difficult to increase selling prices to yield greater revenues. At the same time, operating costs are increasing. Managers are, then, challenged to find ways to achieve financial goals.

- **Maintaining standards.** Successful food service managers must do everything they can everyday to earn the repeat business of their guests. It is very difficult, but important, to consistently meet the operation's quality goals.

- **Ever-present sanitation concerns.** Unfortunately, sanitation problems can cause foodborne illness in any type of operation regardless of whether it is an unknown independent or a well-known brand-name operation. The impact on the health and wellness of victims and on the financial stability of the operation can be almost immeasurable and very difficult to overcome.

- **Increasing government regulations.** Compliance with numerous government regulations and local laws and ordinances are a must! However, it is sometimes difficult for independent business persons to keep up with and even know about these obligations. As well, significant additional time is often required by human resources or other staff specialists in larger operations.

SUMMARY OF CHAPTER LEARNING OBJECTIVES

1. **Describe the basic types of commercial foodservices.**
   Commercial foodservice operations are those that exist to generate profits from the sale of food and beverage products. Restaurants can be classified as upscale (high check average), casual service (midscale), family service, and quick service. Off-site caterers, hotel food and beverage operations (which offer a la carte dining, banquets, room service, and bars and lounges), and retail store foodservices are also commercial foodservice operations.

2. **Discuss the marketing- and operations-related concerns that must be addressed as a menu is planned.**

   Marketing aspects of menu planning focus on the guests. Issues such as the purpose of their visit (in other words, the guests' wants and needs), value (the perceived relationship between selling price and quality), demographic factors, including age, family status, gender, ethnicity, and occupation, along with other factors specific to the individual guests, must all be considered by the menu planner. Operating concerns to be addressed as menus are planned include the consideration of the menu's impact on product purchases (quantity, quality, cost, and availability), personnel needs, property layout and design, equipment availability, and production volumes.

3. **Review each process that must be managed in a comprehensive foodservices system after the menu has been planned.**

   Food and beverage products that are required by the menu must be purchased, received, stored, issued, and produced. (Production may require preparing, cooking, and/or holding.)

Products must also be delivered to the guests by procedures involving serving (moving products from production to service personnel) and service (moving products from service personnel to the guests).

4. **List traits of professional food and beverage servers.**

   Professional food and beverage servers must have a significant amount of knowledge and skill and the proper service attitude. To be professionals, servers must be reliable, responsive, competent, accessible, courteous, understanding, focused, and empowered.

5. **Explain challenges (opportunities) that must be addressed by commercial foodservice operations.**

   Managers in commercial foodservice operations are concerned about addressing the labor shortage, meeting the needs of ever-changing guests' preferences, and attaining financial goals. Other challenges include maintaining standards, successfully confronting sanitation and food safety issues, and maintaining compliance with increasing governmental regulations.

MASTERING YOUR KNOWLEDGE

The chapter makes the point that menu planning is a very important first step in the management of a food and beverage operation. Discuss the following questions.

1. What are some ways that a competitor's menu may affect planning the menu in your operation?

2. How would you describe the types of guests who are most likely to visit the four types of restaurants (upscale, casual service, family service, and quick service) discussed in the chapter?

3. What are some factors you would consider if you were planning a relatively large group function? How would each factor influence your choice of a restaurant, caterer, or hotel?

4. How would the food items planned for the menu be different if that menu was planned for:
   a. Persons dining in an upscale restaurant?
   b. A family including children at a family-service restaurant?
   c. A young couple (mid-twenties) at a mid-scale property?
   d. Customers at a quick-service restaurant?

5. Give several examples of how the menu influences the following:
   a. Product purchases
   b. Personnel (production and serving) needs
   c. Building layout and design concerns
   d. Equipment availability

6. How would you determine the quality of menu items that are most suitable for your operation?

7. What are some ways that food costs can increase unnecessarily at the time of product receiving, storing, and issuing?

8. Think of a recent time when you were a guest in any type of foodservice operation. Describe the positive and negative instances in your interaction with food servers. What were some professional and unprofessional aspects of this interaction? How did the interaction with the server affect your total foodservice experience?

FEEDBACK FROM THE REAL WORLD

Our real-world advice comes from Jim Nuetzl who has served as corporate executive chef, The Capitol Grille, Decatur, Georgia.

Why do some experts say that the financial success of a foodservice operation begins with the menu?

The restaurant's menu is the primary tool that influences guests to dine in your establishment. The most cost-effective menu does no good if it does not appeal to your guests. The menu is also the building block that affects all resources, including labor and food products. Cost control is, then, influenced by what the menu requires you to do and by what it does not allow you to do.

What are some tactics of effective menu planning that can be most helpful?

I have found that the best way to drive menu planning is to meet with and talk to our guests. They know what they want, and they are often anxious to talk to me about what they are looking for in a dining experience in our restaurants. Guests are the reason we are in business, the menu is what brings them into our restaurant, and we want and need their input.

Who should be part of a restaurant's menu-planning team? What role does each member play?

After gathering ideas from our guests, I begin testing ideas on our service teams and managers.

These individuals serve our guests daily, and they have great insights about how we can take a good idea and turn it into a great one. Once they are satisfied, I present the ideas to our regional directors, vice-president of operations, and corporate-level officials. By the time we put an idea in front of them, it has been extensively tested with our guests and staff, and we have objective data about its appeal and profitability. The "numbers" can then speak in support of our proposed menu changes.

What are the most difficult challenges confronting menu planners as they implement changes in an existing menu?

Once the decision is made to implement a menu change, the greatest challenge becomes effective training. With 15 restaurants that are spread throughout the country, a solid method of training is integral to ensure consistency. Training obviously is needed and involves the production staff, who must prepare the new items. However, it also involves the service staff, who must know about the products. Sometimes, as well (especially when new and different ingredients are involved), purchasers must also learn about the new product specifications.

LEARN FROM THE INTERNET

1. Check out the home pages of the following restaurants:
   - Damon's Grill: www.damons.com
   - Johnny Rockets: www.johnnyrockets.com
   - Emeril's New Orleans Fish House: www.emerils.com
   - Olive Garden: www.olivegarden.com
   - Denny's: www.dennys.com

   Looking just at the menu, what are your thoughts about the type of guests whom the restaurant is trying to attract? In what ways is the presentation of menu items attractive and distracting?

2. Check out the home pages of the following foodservice software companies:
   - Cost Guard: www.costguard.com
   - Eatec Corporation: www.eatec.com
   - Micros Systems, Inc.: www.micros.com
   - Food Trak: www.foodtrak.com

How do their products help foodservice managers to control products at the time of purchasing, receiving, storing, issuing, producing, and delivering to guests (serving and service)? Based on its description, which software appears to provide the best overall control of products from procurement to service?

3. Check out the home pages of restaurants in each segment discussed in this chapter:

Upscale

Lettuce Entertain You Enterprises: www.leye.com

Casual Service

Applebee's Neighborhood Grill and Bar: www.applebees.com

Family Service

Pizza Hut: www.pizzahut.com

Quick Service

Hardee's: www.hardees.com

What points do they make about food service and environment as part of their guests' dining experience?

KEY HOSPITALITY TERMS

The following terms were explained in this chapter. Review the definitions of any words with which you are unfamiliar. Begin to utilize them as you expand your vocabulary as a hospitality professional.

commercial foodservices
noncommercial foodservices
restaurant
freestanding (restaurant)
upscale (high check average) restaurants
guests per labor hour
casual-service (midscale) restaurant
family-service restaurant
comfort foods
California-style menu
quick-service restaurant
off-site caterer
commissary
a la carte dining room (restaurant)
banquet
room service
retail store foodservices
a la carte menu
table d'hôte menu
cyclical menu
du jour menu
marketing
competitor
menu planning
value (menu item)
demographic factors
repeat business
word-of-mouth advertising
traffic
overload (equipment)

food (menu) items
ingredients
procurement
quality (of a food item)
theft
pilferage
stockout
value (procurement)
menu engineering
expedite (purchasing)
receiving
storing
issuing
production
standard recipes
"scratch" (food preparation)
convenience food
make or buy analysis
chained recipe
per portion
batch cooking
preparing
cooking
holding
service bar
serving
service
food fads
food trends

Contract Management Company Foodservices

Pearson Education/PH College, Laima Druskis photographer

Children eating lunch in an elementary schoolcafeteria

CHAPTER LEARNING OBJECTIVES

After studying this chapter you will be able to:

1. Recognize that the preferred foodservice management alternative (self-operated or contract management company-operated) must be determined on a by-situation basis.

2. Explain that a win–win relationship between the sponsoring organization and the contract management company is needed.

3. Outline basic steps in the decision-making process to select and utilize a contract management company.

4. Describe the role of a foodservice liaison.

5. Note the importance of and types of communication between the sponsoring organization and the contract management company.

6. Discuss challenges confronting contract management companies.

The authors wish to thank Jeannette Colter, Senior Human Resource Generalist, Sodexho, for her assistance in coordinating the development of this chapter.

FEEDBACK FROM THE REAL WORLD

Pretend that a business manager of a large manufacturing company is concerned about minimizing operating expenses and providing foodservice alternatives that will be enjoyed by his or her employees. The foodservices have been managed and operated by the company's own employees (it has been self-operated), but significant losses have occurred recently. This is a large operation serving several hundred meals to employees six days weekly.

Your contract management company has just received a request for proposal (RFP) from the company that addresses your company's potential interest in managing the foodservices

operation, the services you could provide, and the costs associated with doing so.

What process would you use to develop a winning proposal response? What factors would enable your organization to manage the foodservices more effectively (successfully) than they are currently? How soon after the business is awarded to your company could you tool up to take over the program? What basic steps would be involved in the transition?

As you read this chapter, think about answers to these questions and then get feedback from the real world at the end of the chapter.

---

on-site foodservice a contemporary name for non-commercial foodservices operations

self-operated foodservices noncommercial programs in which the foodservices management and staff are employees of the organization offering the foodservice

contract management company a for-profit business that contracts with an organization to provide foodservices as specified; the management company can be a chain with many contracts or an independent management company with only one or a few contracts

managed foodservices foodservices operations that are managed by a contract management company

---

OBJECTIVE 1
Recognize that the preferred foodservice management alternative (self-operated or contract management company-operated) must be determined on a by-situation basis.

We have defined noncommercial foodservices to be those offered by organizations that exist for some reason other than to make a profit from the sale of food and beverage products. This segment of the hospitality industry is also called **on-site foodservice** in an effort to provide a descriptive name that is less related to its for-profit counterparts. Exhibit 1 shows many of the wide range of organizations that feed people (their employees and/or consumers of their services) for reasons other than to make a profit.

The chart also shows two basic ways that noncommercial foodservices operations can be managed. First, the organization can operate foodservices itself. In a **self-operated foodservices** program, the foodservice manager and his or her staff members are employees of the organization offering the foodservices. An alternative is for the organization to hire a for-profit **contract management company** to operate the foodservices. These foodservice operations are sometimes called **managed foodservices**. In this instance, foodservice managers are employed by the contract management company. Most contracts specify that nonmanagement staff members will also be employed by the contract management company. However, sometimes nonmanagement personnel are employees of the sponsoring organization.

WHICH FOODSERVICE MANAGEMENT ALTERNATIVE IS PREFERRED?

Auto mechanics have had friendly arguments for years about the topic "Which is best, a Ford or a Chevy?" Movie critics have annual debates about the "best movie of the year." Art shows, dog and cat shows, culinary competitions, and craft exhibits are all staged to allow judges and the public to answer the question "Which is the best?" The answer to this question generally relates to some factors that can be measured (the fastest car can be timed; dogs and cats can be compared to exacting breeding standards) and to other factors that are more subjective (car styling and art can be viewed differently by different people).

These points also apply to the question "Which is best: self-operated or contract management company-operated foodservices?" The answer is that it really depends on many factors, most of which are specific to the organization

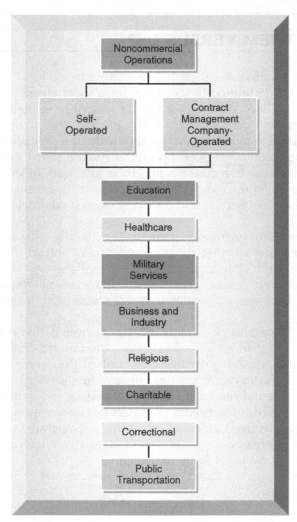

EXHIBIT 1
The World of Noncommercial Foodservices

considering the alternatives. Some concerns are objective (financial statements can indicate whether an operation meets monetary goals), but other factors are more subjective (which alternative offers the best-tasting food?). This distinction (the necessity for service to be offered at minimal cost or employee benefit) represents a fundamental difference in how foodservices are viewed by

This resident in a long-term care facility is eating a meal prepared by the facility's food-service department that could be self-operated or managed by a contract management company.

Pearson Education/PH College, Michal Heron photographer

IS IT THEM VERSUS US?

The history of contract foodservice management probably began when a local restaurant owner or caterer began to provide limited foodservices for a local business. Over the years it has grown into a multibillion dollar business with several large companies offering foodservice management services internationally, others with nationwide **accounts,** and still others with a large regional or community-wide base of operations. Historically, managers of self-operated foodservice programs have disliked contract management companies, in part, because of a concern that their jobs were in jeopardy. The management company brings in its own top-level unit manager(s), because management expertise, of course, is what the organization is buying when it contracts with a foodservice management company.

There is also the matter of profit. An organization operated with public funds, such as a local school district, might question whether the profit paid to a contract management company might be better spent if it remained within the school district. (The contract management company would likely counter that it can yield increased efficiencies that will provide savings to the school district greater than what was paid in management fees to the company.)

So who does the better job of operating foodservices? The answer is that it probably depends just as much on the staff managing the foodservice operation as it does on whether the staff is employed by the sponsoring organization itself or the contract management company. There are no secrets in the process of effective foodservice management. Basic principles are well known and can be applied by all managers regardless of whether they are employees of an organization needing foodservices or a contract management company. Good (and less effective!) managers work for self-operated and for contract management-operated foodservices. A careful mix of creativity, effective operating procedures, and consistent application of basic management principles is a more important determinant of foodservice success than is the type of management operation (self-operated or contract company) used.

account the contract management company's term for the organization that has retained it to operate the foodservices program; also called *client*

representatives of sponsoring organizations. Some factors critical to the "Which is best?" question have both subjective and objective components. (A large management company does have expertise available, for example, to undertake kitchen design work or to do creative graphics for food promotions. However, how much do these services really cost when they are provided as part of a package price for operating the organization's foodservices program?)

OBJECTIVE 2
Explain that a win–win relationship between the sponsoring organization and the contract management company is needed.

A WIN–WIN RELATIONSHIP IS NEEDED

Parties to the **management contract** must both benefit from it. An agreement in which one party wins and the other party loses will likely cause serious operating problems before the business relationship is dissolved. Exhibit 2 highlights potential risks incurred by both parties in a foodservices agreement.

The sponsoring organization may lose control over many aspects of providing its foodservices (and a desire to do so may be an incentive for an organization to retain a contract management company!). Accounts can determine the amount of control they desire. For example, depending on the agreement's terms, the organization may no longer hire or supervise staff or make decisions directly affecting costs. (These operating decisions will likely be made by the contract management company.) The sponsoring organization's staff must be convinced that management and other fees that it must pay will be offset by lowered operating costs. There is always a risk that operating expenses may be higher

RISING STAR PROFILE

Eric Loyall
District Manager
Corporate Services
Sodexho
Cincinnati/Louisville/Atlanta

A "Do Whatever It Takes!" Attitude

What is your educational background?

I graduated with an undergraduate hospitality management degree from the University of Massachusetts.

What is your work experience?

I am a district manager for Sodexho. My district is a bit unusual as I am currently responsible for the Food, Catering, and Vending services at five zoos, one museum, and 10 traditional corporate dining accounts.

What is the most unforgettable moment in your career?

While a student at UMASS, I held a summer job at a food stand inside a regional amusement park. One day management approached me and offered me an increase of 25 cents per hour to be in charge of the food stand. Though I was not sure I wanted to be responsible for others, I agreed. It turned out that, for $10 more each week, I had to do about 10 times the work! At the time, I didn't realize this small step to management would lead to a rewarding career full of unforgettable moments.

What are the most significant challenges facing your segment of the industry? How are they being addressed?

The biggest challenge is the same in all segments: Our customers are becoming more sophisticated (yes, even in the concessions and leisure world!). We address this challenge with more sophisticated menu offerings; themed locations; signature items; package pricing; the use of national, local, and in-house brands; the use of retail-style merchandising; and lots (lots!) of employee training programs.

What, if anything, would you do differently in your career?

I would learn Spanish because it would be very helpful in my efforts to manage a diverse work force.

What is your advice for young people considering a career in your industry?

There is no doubt that the foodservice industry is very exciting. Foodservice combines elements of the manufacturing and service industries, and this creates lots of action. In the course of this action, you will work with and for countless characters in many exciting situations. Hollywood has caught on to the industry's appeal. Just consider the food-related reality shows broadcast on major networks. However, to be successful, one must have what all our successful managers and chefs have: a passion for business, and a "do whatever it takes" attitude.

Elderly person enjoying a meal at a long-term care facility. Its Food and Nutrition Service Department could be self-operated or a managed services account of a contract management company.

Pearson Education/PH College, Michal Heron photographer

management contract a formal, written agreement that specifies the responsibilities and obligations of both the organization sponsoring the foodservices and the management company that provides them; frequently, the company agrees to assume total responsibility for management of the foodservices operation in return for a management fee and, perhaps, other remuneration; the organization provides the building and equipment and may continue to incur legal and economic liability

EXHIBIT 2
Risks in an Arrangement to
Operate Foodservices

deficit or subsidy the amount of expenses that cannot be paid for with revenues generated by a non-commercial foodservice program; called *loss* in a commercial foodservice operation

Organization Risks	Contract Management Company Risks
Loss of total control	Loss of profits
Potential operating cost **deficits** and **subsidies**	Sponsoring organization may become fiscally unsound
Reliance on the contract management company	Lack of input into long-range decisions that affect the foodservice operation
Concerns about lowered priority for its foodservice operation	Potential damage to its reputation
	Possibility that resources used to obtain and manage the account could be better spent elsewhere.

with the management company than without it, and the organization must frequently assume much or all of any operating deficit from the foodservices program. Even if the contract with the management company is terminated, what does the organization then do about its need to offer foodservices? Finally, there is a risk that a management company will reduce the attention it gives to the organization over the life of the contract. This can occur, for example, when it gives priority to efforts to attract and retain more lucrative accounts.

The management company is not without its own risks as an agreement is negotiated and administered. First, the management company risks reduced profit. (It may be possible to increase profits by channeling resources into other more profit generating ventures.) Second, it must assume that the sponsoring organization will remain fiscally sound. Also, the management company generally has little or no input into long-range decisions that affect it. If the management contract is terminated for whatever reason before its term, the management company has lost an account that has cost company resources to build. Also, the management company's reputation can be damaged, and the resources used to obtain and manage the account could have been more effectively used elsewhere.

THE CONTRACT MANAGEMENT DECISION

OBJECTIVE 3
Outline basic steps in the decision-making process to select and utilize a contract management company.

Exhibit 3 reviews general steps that an organization might find useful when making a decision to use a contract management company for its foodservices. Each step in the figure is important, and the steps should be

Elderly persons dining in an upscale retirement center

Getty Images, Inc.-Photodisc, Ryan McVay photographer

NONCOMMERCIAL FOODSERVICES OFFER EXCITING CAREERS

Noncommercial foodservices of both types (self-operated and contract management company-operated) offer exciting career alternatives because they often provide foodservices that are as diverse and challenging as are their commercial (restaurant and hotel foodservices) counterparts. (In fact, some might argue that the challenges are greater in noncommercial operations, because the same audience of potential guests is often at the heart of daily marketing and operating concerns.)

As a case study, consider a foodservices program operated at a world-famous healthcare institution whose main campus comprises many square blocks in a major city. The facility utilizes the services of a contract management company to manage an array of foodservices, including these:

Cash cafeteria operations in several facilities serving thousands of customers on an average day

Regular and special diets served to thousands of patients on an average day

Thousands of meals for employees, including physicians and other medical specialists, daily

Full-service foodservices, including banquets, coffee breaks, off-site catering, parties, and a wide range of other foodservices for employee special events

Special meals for government dignitaries, movie stars, and other personalities (patients) from around the world

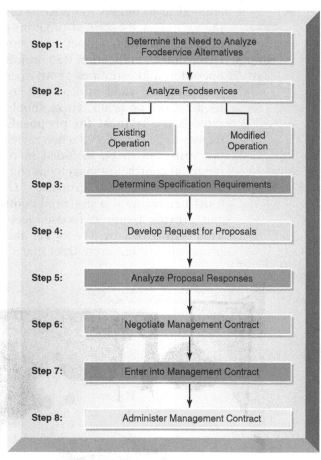

EXHIBIT 3
The Contract Management Decision

The unit manager for a managed services account talks to his area manager.

done sequentially. Let's examine this process.

Step 1: Determine the Need to Analyze Foodservice Alternatives. The organization must consider the factors that it will use to evaluate its own self-operated program and contract management company alternatives. Costs will be important, but so will quality and other standards. These must be defined and used (a) to determine when and if analysis of the current foodservices is needed, (b) to develop performance standards against which to review alternatives, and (c) to suggest priorities for the use of time and other limited resources. (The organization's administrators have many things to do; they need an objective way to determine the most significant problems. Should time be spent analyzing foodservices or, alternatively, is their time better spent on other activities?)

Step 2: Analyze Foodservices. The existing foodservices operation can be carefully reviewed by considering sales, costs, and other factors for which operational data are available. This analysis may generate ideas to modify the existing operation in a way that allows the existing self-operated program to be improved without the need for external (contract management company) assistance.

Step 3: Determine Specification Requirements. Analysis of the existing operation and estimates about operating results if systems are modified can yield information useful in describing an ideal foodservices program. These should be identified and incorporated into a **request for proposal (RFP).** Exhibit 4 identifies factors to be considered when reviewing an existing foodservice program and to be included in requests for proposals from potential contract management companies.

Step 4: Develop Request for Proposals. Organization representatives must determine if a potential contract management company can provide required foodservices in an acceptable manner. They assess this by developing and sending out a request for proposals to eligible contract management companies.

request for proposal (RFP) a formal document that incorporates the organization's needs for foodservices expressed in the form of detailed specification requirements; the objective of the RFP is to define the required foodservices so clearly that prospective bidders (management companies) can develop accurate costs and other estimates used in their proposal responses

A dietitian trains unit managers.

EXHIBIT 4
Essential Foodservice Specifications

Existing foodservices can be examined to assess the extent to which the following factors are satisfactorily met by a self-operated foodservice program. This will suggest information that should be supplied by prospective contract management companies to indicate how they would operate foodservices under a management contract. This basic information includes the following:

Nutritional requirements
Basic meal patterns
Basic portion sizes
Nutritional audits
Revenues, costs, **surplus,** and deficit relative to budget
Standard recipes
Diet modifications (if applicable)
Food purchase specifications
Serving times
Personnel requirements (for foodservice director and operating staff)
Training requirements
Food handlers' health certificates
Staff uniforms
Wage rates
Compliance with all applicable laws and regulations
Responsibilities of the organization and the contract management company
Accountability, records, payments, and fees, including allocation of costs, examination of records, payment of allowable costs and fees, and compliance fees

surplus the amount of revenues that remain after all costs allocated to the non-commercial foodservice program have been paid; called *profit* in commercial foodservices

Step 5: Analyze **proposal responses.** Contract management companies respond to the request for proposals with a formal proposal response. It indicates exactly how the management company intends to meet all the specifications noted in the request for proposal. Organization officials must study proposal responses and compare them with the facility's current operation and with proposal responses submitted by other management companies.

proposal response the information sent by a contract management company to an organization that addresses foodservice specification requirements detailed in the organization's request for proposal (RFP)

The workers in this large cheese production plant will require breaks and a meal period during their shift. These services may be provided by a contract management company.

Bruce Forster © Dorling Kindersley

Step 6: Negotiate Management Contract. The organization cannot enter into a formal agreement with a management company unless and until a contract that specifically outlines the responsibilities and obligations of both parties has been developed. A process to negotiate each point raised by the management company in its proposal response is necessary.

Step 7: Enter into Management Contract. This formal document specifies the expectations, obligations, and responsibilities of both the organization and its contract management company partner.

Step 8: Administer Management Contract. Procedures to require compliance with the contract are essential to assure the organization that the management company "does what it says it would do."

THE FOODSERVICE LIAISON

OBJECTIVE 4
Describe the role of a foodservice liaison.

foodservice liaison a food-service management specialist employed by a sponsoring organization to represent its interests in the ongoing administration of the food-services agreement with a contract management company

Top-level managers of organizations sponsoring noncommercial foodservices are experts in the work they do in education, healthservice, business and industry, and other disciplines. They are not, however, typically experts in managing a foodservices operation within their organization. By contrast, those within the food management company are experts in managing foodservices; after all, it is their business. How can sponsoring organizations level the playing field as they interact with contract management companies?

Some, especially large, organizations may employ a **foodservice liaison** who, with extensive past experience, is a foodservice management specialist. He or she may have worked for many years in a restaurant or hotel's food and beverage operation or even for a contract management company. Increasingly, however, most persons serving as liaisons come from purchasing, human resources, or facility management backgrounds.

Exhibit 5 reviews the possible relationship between the organization and the contract management company when a foodservice liaison is utilized. Note, first, that the foodservice liaison typically reports to a business or finance officer within the sponsoring organization. By contrast, the unit foodservice manager reports to the contract management company's district, regional, or area foodservice director. The foodservice liaison interacts with the unit's foodservice manager on day to day and short-term administration of the foodservice contract. Much of this work involves assuring that both

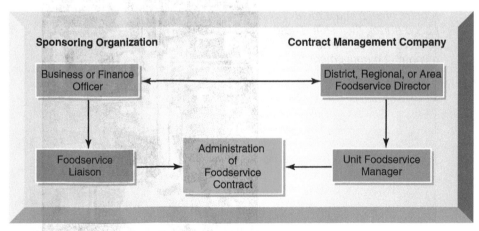

EXHIBIT 5
The Foodservice Liaison: The Link in the Relationship Between the Organization and the Contract Management Company

DID YOU KNOW?

Basketball legend and businessman Earvin "Magic" Johnson is offering his name and image (brand) to contract management foodservices in schools and colleges, sports and recreation feeding venues, and even healthcare facilities.

Themes being planned include "Magic Johnson Sports Bar" for colleges and, for schools and sports venues, "The Magic Johnson Marketplace," a basketball-themed eatery with a large, open grill.

His joint venture is with Sodexho and is being undertaken in efforts to change the "cafeteria-going" experience for consumers in a very large industry that is almost anonymous, even though it serves tens of millions of consumers nationwide.

As of June 13, 2006, no deals had been signed, but a campaign was begun to bring some "pizzazz" into a huge industry that is interested in making itself better known to the public that it serves.

Source: Bruce Horovitz. Johnson hopes to work his image magic with food service. *USA Today.* Retrieved June 12, 2006, from usatoday.printthis.clickability .com

parties comply with terms of the contract and, within these terms, discovering ways to more effectively deliver foodservices to those who utilize them. The organization's business or finance officer interacts with the contract management company's foodservice director as longer-term and special issues arise. For example, issues of agreement noncompliance that cannot be resolved between the foodservice liaison and the unit foodservice manager might be discussed by these officials. The foodservice liaison also provides technical assistance to the organization's business or finance officer as a new foodservice management contract is negotiated.

Omni-Photo Communications, Inc., Frank Siteman photographer

Chef using a grill at the Museum of Science in Boston

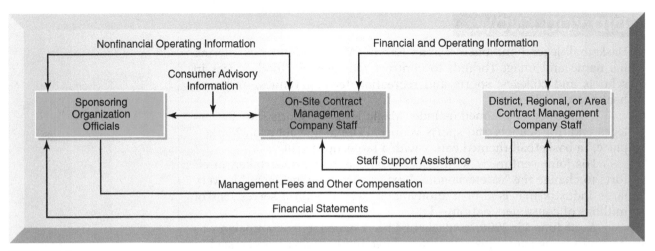

EXHIBIT 6
Relationship Between Organization and Contract Management Company Under a Foodservice Agreement

MANAGING THE MANAGEMENT CONTRACT

Exhibit 6 reviews the relationship between the sponsoring organization and the contract management company after a foodservices contract has been agreed on. The relationship between the organization and on-site management is primarily of a nonfinancial nature. Also, there is often ongoing input to the sponsoring organization and on-site management from an advisory group of consumers. By contrast, much of the relationship between the organization and off-site contract management company personnel relates to financial matters. The organization pays fees and compensation to the company, which, in turn, provides financial statements to the organization.

Exhibit 6 also illustrates the relationship between the on-site management staff and the off-site (district, regional, or area) management company staff: financial and operating information flows between these personnel, and the off-site office provides staff support and assistance as needed.

There are numerous ways that sponsoring organization and contract management company personnel communicate. These are important to recognize, because effective ongoing communication is a critical factor in a successful agreement between the two parties. In an effective relationship, personnel from both the organization and the company will actively manage the agreement, identify operating and other problems, and work cooperatively to address them. Exhibit 7 reviews the types and frequency of communication between sponsoring organizations and the management companies who operate their foodservices.

Pearson Education/PH College, Michal Heron photographer

The unit manager of a healthcare food and nutrition services department meets with her district manager.

EXHIBIT 7
Communication Between
Organization and Contract
Management Company

Type of Communication	Frequency of Communication
A. Telephone, e-mail, and facsimile (fax)	
1. Organization to on-site management staff	1. Anytime
2. Organization to district- or regional-level management company staff	2. Anytime
B. Meetings	
1. With organization's consumer advisory committee	1. At least monthly
2. Between organization and district- or regional-level management company staff	2. At least bimonthly
3. Between organization and on-site management staff	3. Anytime
C. Written **pro forma projections**	
1. Provided by the contract management company to the organization	1. At least quarterly
2. Annual budget (comparison of projected and actual to-date expenses)	2. Annually
D. Written financial statements	
1. Monthly operating statement (for month and year to date)	1. Monthly
2. Weekly revenue and cost report	2. Weekly
E. Written audit report	
1. Audit report of district or regional staff visit to organization	1. At least bimonthly
F. Informal oral conversation	
1. Between organization and on-site management staff	1. Anytime

pro forma projection
estimates of financial performance done in advance of a
fiscal period

CHALLENGES! CHALLENGES!

OBJECTIVE 6
Discuss challenges
confronting con-
tract management
companies.

The future of this industry segment and the challenges that will likely confront it can be considered from the perspectives of its customers, programs,
clients, and work force.[1]

Customers

The typical customer continues to evolve. Globalization along with an increased
presence of multinational companies and demographic changes in our own communities have made the customer base of contract management companies increasingly diverse. This base represents every culture and ethnic background
and includes many persons whose dining preferences are not traditional U.S.
cuisine. To attract and retain their business, we must identify and meet their
needs. As well, our traditional customers are learning about new and different
cuisines, and they are demanding a wider variety of dining options.

---

[1] This section was contributed by Stephen Di Prima, Division Vice-President, Sodexho's Corporate Services Division, Central Region, who also provided the "Feedback from the Real World" at
the end of this chapter.

Along with dining preferences, work habits are also changing. Some changes are being mandated from the boardroom, but just as many are being driven by the front-line workers themselves. **Offshoring**, virtual offices, flex hours, increased productivity, and technology improvements have all had an impact on noncommercial foodservice operations. In many cases, fewer workers are in buildings, and others maintain work schedules that don't align with traditional dining service operating hours. Contract management companies are aggressively addressing this issue and working even harder to build sales.

A third interesting dynamic is wellness and healthy dining in the workplace. There will always be fads (remember low-carbohydrate diets?), but an increasing number of customers are shifting their personal dining habits with health in mind. They want options that allow them to meet specific dietary goals, such as low salt, low fat, and high fiber, and they no longer want their healthy food decisions to be punitive, that is, to require the purchase of unappealing and bland foods. They expect wellness offerings to be integrated into all points of service and are not willing to sacrifice quality or taste as this occurs.

The impact of inflation, especially higher gasoline prices, also affects our customers, and operations. While income levels make a difference, more customers are demanding more value selections or choosing to bring meals from home. This is an ongoing issue that will continue to evolve with the economy and geopolitical environment.

Programs

Contract management companies are aggressively moving to address the changing profiles of their customers. No longer do companies look at each other as the competition for the customer. Increasingly, the competition is viewed as nearby casual- and quick-service restaurants and the brown bag. Contract management companies continue to partner with well-known national and regional brands, but they are also working hard to develop internal concepts with a retail "feel." For example, Sodexho continues to roll out innovative programs that are comparable to public venues with regard to what is offered and how it is packaged. Today's demanding workplace requires us to look at different ways to serve our customers. For example, credit cards are now the norm, and express lines, office delivery, **grab and go**, and take-home meals have become a standard part of our program.

Sustainability is another trend emerging in our market. Global environmental issues are becoming more important to our customers and clients. While recycling is important, these concerns go well beyond that. Locally grown products are capturing more interest, as is energy conservation. We have an operation in North Carolina that converts used frying oil to biodiesel fuel used to power vehicles on site. Locally grown products demonstrate a support for local industries and provide a higher level of perceived quality. This is a trend that will continue to evolve and grow.

Clients

Our **clients** are proxies for the economic activity that is happening around the world. Many, if not most, of our client companies are affiliated with international companies or offshore jobs or have foreign subsidiaries. Clients continue to look for ways to reduce suppliers and often move to single-source solutions or a short list of preferred providers. This means that they are looking for companies with global footprints that can follow them wherever they go and that offer the expertise and experience required to work around the

offshoring the relocation of some business functions such as production or manufacturing to a lower cost-location, typically overseas

grab and go the foodservice option in which a customer selects a prepackaged food item for consumption away from the site

sustainability the concept that the needs of today's population can be provided for without damaging the ability of future generations to meet their needs

client (of contract management company) the organization that negotiates and administers the foodservice contract with the management company

globe. Client expectations are for a single point of contact, master contracts, and program consistency. Contract management companies that do this well will grow, and those that don't will miss out on opportunities.

Management contracts are also changing. Traditionally, contracts were agreements that allowed companies to receive a fee for operating the foodservice program. Often these programs operated at a loss that was absorbed by the client. Today, fewer companies are willing to subsidize their programs. They structure contracts in which the management company takes the risk as it retains profits, but also assumes responsibility for losses.

Work Force

Internally, the greatest challenge foodservice management companies will face in the future is the same challenge that confronts them today: finding qualified people with a passion for the business and the desire to make this industry their career. This is true for every level, from the grill cook to boardroom executives. Foodservice professionals must also give back to their industry by supporting educational institutions, mentoring aspiring managers, and becoming personally involved in industry alliances and professional organizations.

SUMMARY OF CHAPTER LEARNING OBJECTIVES

1. **Recognize that the preferred foodservice management alternative (self-operated or contract management company-operated) must be determined on a by-situation basis.**
   There are pros and cons to both self-operated foodservice programs and those operated by contract management companies. The specifics of each situation must be carefully evaluated by decision makers to determine which alternative is best for the organization that sponsors the foodservice program.

2. **Explain that a win–win relationship between the sponsoring organization and the contract management company is needed.**
   Both parties to a management contract must benefit from it for a long-term relationship to evolve. Both the organization and the foodservice management company assume risks, and these must be assessed before and during the time of the contractual relationship.

3. **Outline basic steps in the decision-making process to select and utilize a contract management company.**
   Basic steps to select and utilize a management company include the following:
   - Determine the need to analyze foodservice alternatives
   - Analyze foodservices
   - Determine specification requirements
   - Develop requests for proposals
   - Analyze proposal responses
   - Negotiate management contract
   - Enter into formal agreement
   - Administer management contract

4. **Describe the role of a foodservice liaison.**
   A foodservice liaison is a representative of the organization sponsoring a noncommercial foodservice operation. He or she represents this organization in the administration of the agreement with the contract management company and may or may not have foodservices management experience.

5. **Note the importance of and types of communication between the sponsoring organization and the contract management company.**
   Organization officials generally interact with on-site contract management company staff relative to nonfinancial operating information. Financial aspects of the relationship involve interaction between organizational officials and off-site (district, regional, or area) contract management company staff members. Numerous types of telephone, e-mail, facsimile, meeting, written pro forma projections, written financial statements, written audit reports, and

informal oral conversation help to assure that communication is timely and effective.

6. **Discuss challenges confronting contract management companies.**

Customers are becoming increasingly diverse, and a wider variety of needs must be successfully met to retain the business. As well, changing work habits (for example, virtual offices and flex hours), an increased interest in healthy foods, and the ever-present demand for value in food purchases are becoming more important. There is increased competition from off-site foodservices that is being addressed by companies as they partner with national and regional brands and as they roll out innovative internal concepts. Environmental concerns are now very important and must be addressed. Large clients often want to interact with preferred suppliers who, increasingly, have global footprints, as do their large clients. Today, fewer companies want to subsidize foodservices, so profit and loss contracts are popular. The largest internal challenge of management companies continues to be the search for qualified personnel with a passion for the business.

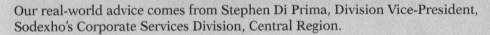

FEEDBACK FROM THE REAL WORLD

Our real-world advice comes from Stephen Di Prima, Division Vice-President, Sodexho's Corporate Services Division, Central Region.

In his current position, Steve's responsibilities include overseeing operations in 20 states and over $400 million in annual revenues. Steve has an undergraduate degree and more than 20 years of foodservice industry experience in both sales and operations. Steve maintains a key focus on client relations, team enhancement and management training, and development activities.

What process would you use to develop a winning proposal response?

Many factors combine to create a winning proposal: one that is customer focused and aligned with the client's needs and objectives.

Long before we develop our response, we employ a strategic process to confirm client objectives, identify creative solutions to meet their needs, outline measurable outcomes, and incorporate proof statements. Throughout this phase, we challenge ourselves to truly differentiate our ideas and proposal. We assign a strategy team for each project made up of individuals with the best skill set to address each new business opportunity.

In some cases, our response must follow a required format (request for proposal), and in other cases, the format is left to our discretion. In either case, the response itself usually includes an executive summary, recommendations, financial projections, and references. The document must be clear, concise, and error free, and must offer a compelling reason to choose our company.

Executive summaries communicate our message and may be the only part of the proposal the decision makers will read. They must be able to see why our company should be selected in a few, well-written pages.

Our clients often tell us that they appreciate our proposals for the following reasons:

- Well-organized and easy to find key information
- Attractive and professionally presented
- Thoroughly demonstrates how well we understand them and their needs
- Customized presentation, rather than a boilerplate document

- Innovative solutions
- Competitive offer

The single most important factor in developing a winning proposal is to clearly understand the client's objectives and to use these to guide your strategy and response.

What factors would enable your organization to manage the foodservices more effectively (successfully) than it is currently?

Numerous factors enable a contract management company to more effectively manage a foodservice operation. Management depth, organizational support, technical expertise, and economy of scale are all advantages that management companies enjoy.

A self-operated organization typically offers limited promotional opportunities for foodservice managers within their field of expertise. In addition, management turnover can have a significant impact, since the transition can require an organization to bring in a candidate from the outside. Support during the transition can be limited. Also, the person being replaced may be the only experienced foodservice management person in the organization.

Conversely, a management company is better able to attract and retain quality candidates because of the clear career path offered by the organization. This career track also provides a ready pool of qualified candidates to replace promoted or reassigned managers.

A management company also has the ability to allocate resources. If, for example, an account has a major event or is opening a new facility, the management company can direct additional managers or specific expertise to support the operation. These resources can include marketing, culinary support, and training, as well as many other areas.

An operation often requires additional technical expertise not available on-site. Sourcing this expertise can be challenging for a self-operated program, and it can be difficult to find and expensive. Management companies that operate a large number of sites typically have faced similar issues in other locations and can share that experience in subsequent situations. Even more importantly, they have the technical resources to support the actions necessary to address these issues.

Finally, a management company can leverage its scale to the advantage of individual accounts. Purchasing power, manufacturer support, distributor marketing, and training are all areas in which a management company can have a positive impact on an individual account.

How soon after the business is awarded to your company could you tool up to take over the program?

There is no standard timetable for transitioning an account. Based on expectations and circumstances, a contract management company can open a new program in two days or two months. Ideally, the organization wants to open with all its new programs and concepts in place. Ultimately, the client determines the speed of the transition.

Factors to consider for the client include current contract terms, company calendar, expectations for service, and upcoming events. Items that the management company must consider include status of current employees, the management selection process, number of locations, renovations, and contract negotiations.

The most successful transitions occur when both sides work together to forge a win–win relationship. Early and candid communication is crucial to a successful transition. This includes a clear understanding of expectations and joint development of performance requirements.

What basic steps would be involved in the transition?

The basic steps in the transition are these.

- Have regular and ongoing communication with client and team
- Review and establish mutual understandings about performance expectations
- Develop and execute bound contract
- Name the opening team and front-line workers
- Develop program specifics
- Requisition equipment
- Identify corporate resources required for the opening
- Renovate and merchandise as necessary
- Conduct preopening surveys and focus-group sessions (if client permits)
- Orient employees
- Train employees

MASTERING YOUR KNOWLEDGE

Discuss the following questions.

1. If you were the manager of a self-operated food-services company, what reasons would you cite to emphasize that self-operated foodservices are the preferred alternative for your organization?

2. If you were a district foodservices director for a contract management company making a sales call on a prospective organizational client, what points would you address that speak in favor of using your company to operate the organization's foodservice program?

3. What are the advantages and disadvantages of using a foodservice liaison from the perspective of the organization and the contract management company?

4. What kinds of day to day operating problems do you think are most likely to arise when an organization enters into a foodservice agreement with a contract management company?

5. How, if at all, does an emphasis on pleasing the consumer and attaining quantity and quality standards change when a self-operated foodservice program ends and a program offered by a contract management company begins?

LEARN FROM THE INTERNET

1. Check out the websites for the following contract management companies:
   - Delaware North Companies: www.delawarenorth.com
   - Centerplate: www.centerplate.com
   - Gluckenheimer Enterprises: www.gluckenheimer.com

   What selling points do they utilize to emphasize how they can benefit organizations who employ them?

2. Review the websites for the following contract management companies that were the top revenue producers in 2005.
   - ARAMARK: www.aramark.com
   - Compass Group, The America's Division: www.cgnad.com
   - Sodexho: www.sodexho.com

   What do you think are some of the personal and professional advantages to working for one of these Big Three companies relative to other organizations that generate smaller revenue levels? What are possible disadvantages?

3. Check out the website addresses for the following hotel contract management companies:
   - White Lodging Services Corporation: www.whitelodging.com
   - Hostmark Hospitality Group: www.hostmark.com
   - Tharaldsen Lodging Companies: www.tharaldsen.com

   What are the similarities or differences in (a) the way they approach prospective clients and (b) the benefits they suggest will accrue to owners compared to their counterparts who are foodservice management companies?

KEY HOSPITALITY TERMS

The following terms were explained in this chapter. Review the definitions of any words with which you are unfamiliar. Begin to utilize them as you expand your vocabulary as a hospitality professional.

on-site foodservice	surplus
self-operated foodservices	proposal response
contract management company	foodservice liaison
managed foodservices	pro forma projection
account	offshoring
management contract	grab and go
deficit or subsidy	sustainability
request for proposal (RFP)	client

Private Club Management

Shaen Adey © Dorling Kindersley

Private golf club in Point Elizabeth, South Africa

CHAPTER LEARNING OBJECTIVES

After studying this chapter you will be able to:

1. Explain why many persons join private clubs.
2. Review two basic ownership structures for private clubs.
3. Describe common types of private clubs.
4. Describe how equity clubs are organized.
5. Review an organizational chart for a typical private club.
6. List the competencies required to be an effective club general manager.
7. Review unique aspects of private club food and beverage operations.
8. Review challenges confronting the private club industry.

From Chapter 22 of *Discovering Hospitality and Tourism: The World's Greatest Industry*, Second Edition, Jack D. Ninemeier, Joe Perdue. Copyright © 2008 by Pearson Education, Inc. Published by Pearson Prentice Hall. All rights reserved.

FEEDBACK FROM THE REAL WORLD

There are many great employment opportunities throughout the vast world of hospitality management. A common denominator typically involves interaction with a large number of persons: employees and guests of the operation. Private club management is no exception.

What are the rewards and challenges of interacting with club members who, unlike many of their counterparts at hotels and restaurants, are likely to be very frequent visitors to their clubs? How, if at all, does a club manager interact differently with a relatively new member and one who has been a member of the club for many decades? What tactics can a club manager use to interact with a building superintendent whose knowledge and skills in very technical areas are vastly different from those of the club manager?

As you read this chapter, think about answers to these questions and then get feedback from the real world at the end of the chapter.

private club a membership organization not open to the public; persons join a club after being accepted by its membership and must typically pay an initiation fee and monthly membership dues; they must also pay for products and services purchased at the club that are not included as part of membership dues

The world of **private club** management offers opportunities for those with knowledge and skills in hospitality management, and this segment is unique in numerous respects. Its modern history can be traced back to the mid-1700s when social clubs developed in England and when the origin of golf in Scotland brought people together to pursue their interest in this new sport.

In the past, only relatively wealthy persons joined private clubs. By contrast, today clubs are of interest to and within the financial ability of a large percentage of the population,

What is the world of club management all about? Why is membership in private clubs becoming increasingly popular? What do club managers do? These are among the issues addressed in this chapter.

OBJECTIVE 1
Explain why many persons join private clubs.

WHY JOIN A PRIVATE CLUB?

People join private clubs for numerous reasons, including the following:

- *Access to recreational facilities.* Persons who join country (golf), tennis, and yachting clubs, for example, may find private club facilities to be

Private clubs frequently provide tennis facilities for members and guests.

Guy Drayton © Dorling Kindersley

much better than those available to the general public elsewhere in the community.

- *Convenience.* Ready access to a dining room table or a golf tee at busy times is typically easier in a private club than in a public facility.
- *Business reasons.* Conducting small business meetings and entertaining business clients in a private club are very useful tactics for many businesspersons. Club environments also provide the opportunities for businesspersons to interact socially with others who might be influential in their businesses.
- *Employment benefit.* Some organizations provide private club membership as a benefit to selected executives and others.
- *Family tradition.* Some families may have been members of a specific club for many generations; club membership is a tradition.
- *Friendly atmosphere.* Many people enjoy the recognition and service provided by club managers and staff, which are enhanced by personal relationships formed during their numerous visits to the club.
- *Statement of social status.* Some clubs are very exclusive, with high initiation and membership fees (and very long waiting lists to join!), which make them available to only the very affluent.

WHO OWNS THE CLUB?

OBJECTIVE 2
Review two basic
ownership structures
for private clubs.

Private clubs can be member owned or nonmember owned. Clubs of either type of ownership can be operated by a contract management company whose personnel interact with the club owners (members in equity clubs and the owners in nonequity clubs) in much the same way that management companies operate lodging properties for their owner(s). Let's look at both types.

Equity Clubs

Equity clubs are owned by their members and are governed by a board of directors elected by the members. Each member is a shareholder and owns equal equity in the club. Voting members elect board members from among their peers, who then make major club decisions. A club manager, then, works directly for the members since they own the club. Most private clubs are equity clubs. As such, they are nonprofit corporations exempt from federal income taxes and some state and local taxes.

equity clubs (private clubs)
private clubs owned by their members and governed by an elected board of directors

Nonequity Clubs

Nonequity clubs are owned by an individual or corporation, rather than by club members. Members have much less decision-making authority than do their counterparts in equity clubs. Most nonequity clubs are not tax exempt because they are typically for-profit organizations. These clubs are typically owned by developers (for example, of a real estate project) or by corporations. Club managers in nonequity clubs do not work for club members; they work for the club's owner.

nonequity clubs (private clubs) clubs owned by an individual or corporation that are generally not tax exempt; most are corporate- or developer-owned clubs

COMMON TYPES OF PRIVATE CLUBS

OBJECTIVE 3
Describe common
types of private clubs.

Exhibit 1 shows several common types of private clubs. Let's take a close look at each of these.

RISING STAR PROFILE

Michael W. Graney
General Manager and Chief Operating Officer
The Country Club at Muirfield Village
Dublin, Ohio

Michael received an undergraduate degree in political science from Miami University (Ohio) and then returned to school to receive an associate's degree in culinary arts from Columbus State Community College in 1996. He offers some interesting insights for persons studying hospitality management today.

What is your most unforgettable moment in the hospitality industry?

In 2003, I was the executive chef at The Country Club. I applied for the position of general manager for the club and was awarded the job. I will never forget the day the announcement was made, and I became the supervisor of the persons who had been my peers: other department heads. While I may have lacked a little confidence about my leadership abilities at that time, I discovered that my staff members were ready to work with me, and we became a great club management team. I am blessed with great employees, but it seems I always have been. Luck and timing are important factors in career success, but I believe that teams follow captains for a reason.

What are the most significant changes that have occurred in private clubs?

Competition for our members' luxury time is a very significant challenge that we all face in the club industry today. Time is becoming the most valued asset for many of our members. Most of them have the financial and time-related abilities to do most anything they wish, but it has to be convenient for them to do so. If our products, services, and facilities are convenient and time efficient, then we will succeed and outperform our competition, and their luxury time will be spent with us.

What, if anything, would you do differently in your career?

I should have traveled more at the beginning of my working career to experience the different regional cultures in the United States. I am always amazed about the similar behavior and reactions of people from the same part of the country.

What is your suggestion for those interested in a career in the hospitality industry?

I recommend that one begin a career in the industry in a position such as a restaurant server. If you do not enjoy the immediate gratification of exceeding a member's or a guest's expectations, then hospitality management is probably not going to provide an enjoyable career. If you cannot hear a complaint straight from the customer's mouth and immediately decide how you will remedy the situation, you cannot think on your feet well enough to succeed in the industry. If you begin your working career as a server or in another high-guest-contact position, these two issues will be addressed very quickly.

Country Clubs

country club   a private club with a clubhouse, golf course, and typically other recreation facilities, along with food and beverage outlets, pro shop, locker facilities, and other amenities; also commonly called a *golf club*

Country clubs have a **club house** and a golf course; many have other sports facilities, such as tennis courts and a swimming pool. Country clubs typically offer one or more food and beverage outlets, pro shop (for selling golf and other sporting equipment, logo merchandise, and other items), and locker rooms. There are more country clubs than any other type of private club in the United States.

City Clubs

club house   the club facility used for primary food and beverage production and service, social functions, swimming pool and lockers, and the club's administrative offices, among other purposes

City clubs are typically located within a city's business area or a suburban office complex. Services range from clubs with food and beverage outlets to others

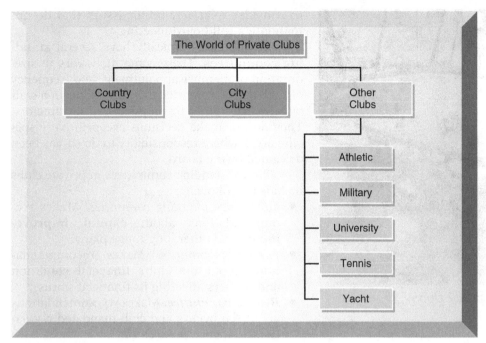

EXHIBIT 1
Types of Private Clubs

with conference rooms, indoor sport facilities, and sleeping rooms for members and guests. These clubs typically exist to meet the business, entertainment, and social needs of club members in a city or suburban environment.

Other Types of Clubs

There are various other types of clubs as well.

- *Athletic clubs.* Fitness or sports facilities are provided for members.
- *Military clubs.* Each branch of the U.S. military offers clubs for officers and enlisted personnel. Most are similar to city clubs; some offer additional services.
- *University clubs.* These clubs serve university communities, including graduates, faculty, and staff. Facilities typically include food and beverage outlets, meeting and banquet areas, and sometimes fitness facilities and other accommodations.
- *Tennis clubs.* These clubs offer tennis courts and related amenities. Many offer food and beverage services, including banquet rooms.
- *Yacht clubs.* These clubs address the needs of boaters and offer marina services (storing, refueling, and dock services). Some have a clubhouse, food and beverage services, and swimming pools.

ORGANIZATION OF EQUITY CLUBS

You have learned that most private clubs are equity clubs. Exhibit 2 illustrates a common way that equity clubs are organized. An elected board of directors develops club policies and provides overall governance and direction for the club. Officers typically include a president, vice-president, secretary, and treasurer. Many clubs have an **executive committee** comprised of these officers. Its function is to, if necessary, address emergencies and/or

city club a private club within a city's business area or suburban office complex that offers food and beverage services and, often, conference and indoor sports facilities; some offer sleeping rooms

OBJECTIVE 4
Describe how equity clubs are organized.

executive committee (private clubs) a group composed of a club's president, vice-president, secretary, and treasurer who, if necessary, address emergencies and/or consider relatively minor issues that do not mandate a full board meeting

Poolside a la carte dining at a private club

Getty Images, Inc.-Taxi, Ron
Chapple, photographer

standing committee (private club) a permanent committee that provides advice to the board of directors about matters within the area of their assigned responsibilities

capital improvements remodeling and/or building or facility additions, changes in land use and other projects requiring substantial sums of money

to consider relatively minor issues that do not mandate a full board meeting.

Private clubs typically have several **standing committees.** These committees vary in size, duration of member appointment, and frequency of meetings. Committee members serve in a staff or advisory role to the club's board of directors. They do not make decisions except in very specific areas where responsibility to do so has been delegated by the board.

Typical standing committees in private clubs include the following:

- *Long-range planning committee.* Makes recommendations about **capital improvements** and other long-range plans.
- *Finance committee.* Makes recommendations about the club's financial condition and matters affecting its financial status.
- ***Bylaws committee.*** Makes recommendations about the bylaws and club-mandated regulations that govern the club.
- *Nominating committee.* Makes recommendations about the candidates to be considered for election to the board of directors.
- *Membership committee.* Makes recommendations about candidates for club membership and about the membership status of club members.
- *House (club house) committee.* Makes recommendations about the maintenance of the club house, the grounds that surround it, and the food and beverage operations.
- *Social committee.* Makes recommendations about the entertainment activities of the club.

PRIVATE CLUBS OFFER NUMEROUS MEMBERSHIP CATEGORIES

Members of a private club do not all have the same rights and privileges. Among the most common membership categories are the following:

Regular membership. The member has full use of all club facilities and amenities and has voting rights and the right to hold an elected office within the club.

Social membership. These members have use of the clubhouse and its food and beverage facilities, but may have limited use of facilities such as the swimming pool, tennis courts, and fitness centers. There may be no or very limited use of golf facilities.

Nonresident members. Those living beyond a specified distance may be allowed to pay lower dues than regular members.

Junior membership. These members, generally children of regular members, are granted membership on the basis of their parents' affiliation but have not yet attained the age required for regular membership.

Senior membership. This category is reserved for members who have been affiliated with the club for a specified number of years and who have reached a specified age.

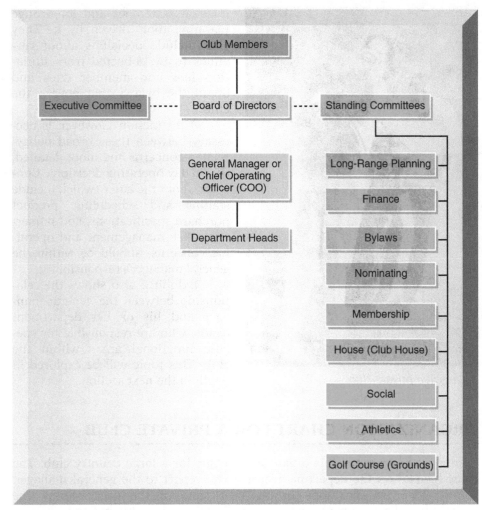

EXHIBIT 2
How Equity Clubs Are Organized

bylaws committee (private club) a committee in a private club that makes recommendations about regulations that govern the club

- *Athletic committee.* Makes recommendations about athletic concerns. Many large clubs typically have separate athletic committees addressing golf, tennis, swim, and fitness activities.
- *Golf course (grounds) committee.* Makes recommendations about golf course maintenance, course irrigation, and policies to regulate play.

Exhibit 2 also indicates the relationship between the general manager and the board of directors in an equity club: the general manager reports to this governing body.

The **Club Managers Association of America (CMAA)** is the association that serves the needs of private club managers. It emphasizes the need for a business model to guide the relationship between the club's board of directors and the general manager. In effect, the club's board develops the broad policies that should govern the management and operation of the club. The general manager should serve as the club's chief operating officer (COO) to implement programs and procedures in concert with the policies developed by the board.

The need to constantly recognize and follow the model of the club's general manager as COO is important. The board of directors represents the members who own the club and should make decisions about the most important matters affecting the club. These include the development of the

Club Managers Association of America (CMAA) the association that serves the needs of private club managers

mission statement and long-range planning tools driven by it. They also include decisions about revenues to be collected from initiation fees and member dues and about the bylaws that govern the club.

A distinction, however, is necessary between these broad policy-related concerns and more detailed, day to day operating decisions. Concerns about the latter (which include staffing and scheduling, product purchase specifications, and numerous other management and operating concerns) should be within the general manager's responsibility.

Exhibit 2 also shows the relationship between the general manager and his or her department heads, who are responsible for specific functional areas within the club. This topic will be explored in depth in the next section.

Golfers at a private club

ORGANIZATION CHART FOR A PRIVATE CLUB

OBJECTIVE 5
Review an organizational chart for a typical private club.

Exhibit 3 shows a possible organization chart for a large country club. The chart focuses on the department heads who report to the general manager. It also identifies positions in the next rung of the organization, the intermediate-level managers who report directly to department heads.

Notice that the general manager directs the work of 10 department heads. Five of these (food and beverage director, director of human resources, controller, membership director [Marketing], and director of purchasing) involve responsibilities that are similar to those of counterpart positions in large lodging organizations. Notice, however, that a new position, assistant general manager (Club House Manager), manages the work of

Golfer at a private club's pro shop

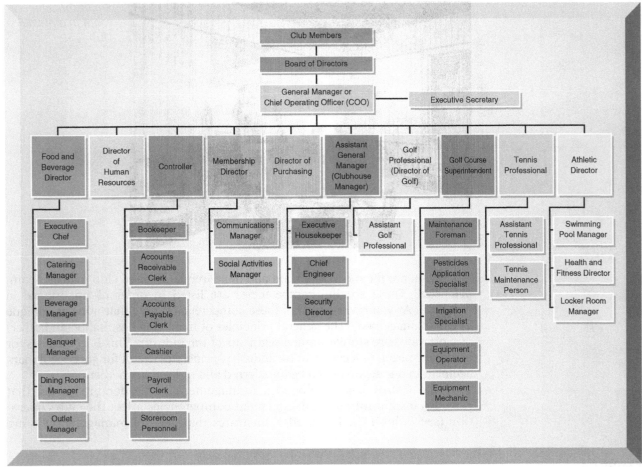

EXHIBIT 3
Organization Chart for a Large Country Club

three department heads (executive housekeeper, chief engineer, and security director) typically found in a hotel.

Four other positions (golf professional, golf course superintendent, tennis professional, and athletic director) are generally found only in private club management, although resorts may have some or all of these positions as well.

COMPETENCIES FOR CLUB MANAGER SUCCESS

The Club Managers Association of America has conducted extensive research to identify **competencies** required for successful club managers. These fall into the following nine broad categories, listed in order of importance:

- Management
- Accounting and finance
- Human and professional resources
- Food and beverage management
- Club governance
- Building and facility management
- Marketing
- Sports and recreation management
- External and governmental influences

OBJECTIVE 6
List the competencies required to be an effective club general manager.

competency a requirement that specifies what an individual must know and/or be able to do to be successful in a position

107

Small-function room in a private club

Art Resource, N.Y., Giraudon photographer

What are the most important and most frequently used club manager competencies? These specific competencies are listed in order of importance in Exhibit 4. As you review each of these competencies, note that none are unique to club management. The general principles of managing hospitality (and other) organizations are similar among segments of the industry. This is good news for persons aspiring to a career in the industry: principles useful for successful management in one segment can be transferred and utilized in another.

The CMAA has developed a Management to Leadership model that provides insight into how management competencies affect the club's operation (see Exhibit 5). The model illustrates that general managers/COOs are

EXHIBIT 4
Most Important and Most Frequently Used Club Manager Competencies

Competency	Competency Domain
Budgeting	Accounting and Finance
Financial Statements	Accounting and Finance
Communication Principles	Human and Professional Resources
In-House Communications	Marketing
Cash Flow Forecasting	Accounting and Finance
Employee Relations	Human and Professional Resources
Balancing Job and Family	Human and Professional Resources
Time Management	Human and Professional Resources
Supervision Tactics	Human and Professional Resources

EXHIBIT 5
Management to Leadership
Source: Club Managers Association of America

Leadership

Culture

Asset management

Operations

Management

108

HOW IMPORTANT IS GOLF IN COUNTRY CLUBS?

You have learned that country clubs comprise the majority of private clubs in the United States. Most members join these facilities for access to golf. The responsibilities of the golf professional and golf course superintendent are, therefore, absolutely critical to the success of the club. Some country clubs that do not use the COO concept have an organizational structure in which three persons report directly to the board of directors: the general manager (responsible for food and beverage operations and business aspects of the club), the golf professional, and the golf course superintendent. While the responsibilities of these three professionals are obviously different, numerous operating problems arise when more than one person with general operating responsibilities directly reports to the board. These problems are best resolved when an organization similar to that illustrated in this chapter is used.

responsible for three major areas: operations, assets and investments, and club culture. The building and perfecting of skills and competencies is ongoing.

The foundation of the model is the successful management of club *operations* that are defined in the core competencies identified in Exhibit 4. The second tier of the model involves mastering the skills of *assets management*. The general manager/COO must be able to manage the club's physical property and the financial well-being and human resources of the club. The third part of the model involves preserving and fostering the *culture* of the club: its traditions, history, and vision.

CLUB FOOD AND BEVERAGE OPERATIONS

OBJECTIVE 7
Review unique aspects of private club food and beverage operations.

Several aspects of a foodservice operation in a private club often set it apart from some of its counterparts in other segments of the hospitality industry. Let's look at several of these.

Number of Food and Beverage Outlets and Range of Products Offered

Large private clubs typically have several (or more) a la carte dining outlets serving everything from ice cream cones (at the pool snack bar) to gourmet dinners in an upscale dining room. All or most of the food products for this diverse range of outlets would likely be prepared in the same kitchen, and a single manager might have general oversight for all food and beverage operations. Other staff might be cross-trained to work in all or several of these outlets, and the club's standards must be consistently attained within each outlet.

Meeting Club Members' Needs and Requirements

Many members join their club because of the recognition they receive. Referring to guests by name, seating them at a preferred table, remembering special occasions, and allowing members

Getty Images, Inc.-Photodisc, David Buffington photographer

Banquet setup in a private club

DID YOU KNOW?

The unique appeal of private clubs is founded on service. People can get elsewhere the many things that clubs offer—fine dining, catering, golf, tennis, fitness facilities, and so on. What they can't find in a public facility is the level of service they can expect from a private club. Most private clubs are willing to absorb the labor costs and hire the staff members it takes to provide extraordinary service.

A moment of truth happens with every encounter a member has with the club. It can be an encounter with a staff person, a product, or some aspect of the club's physical facilities. Did the server greet me courteously? Are the golf cars charged, clean, and ready to go? Are the rest rooms clean? Did the employee in the pro shop answer the phone right away? Service is about details, so club managers must train the club's staff to take care of the details. An attendant at the club's pool, for example, must be trained to go get a towel for a member who forgets to bring one, rather than just tell the member where the towels are located.

The service goal is to make the members say "wow." A club should try to exceed member expectations. This is harder to do in a club than in a hotel or restaurant. Hotels and restaurants have different people in every day. A club member might be at the club several times a week, year after year. This makes it harder to provide "wow" service. The club has to constantly work to keep the service level high.

One of a club manager's primary tasks is to make sure staff members have what they need to do the job properly. If you are not directly serving members, you should be serving the people who are. Club managers should talk to staff members frequently to find out about obstacles that are hindering them from providing great service. An obstacle can be a flawed process or something physical—it can be as simple as a piece of furniture that's in the way. Club managers should make the work environment as efficient as possible so that employees are not frustrated, because employee frustration can get taken out on club members.

A club's management team is small relative to the number of employees. Because of that, it's important that club managers give each employee the proper training. Training is an ongoing management function; it's a cycle. Club managers set the standards, communicate the standards to the staff, provide the tools and training, and then gather feedback from members to make sure the standards are right and the training is working. Of course, the most important measure of staff performance is member satisfaction. Taking a membership-satisfaction survey on an annual basis provides wonderful feedback. A manager should work to constantly raise the level of satisfaction.

A feature of private clubs, one that makes providing great service both easier and at times more challenging, is that there is a finite number of members. Over time, club managers are able to get to know members and their families and can provide very personalized service. Not only can club managers smile, say hello, and call members by name, they can also ask them about the grandchildren, the new house, or the bank merger. Members like to talk about themselves, but not on a superficial level. They don't want a generic "How are you?" from a club manager.

One of the biggest service challenges clubs face is the basic fact that clubs deal with people. Communication is not always perfect. You've got to meet or exceed what members expect again and again. It is very difficult to maintain standards so high that members are impressed every time they walk in. That's the service challenge that club managers face every day.

Cathy Gustafson, PhD, CCM
Professor, University of South Carolina
Former General Manager of The Faculty House of Carolina,
Columbia, South Carolina

Source: Contemporary Club Management. Joe Perdue, ed. Alexandria, VA, Club Managers Association of America, and Lansing, MI, Educational Institute of the American Hotel & Lodging Association, 1997 (pp. 97–98).

to order special items (even if they are not on the menu!) are among the ways that club food and beverage personnel address their members' special concerns.

Other Food and Beverage Services

Club members may request a special menu for small or large groups. Outdoor picnics, food and beverage cart service on the golf course, and parties at poolside are examples of opportunities that club food and beverage managers have for implementing their creativity.

Boardroom in a private club

Getty Images, Inc.-Photodisc, Keith Brofsky photographer

Food and Beverage Service Issues

Turnover in private clubs is frequently lower than in other segments of the hospitality industry. Advantages are obvious, including the employees' familiarity with the club's policies, members, and procedures. It is thus easier to attain efficiency and quality service goals.

Long-term employment can also create some difficulty in retraining, resistance to changed procedures, and the possibility that poor work habits evolve over time. Also, when compensation is, in part, based on seniority, there can be a wide range of differences in wages or salaries paid to beginning and more senior staff members. Clubs that do not offer retirement packages may have another difficulty: some employees may work beyond when they should. If they become inefficient, morale problems can result as they interact with new staff members who receive less compensation. Long-term employees may also be tempted to become too familiar with members and not respect the professional distance that should be kept between the club's members and employees.

THE ROLE OF FOOD AND BEVERAGE IN A CLUB

The food and beverage department in a private club is critical to its success. First, it helps to attract new members. For example, a nonmember's first experience in a club may be as a guest in its dining room or at a banquet function. Consistent food quality and service are factors that are important to prospective club members, and the reputation of a club's food and beverage service is an important marketing tool.

(continued)

Careful attention to members' needs is very important in all clubs, and member satisfaction with food and beverage services is an important aspect in member retention. Food and beverage products and services must be of consistently high quality. This is achieved by recruiting, selecting, and retaining the very best personnel and by establishing and working toward the attainment of food quality standards that consistently meet or exceed the members' expectations.

Financial concerns are also important. In some clubs, the food and beverage department generates the primary source of revenue. At others, the revenue generated is much less. Depending on the specific club, the financial goals of the food and beverage department may be to make money, break even, or even to lose money. (Some outlets, such as the snack bars and "halfway house" facilities in country clubs, exist solely to serve the membership. They must be subsidized with revenue from other sources.) A mix of pricing factors and the volume of food and beverage services provided in a la carte and banquet dining functions help to determine the profitability of a club's foodservices.

OBJECTIVE 8
Review challenges confronting the private club industry.

CHALLENGES! CHALLENGES!

Several important challenges, discussed next, confront private club managers today and will likely do so in the future.

Need to Continually Provide Value to Members

Private club members, like their counterparts utilizing the services of other hospitality operations, desire value for the money they spend on meals, services, and recreation away from home. Club managers must find ways to reduce costs and maintain reasonable selling prices to attract new and to keep existing members.

Competition with Other Hospitality Operations

Private clubs do not just compete with other private clubs. Rather, organizations such as restaurants, public sports facilities, and other entertainment venues all provide alternatives for club members. Club managers and their staffs must continually find ways to delight their members. This becomes especially challenging with those who have been members of a club for many years.

Las Vegas National Golf Club, Las Vegas, Nevada

© Dorling Kindersley, Courtesy of the Desert Inn, Las Vegas

Competition for the Best Possible Staff Members

Private clubs, like other operations in the hospitality industry, must recruit and retain the very best employees. To do this increasingly involves a close look at compensation programs and all methods used to supervise employees.

Getty Images, Inc.-Stone Allstock, Brian Stablyk photographer

Royal Vancouver Yacht Club, Vancouver, British Columbia, Canada

Implementation of quality efforts, including empowerment, appeal to the new generation of better-educated people with more job employment opportunities than were available to yesterday's employees.

Ways to Reduce Costs with Increased Utilization of Technology

Club members continue to want service delivered by hospitable staff members. Reductions in staff levels in these service-related positions may be difficult. However, just as managers of hotel, restaurant, and other hospitality organizations are looking at technology to increase revenues and reduce costs without sacrificing quality, so too are private club managers. One example: many clubs are developing creative websites to inform members of club activities and to allow them to book reservations for desired events online.

SUMMARY OF CHAPTER LEARNING OBJECTIVES

1. **Explain why many persons join private clubs.**
   Reasons why people join private clubs include access to recreational facilities, convenience, business reasons, as an employment benefit, as part of a family tradition, for the friendly atmosphere, and as a statement of social status.

2. **Review two basic ownership structures for private clubs.**
   Equity clubs are owned by their members and are governed by a board of directors elected by the members. Each member is a shareholder owning equal equity in the club. By contrast, nonequity clubs are owned by an individual or corporation, and members have much less decision-making authority.

3. **Describe common types of private clubs.**
   Country clubs (also called golf clubs) are the most common type of private club in the United States. Other examples of clubs include city, athletic, military, university, tennis, and yacht.

4. **Describe how equity clubs are organized.**
   In one common type of organization, equity club members elect a board of directors who, in turn, retain the services of a general manager (chief operating officer) who supervises the work of department heads. The board of directors utilizes an executive committee and numerous standing committees to provide input about specific club-related concerns. The Club Managers Association of America recommends

that the board of directors develop broad policies to govern the management and operation of the club. The general manager, in turn, serves as the club's chief operating officer.

5. **Review an organizational chart for a typical private club.**

The club's general manager typically supervises the work of department heads with responsibilities for food and beverage, human resources, finance, membership, purchasing, golf, golf course maintenance, tennis, and athletics. Also, a club house manager is supervised by the general manager and is responsible for housekeeping, engineering, and security.

6. **List the competencies required to be an effective club general manager.**

The nine most important and frequently used club manager competencies relate to budgeting, financial statements, communication principles, in-house communications, cash flow forecasting, employee relations, balancing job and family, time management, and supervision tactics.

7. **Review unique aspects of private club food and beverage operations.**

Aspects of a club's foodservice operation that set it apart from other segments of the hospitality industry may include the number of food and beverage outlets and the range of products offered, the need to meet club members' needs and requirements, different food and beverage services, and special food and beverage service issues.

8. **Review challenges confronting the private club industry.**

Several important challenges include the need to continually provide value and satisfaction to members, competition with other hospitality operations, competition for the best possible staff members, and the discovery of ways to reduce costs with increased utilization of technology.

FEEDBACK FROM THE REAL WORLD

Our real-world advice comes from Peter Schaub, CCM, Executive Assistant Manager, The California Club, Los Angeles, California.

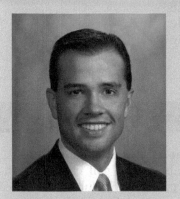

Peter received his undergraduate degree in hotel and restaurant management. He joined the management team at Houston Country Club in Houston, Texas, as an assistant manager. Since 1998, Peter has served as the executive assistant manager at The California Club in Los Angeles, California.

Both prior to and during his university studies, Peter held internship positions at Oak Ridge Country Club in Hopkins, Minnesota, Woodhill Country Club in Wayzata, Minnesota, and Twin Orchard Country Club in Long Grove, Illinois.

It is worth noting that Peter is a second-generation club manager. His father, Hans J. Schaub, CCM, is the general manager at The Minneapolis Club in Minneapolis, Minnesota.

What are the rewards and challenges of interacting with club members who, unlike many of their counterparts at hotels and restaurants, are likely to be very frequent visitors to their clubs?

The most rewarding aspect of having frequent "visitors" (our club members) is the ability we have to anticipate our members' needs. If proper attention is given to every detail, our staff can learn the likes and dislikes of every member. This al-

lows us service opportunities that are not typically available in hotels and restaurants, such as serving a member his favorite drink as soon as he is seated or handing a member her favorite newspaper as she walks through the front door each morning on the way up to the health club.

It is important to remember that personal attention is a major reason why people join private clubs. An obvious challenge is that our members' expectations may change often and we, as club managers, must always strive to meet and exceed these ever-changing expectations each day. Consider, for example, a member who originally joins the club to have a place to conduct business. He soon marries, and the club must now also fulfill the needs of his spouse. Later, the couple may have a child, and their needs once again shift to include a family-friendly environment. If the club is unable to fulfill these changing needs, the chances of losing an important member increase.

How, if at all, does a club manager interact differently with a relatively new member and one who has been a member of the club for many decades (or longer)?

From a professional standpoint, nothing should be different. Both the long-standing club members who joined 50 years ago and the member who joined last month deserve the utmost respect.

It is, however, extremely important that a club manager pay close attention to a new member. Each member joins for a different reason, and each has different expectations of her or his club experience. Each member has different likes and very different dislikes. The sooner we, as managers, can pinpoint their needs and preferences, the sooner we can exceed their expectations. The sooner we are able to exceed their expectations, the more they will use the club, grow with the club, and bring new members to the club.

What tactics can a club manager use to interact with a building superintendent whose knowledge and skills in very technical areas are vastly different from those of the club manager?

The technical knowledge it takes to work as an engineer in a building built in 1929 is obviously great. The details one must learn to work on pipes, electrical issues, boilers, and refrigeration, for example, are enough to fill many books in the engineering school's library, and this is obviously time that a club manager does not have.

To interact properly with an engineering staff, a club manager must understand enough to know what is being discussed and how to explain it to the applicable committee(s) and have the ability to make an educated decision when necessary. The best people to learn from are those who know best: the engineering staff. A club manager must ask plenty of questions, learn the lay of the land from his or her staff, and not be afraid to get dirty if it means learning more about the physical plant and how things work.

MASTERING YOUR KNOWLEDGE

Discuss the following questions.

1. What factors or features would be of greatest interest to you if you were evaluating alternative clubs for membership? What features would be important in your decision to maintain or give up your membership?
2. What role, if any, would you as the general manager want to have in interacting with a private club's standing committees? Why?
3. How important to a club's success is the Club Managers Association of America's model of the club manager as the chief operating officer (COO)?
4. How would you as a club manager direct the work of the club's golf professional and golf course superintendent, given that the knowledge and skills required for these positions would be significantly different from your own?
5. What are examples of activities in which club managers employ the most important and most frequently used competencies described in this chapter?

LEARN FROM THE INTERNET

1. Review the websites of several types of clubs (or look up private clubs in your area) by typing the following in your favorite search engine:

   - Private university clubs
   - Private golf clubs
   - Private city clubs
   - Private yacht clubs

   What kinds of products and services do they note to be available? Why should someone belong to the club?

2. Check out the website of the Club Managers Association of America: www.cmaa.org. What kinds of issues of interest to club managers are being addressed? How, if at all, do these issues differ from those that would interest managers in other segments of the hospitality industry? How does the CMAA help the private club industry?

3. Check out the websites of the following hospitality industry-related trade magazines:

   - *Club Management:* www.club-mgmt.com
   - *Club Director:* www.natlclub.org
   - *Restaurant Business:* www.restaurantbiz.com

   What are examples of issues noted that would be of concern to all private club managers? To those in specialized types of clubs?

KEY HOSPITALITY TERMS

The following terms were explained in this chapter. Review the definitions of any words with which you are unfamiliar. Begin to utilize them as you expand your vocabulary as a hospitality professional.

private club
equity clubs (private clubs)
nonequity clubs (private clubs)
country club
club house
city club

executive committee
standing committee (private club)
capital improvements
bylaws committee (private club)
Club Managers Association of America (CMAA)
competency

Cruise Lines
A Close Look at Resorts on Water

Peter Wilson © Dorling Kindersley

The ship's captain on the bridge

CHAPTER LEARNING OBJECTIVES

After studying this chapter you will be able to:

1. Present a brief history of cruising.
2. Explore typical reasons why people cruise.
3. Review basic features of modern cruise ships.
4. Describe common ship- and land-based management positions in the cruise industry.
5. Explain procedures used to sell cruise vacations.
6. Note basic sources of revenues on cruise ships.
7. Consider challenges confronting the cruise line industry.

This chapter was authored by Bernard N. Fried, EdD, CHAE, Associate Professor, Tourism and Convention Department, William F. Harrah College of Hotel Administration, University of Nevada, Las Vegas.

FEEDBACK FROM THE REAL WORLD

Cruise lines require many persons working on ships and on the shore. Many persons have a stereotype of jobs with glamour and adventure when they think about employment in the cruise industry. There are great positions in the industry but, as in all other segments of the hospitality industry, hard work and extensive knowledge and skills are required to be successful.

Why are travel agencies the biggest generator of cruise sales? How do travel agents interact with the cruise lines as they sell cruises? Do discounts and agency rebates help to generate cruise business? What types of positions are available in travel agencies specializing in cruise sales? From the perspective of a travel agent, what do you see to be the future of the cruise industry?

As you read this chapter, think about the answers to these questions, and then get feedback from the real world at the end of the chapter.

What do you think of when you see advertisements for cruises and/or learn that one of your friends will be taking a cruise? Do you think about travel to unique locations, great onboard luxury accommodations, and spectacular (and seemingly never ending) food and beverage services including midnight buffets? Do you think about meeting new people, romance and/or participation in numerous onboard activities, including gaming, lounging around the swimming pool(s), and/or dancing until the very late hours (or later)? Today's cruises offer all of these and much more.

Many people in many different positions are required both on the **cruise ship** and on shore. Many of these are in guest (passenger) contact positions. However, just as is true in other segments of the hospitality industry, many positions unnoticed by the traveling public are, at the same time, absolutely critical to the success of the organization.

In this chapter, you will learn basic background information about the cruise line industry. It is a very large and fast-growing segment and provides employment opportunities for many people from around the world. Perhaps, after studying this chapter, you will have an interest in becoming one of them!

cruise ship a passenger vessel designed to provide leisure experiences for persons on vacations

OBJECTIVE 1
Present a brief history of cruising.

HISTORY OF CRUISING

Humans have historically used coastal waterways, rivers, and lakes for commerce, warfare, and exploration and to travel for business purposes. It has been relatively recently, however, that the oceans and other large bodies of water have been used as a medium for persons to enjoy their leisure time.

The first scheduled passenger sailing across the Atlantic took nearly 28 days in 1818. The world's first propeller-driven passenger vessel was launched in the early 1840s. By the early 1900s, transatlantic ocean travel was relatively common, but not always safe (remember the *Titanic*!). Early cruises were very expensive voyages that provided those who could afford it a holiday as they traveled from one destination to another.[1]

---

[1] Roger Cartwright and Caroline Baird, *The Development and Growth of the Cruise Industry*. Oxford, England: Butterworth Heinemann, 1999. Information about the history of ship travel is from Marc Mancini, *A Guide to the Cruise Line Industry*. Albany, NY: Thompson Learning, 2000.

Ocean liners of the early 1900s were basically built to transport immigrants. The wealthy who could afford it traveled first class, but the vast majority of persons on board traveled in steerage class. After World War I (1914–1918), during which most available ocean-crossing ships were used for troop transport, ocean liners became bigger and started to provide more of the amenities that are part of today's cruising experience.

In 1958, commercial jet service began across the Atlantic, and travel between the United States and Europe took hours rather than days. Ships whose primary objective was to provide transportation were much less popular. During the 1970s and 1980s, the concept of leisure cruising evolved rapidly. Air conditioning, swimming pools, dance floors, and superb food and beverage services, among many other amenities, made "floating vacations" more popular. By the 1990s, **megaships** carrying 2,000 or more passengers were being built.

In fact, increasingly large cruise ships continue to be built. *Freedom of the Seas*, a Royal Caribbean Cruises Ltd. liner, was christened in May 2006, in New York Harbor. It is 237 feet tall and 1,112 feet long, with 15 passenger decks. It can cruise with more than 4,000 passengers.*

A cruise ship sailing at night is a majestic sight.

Rob Reichenfeld © Dorling Kindersley

megaship a cruise ship that carries 2,000 or more passengers

*Largest passenger ship christened in New York Harbor. cnn.com. Retrieved May 13, 2006, from www.cnn.com/2006/travel/05/12.

ALL ABOUT THE CRUISING EXPERIENCE

Cruise lines offer cruises that last from a very few days to several months (or longer). Typical schedules involve at-sea and at-port times, with activities that permit passengers to be just as active or inactive as they wish for almost every moment during the journey. Some itineraries are round trip; the cruise ship leaves from a port, cruises and visits other ports of call, and returns to the port from which it left. Some cruise lines offer one-way itineraries; a cruise ship leaves from one port and ends its cruise at another. (Passengers leave the ship, or disembark, and use another means of travel to their next destination.) Some cruises offer pre- and/or postcruise packages that allow passengers to select options to have hotel and perhaps land excursion activities before or after the cruise.

Where can one cruise? Almost anywhere that there is deep water! Popular cruises include those to Alaska, within the Caribbean, the western and eastern Mediterranean and throughout Europe, Africa, and in the Pacific, among numerous destinations.

Cruise ships are normally redeployed (repositioned) to make them available for popular cruising seasons in different places at different times throughout the year. For example, cruise ships visiting Alaska during the summer months may then cruise across the Pacific to Hawaii and then on to the South Pacific until warm weather cruises again become popular in Alaska.

Casino on a cruise ship

Alan Keohane © Dorling Kindersley

WHY PEOPLE CRUISE

There are several common reasons why cruises are popular vacation choices for many people:

- *Relaxation.* Passengers can unpack and enjoy their cruise with few, if any, responsibilities until its conclusion. There are no worries about where to go, how to get there, or what to eat. The wide range of activities means that there is something for everyone whenever they want to enjoy it. Passengers are pampered with service to the extent they wish to be.
- *Travel and education.* Cruises typically cover long distances and allow passengers to see and experience places they have only dreamed about visiting. Many tourists think about ports of call they have visited during cruises when they consider potential sites for future vacations. Opportunities to learn about the sites visited are extensive both on the ship before it arrives and during the port-of-call stop.
- *Social.* One can make new friends or enjoy a romantic experience. Many newlyweds celebrate their marriages by taking cruises.
- *Status.* The cost of cruising has declined dramatically over the past decade; almost anyone who can afford to take a vacation can find a cruise package within his or her budget. However, relatively few people have been on cruises, and the "bragging rights" that accrue are an incentive for some persons to take cruises.
- *Safety.* Traditionally, cruises have been seen as a safe vacation choice. The controlled environment, shipboard safety and construction features, and ready access to medical personnel have been a plus for many travelers.
- *Family tradition.* Some persons take all (or almost all) of their holidays on cruises. Some veteran cruisers have taken 30 or even more cruises and plan their next one while on the current one.

A CLOSE LOOK AT MODERN CRUISE SHIPS

Modern cruise ships are vastly different from ocean liners built just a relatively short time ago. Space, not speed, is a prime concern to accommodate many large **staterooms** (guest rooms) and the large number of public spaces for activities available to the passengers. Modern cruise ships are carefully planned

stateroom a guest room on a cruise ship; also called *cabin*

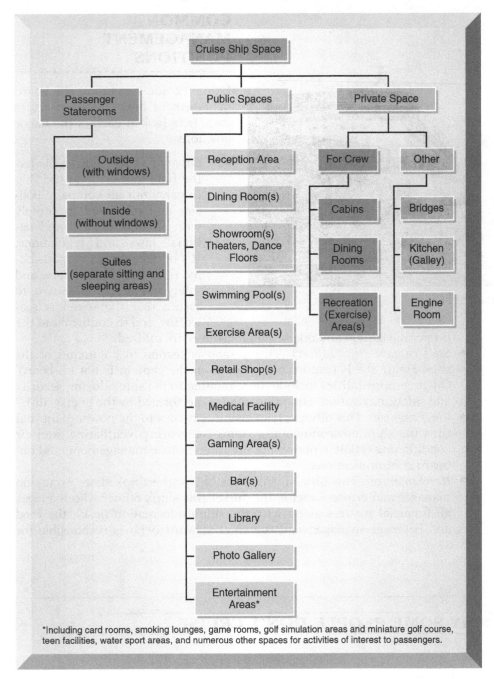

EXHIBIT 1
Classification of Spaces Available on Cruise Ships

to facilitate passenger **embarkation** and **debarkation** and for movement once persons are aboard the ship.

How is the space on a cruise ship classified? Exhibit 1 helps to answer this question. Space is allocated for passenger staterooms (these are typically suites, which are outside cabins with windows and, sometimes, private external sitting areas, and other sleeping rooms without windows in terms of decreasing costs). Public spaces include all areas of the cruise ship to which passengers have normal access. Private spaces exist for the crew and for other purposes, including the bridge (from which the captain commands the ship), the ship's kitchen (galley), and the engine room.

embarkation the process of boarding a cruise ship

debarkation the process of exiting a cruise ship

Chris Stowers © Dorling Kindersley

Cruise ship docked at an ocean terminal

OBJECTIVE 4
Describe common ship- and land-based management positions in the cruise industry.

COMMON MANAGEMENT POSITIONS

Exhibit 2 notes common shipboard management positions on a cruise ship. Let's look at each of the major positions.

- *Captain.* This individual has the final authority on the ship to carry out all company policies and rules and to comply with all international and national laws and regulations. His or her primary responsibility is to see to the care and safety of everyone on board, to assure that the vessel is seaworthy, and to confirm that the proper navigation and operating procedures are utilized.
- *Staff captain (first officer).* This person is second in command of the ship. He or she is responsible for it when the captain is not on board. Other responsibilities include those relating to the ship's doctor, security and safety, navigation, and maintenance (performed by the boatswain).
- *Chief engineer.* This officer's responsibility relates to the power plant that runs the ship; environmental systems for heating, ventilating, and air conditioning (HVAC); plumbing; fire safety; waste management; and on-board communications.
- *Hotel manager.* This official is responsible for the ship's shore excursion manager and cruise director, the purser (the ship's officer who manages all financial matters along with the ship's information desk), the food and beverage manager, and the chief steward (who is responsible for

---

WHY SOME PEOPLE DON'T CRUISE

Perceptions are reality, and some people are not interested in cruises because of their perceptions about the following:

- Expense
- Exclusivity (cruising is thought to be an upper-class pastime)
- Single and adult market (the belief that cruises are not suitable for families with children)
- Confined space and lack of quiet spaces
- The prevalence of sea sickness and other discomforts
- Schedules that must be tightly adhered to; concerns about dining at specified times and spending a required amount of time at a port-of-call are examples of routines that disinterest some persons

The cruise line industry is working to educate the public about what the cruise is and what it is not. As it becomes more successful, more persons will likely try and enjoy cruise experiences.

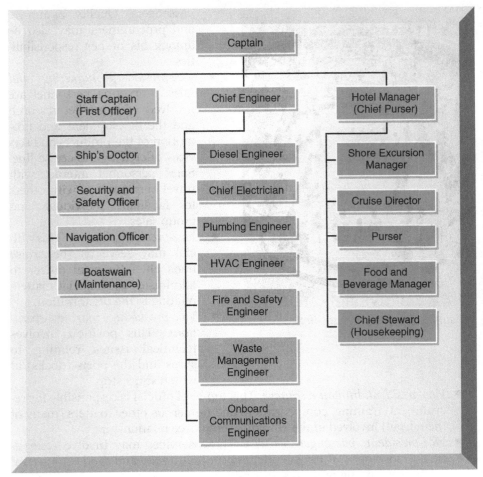

EXHIBIT 2
Common Management Positions on Cruise Ships

housekeeping). (Hospitality management graduates are most likely to obtain onboard positions within the hotel manager's department.)

Management positions needed for the land-based support of cruise line organizations are basically divided into the same functional areas as in other large hospitality operations. Exhibit 3 identifies some of these. Let's look at each of these positions.

- *Vice-president, hotel operations.* This position relates to planning and coordinating onboard guest services and land programs made available to

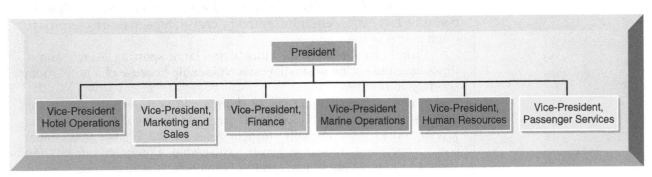

EXHIBIT 3
Common Land-Based Management Positions in the Cruise Line Industry

Getty Images Inc.-Stone Allstock, Jonathan Morgan photographer

Swimming pool on a cruise ship

passengers. Quality assurance and procurement may also be among his or her responsibilities.

- *Vice-president, marketing and sales.* Marketing personnel are involved with market research and the development and promotion of the products and services offered by the cruise line. Sales personnel interact with travel agencies and with others to facilitate individual and group sales.
- *Vice-president, finance.* This official may serve as the cruise line's chief financial officer to administer all financial matters relating to the organization.
- *Vice-president, marine operations.* This position involves technical issues relating to ships and the ports (docks) at which ships stop.
- *Vice-president, human resources.* This top-level official is responsible for recruitment, training, compensation, and numerous other matters (many of them legal) involved in the employer–employee relationship.
- *Vice-president, passenger services.* These services may involve reservations, movement of luggage, and coordinating air and land and arrival schedules, among other responsibilities.

OBJECTIVE 5
Explain procedures used to sell cruise vacations.

SELLING THE CRUISE EXPERIENCE

Some seasoned cruisers enjoy one or more holidays at sea every year. Planning and arranging their cruise experience require less time and difficulty than the efforts required for noncruisers, who typically do much preplanning for a land-based vacation by automobile with their family. By contrast, other,

DID YOU KNOW?

Cruise ships have been and are being used for nontraditional purposes. For example, cruise ships were used as temporary shelters for persons affected by Hurricane Katrina in the New Orleans area after it made landfall in the fall of 2005. Visitors and others in Lebanon during the events of July 2006 were transported by cruise ships to nearby Cyprus to catch planes to their homes.

Visitors to Jacksonville, Florida, for large sporting events, sometimes have the option of staying on a cruise ship because of a hotel room shortage in the area.

A new concept: *condo cruise ships*. Condo cruise lines are selling condo suites on cruise ships. Owners pay a standard condo fee (between $7,000 and $10,000 annually) to help generate the $15,000,000 annual cost to operate a mid-sized luxury cruise ship. For more information about this lodging alternative, go to www.condocruiselines.com.

CRUISE SHIPS: WHO IS IN CHARGE OF WHAT?

Some cruise lines retain **concessionaires** to provide some of the ship's services. Examples of such services include photography, beauty salons, and retail gift shops. Some cruise lines subcontract almost every service, including casino management, food and beverage operations, and entertainment. (When extensive use is made of concessionaires, the ship's hotel manager may be responsible only for housekeeping and social activities.)

especially first-time, cruisers consider cruise holidays to be very significant events for which extensive planning is important.

Cruise lines typically develop very colorful and informative brochures to advertise cruises far in advance of the actual event. In fact, many passengers book their cruise vacations more than one year in advance of the cruise. While some cruisers book directly with the cruise line company (and the number may increase because of the Internet), the vast majority of passengers utilize a travel agency or other intermediary to help in making selection decisions and arrangements for their cruise.

Why do many passengers book their cruises through travel agencies? The answer is that, unfortunately, booking a cruise is more complicated than making a reservation for an airplane flight or a hotel room (which travelers increasingly do themselves). A significant amount of information is needed, which, historically, many travel agents have been able to provide. As well, some, especially first-time prospective cruisers, desire advice about the cruise that is best for them. Numerous cruise lines offer cruises to many destinations, and onboard cruising environments make the decision-making task even more daunting; many persons do not know where to find information to answer their questions other than a travel agent.

Consider just one variable: cost. There can be 30 or more different charges for one specific cruise depending on cabin size and location and pre- and post-cruise packages. Cruise lines utilize **yield management** practices, which also have a significant impact on costs for a cruise. The extent of discounting, if any, from brochure-stated prices also affects ticket price. Cruise lines have historically offered numerous and very creative discounting plans that create wide differences between brochure and actual cruise prices and even between what two passengers in neighboring cabins pay for the same cruise.

concessionaire a for-profit business that has been granted the right to provide agreed-on products and services to the organization's (cruise ship's) passengers (customers)

yield management a demand forecasting system designed to maximize revenue by maintaining high rates (charges) during times of high demand and by decreasing rates (charges) when there is lower demand

Buffet on a cruise ship

PhotoEdit, Jeff Greenberg photographer

NAUTICAL GLOSSARY

Aft   Toward or near the stern (back) of the ship.

Air/sea package   A single price charged a tourist for airfare to and from the point of departure, the airport-to-dock and return), the cruise and, perhaps, lodging before or after the cruise.

Basis two (also called *double occupancy*)   Pricing per person based on two passengers sharing a stateroom designed to accommodate two or more passengers.

Beam   The width of the ship at its widest point.

Berth   A bed on a ship; also can refer to the docking space of a ship at port.

Boat deck   The deck where the lifeboats are located.

Bow   The front of the ship.

Bridge   Place on the ship from where it is controlled.

Bulkhead   An upright partition or wall dividing the ship into cabins and compartments.

Cabin itinerary (also called *round-trip itinerary*)   The route with ports of call (stops) for a ship leaving from and returning to the same port.

Cabin steward   The person who maintains staterooms.

Course   The direction in which the ship is headed; usually expressed in compass degrees.

Cruise Lines International Association (CLIA)   A trade organization that consists of representative cruise lines and travel agency affiliates.

Cruise-only trip   Cruise with no associated arrangement for air transportation.

Deck   The equivalent of a story (floor) in a building.

Deck plan   The ship's floor plan showing cabins and public spaces.

Disembarkation (also called *debarkation*)   Exiting the ship.

Dock   A berth, pier, or quay.

Embarkation   Boarding the ship.

Fathom   A measurement of distance (usually depth) in the water; equal to 6 feet.

First seating (or *sitting*)   The earliest of two meal times in the ship's dining room.

Forward   Toward or near the bow (front) of the ship.

Free port   A port or place free of custom's duty and regulations.

Funnel   A smokestack (chimney) of the ship.

Galley   The ship's kitchen.

Gangway   The opening through the ship's side and the corresponding ramp by which passengers embark or disembark.

Gross registered ton (GRT)   A measurement of 100 cubic feet of enclosed revenue space within a ship.

Hold   Interior space below the main deck for storage or cargo where passengers are not allowed.

Hull   The part of the ship that rests in the water; the frame or body of the ship, exclusive of the superstructure.

Inside cabin   Passenger accommodations without a window or porthole; located in the interior of a ship.

Knot   A unit of speed equal to one nautical mile (6,076 feet) per hour, as compared to a land mile of 5,280 feet.

Lido deck   Pool deck area that offers informal, buffetlike dining, both indoors and outdoors.

Manifest   A list or invoice of a ship's passengers, crew, and cargo.

One-way itinerary   Itinerary with the ship starting at one port and finishing at another.

Open seating (or *sitting*)   A dining plan in which passengers may sit anywhere in the dining room; tables are not assigned.

Past passenger rate (also called *alumni rate*)   A discounted rate given to persons who have previously sailed a cruise line.

Pax   The industry abbreviation for "passengers."

Port When facing forward, this is the left side of the ship.

Port charge What ports charge to dock a ship.

Port day A day when the ship stops at a port of call.

Postcruise package A package that includes lodging at the ship's arrival port after the cruise.

Precruise package A package that includes lodging at the ship's departure port before the cruise.

Pitch The front-to-back (bow-to-stern) motion of a ship.

Porthole Round window or opening on the side of the ship.

Quay (pronounced *key*) A berth, dock, or pier.

Registry The country whose laws the ship and its owners are obliged to obey, in addition to complying with the laws of the countries where the ship calls and/or embarks passengers.

Repositioning cruise A cruise during which the ship moves from one general cruise area to another.

Roll The side-to-side motion of the ship.

Seating times Scheduled times when certain meals are served in the formal dining room of a ship. Usually there are two seatings: main (early) and second (late).

Shore excursion A port-based tour or activity.

Space ratio A measure of how much space is occupied by one passenger if a full complement of passengers is sailing; equals GRT divided by standard passenger capacity.

Stabilizers Finlike, gyroscopically operated devices that extend from both sides of the ship below the waterline to provide a more stable motion.

Stack A funnel from which the ship's combustion gases are exhausted to the atmosphere.

Starboard When facing forward, the right side of the ship.

Stateroom (also called *cabin*) A guest room on a ship.

Stern The back end of the ship.

Suite The most expensive type of passenger accommodation; generally consists of a sitting area, one or two bedrooms, a bathroom, a kitchenette, and a verandah.

Superstructure The part of the ship above the hull.

Table assignments Assigned tables in the dining room for scheduled meals that accommodate two to ten people.

Tender A small boat that ferries passengers between port and ship.

Weather deck Any deck open to the outside.

Windward Toward the wind.

A 24-hour pizzeria on a cruise ship

Carnival Cruise Lines

LAND OR CRUISE VACATIONS: WHICH ARE MORE EXPENSIVE?

Many persons have a perception that cruises are much more expensive than land vacations. Is this correct?

When a tourist thinks about a land vacation, he or she typically thinks about the (relatively) low hotel room rental price, but may disregard the (relatively) high additional costs for meals, land transportation, entertainment, and other charges. By contrast, most charges for a cruise are **bundled** (all-inclusive), which suggests a relatively high initial purchase price, but relatively fewer additional costs. This creates, for many, "sticker shock" at the first step of price comparison.

Most persons consider more than costs when making vacation plans. However, when cost differentials are significant, this factor is important. Cruise lines, their industry association (Cruise Lines International Association), and knowledgeable **travel agents** are working to educate consumers about the real costs of this holiday alternative.

The cruise industry is increasingly being challenged by land vacations that are all-inclusive. Some land resorts, such as Club Med and Sandals, offer packages including room, food and beverages (including alcoholic beverages), beach, entertainment, and other activities and even have no-tipping policies. The number of vacationers purchasing all-inclusive land vacations is increasing each year.

bundled (charges) costs for several (or more) products or services in an all-inclusive charge

travel agent a person or company (travel agency) that sells travel products and services to the public and is compensated for this service by fees charged to the buyer and/or by commissions paid by the travel supplier

OBJECTIVE 6
Note basic sources of revenues on cruise ships.

Some travel agencies are full service. As the name implies, they sell any travel product or service available to the public. By contrast, others specialize in one product or service. For example, some agencies primarily sell cruises and have a great deal of knowledge about this special travel product. The best (usually higher-volume) agencies may have relationships with one or more cruise lines that enable them to pass on discounts and value-added benefits (such as stateroom upgrades) to their clients.

Omni-Photo Communications, Inc., Jeff Greenberg photographer

Guests dining on an observation deck of a cruise ship

GENERATING REVENUE ON THE CRUISE

As you have learned, many charges that one would incur on a land-based vacation are bundled into their cruise costs; however, cruise lines still generate significant amounts of revenues from most passengers. Let's see how.

- *Alcoholic beverage sales.* Sale of alcoholic beverages is the single biggest source of onboard revenue on many cruise ships. Modern liners are designed to have numerous beverage outlets conveniently available, highly visible, and opened at the times when passengers are most likely to utilize them.
- *Photographs and videos.* Photographers are available on many cruise ships from the time one embarks to when one debarks and at many

times in between. Photo opportunities occur during the captain's reception, at the dinner table, and frequently at other times when candid photo opportunities arise.

- *Ship's casino.* While most passengers do not take a cruise primarily to gamble (some do!), some passengers do gamble and many others like to watch. Some cruise lines market to high-rollers, and other companies schedule special cruises catering to passengers who enjoy gambling.
- *Merchandise with the ship's logo, souvenirs, and necessities.* These suggest the range of items sold in retail shops on cruise lines. Revenues may also be generated from onshore shops that are promoted by cruise line personnel as ships enter a port of call.
- *Beauty salons and spas.* Passengers can have massages, facials, hair styling, and even mud baths onboard cruise ships.
- *Shore excursions.* Some cruise lines own buses and boats, for example, that passengers utilize for extra-cost activities.

RISING STAR PROFILE

Mike Laundry
Hotel Director
Pride of Aloha (Hawaii)
Norwegian Cruise Lines–America

Mike received an undergraduate degree in marketing and management with a minor in accounting from North Adams State College in Massachusetts in 1992.

Although he spent six months working in a hotel in Miami, he basically came right out of college and went right onto the ships. "I wasn't sure exactly how I was going to like working and living on a cruise ship, but once I got on board I realized that a life at sea could be very rewarding and fulfilling, both personally and professionally. I started out as a junior purser and, after working my way up through the ranks, became a hotel director earlier this year. I am responsible for all of the ship's hotel systems, including cabins, food and beverage, entertainment, and spa. Depending on the size of the ship, I am responsible for the management of upward of 800 employees.

"I joined Carnival Cruise Lines in 1994 and participated in the launch of three new ships, including the 2,052-passenger *Imagination* in 1995, the 2,642-passenger *Carnival Destiny* in 1996 (at the time the world's largest cruise ship), and the 2,124-passenger *Carnival Pride* in 2002. For these ship introductions, I traveled to shipyards in Italy and Finland and then sailed across the Atlantic to the United States. The launch of a new ship is a massive undertaking with a great deal of responsibility and provides an excellent opportunity to

showcase my job skills. Above all, these ship introductions provided me with unforgettable memories for years to come."

In his present position, Mike is onboard the Pride of Aloha, a cruise ship that makes inter-island cruises around the Hawaiian Islands.

Mike commented on the most significant challenges facing the cruise industry: Only a relatively small percentage of the population has ever taken a cruise. This means that there is tremendous room for growth. Today's massive cruise ships are dramatically different than even just a few years ago. They offer more and varied dining, entertainment, and activity options than ever before. The industry must continue to push the envelope in terms of onboard amenities in efforts to find ways to attract new cruisers."

Mike was asked about changes he would make in his career: "I wouldn't change a thing. I have put in a lot of hard work over the years, and it has definitely paid off. I have worked with very talented people from all over the world, including an excellent management team that has provided encouragement and allowed me to learn and grow in my professional career."

He also provided advice for young people considering a career in the cruise industry: "A life at sea can be very rewarding. Modern cruise lines provide a comfortable working environment. Granted, there is lots of hard work; cruise ships operate on a 24/7 basis. However, working aboard ship provides a unique opportunity to help guests' vacation dreams come true, to see the world, and to interact with people from all walks of life. Not many jobs can make that claim!"

OBJECTIVE 7
Consider challenges
confronting the cruise
line industry.

CHALLENGES! CHALLENGES!

Several challenges that confront the cruise line industry must be effectively managed to help to assure the short- and long-term success of the industry.

Getty Images, Inc.-Photodisc, EyeWire Collection

Cruise ship at port

Increased Competition

Larger and larger capacity cruise ships are on order and being delivered. Cruise line companies will need to more aggressively compete for cruise line passengers. A key element in this competition will be the tactics used to encourage first-time cruisers to consider this holiday alternative and to convert their potential interests to cruise ticket sales.

Competition will also come from land-based vacation alternatives offering all-inclusive prices. Since most or all of these resorts are at oceanfront locations, they can offer many of the same type of water-related activities as do their cruise ship counterparts.

Increasing Incremental Revenues

How can cruise lines encourage cruisers to spend more while on the ship? Upgrading (to higher-priced staterooms) and tactics to encourage cruisers to purchase noninclusive amenities available on the ships will be very important in helping to assure the long-term success of specific cruise line organizations.

Holland America Line

Dining room on a cruise ship

At-Sea Security Concerns

The possibility of terrorist acts now confronts all segments of society, including the hospitality industry in general and cruise liners more specifically. The very large numbers of passengers and crew on many cruise ships makes these ships attractive to those who would commit terrorists acts. Increased passenger and baggage screening and ship protection while at port are among the tactics that will be increasingly used to protect ships and their passengers and crew.

DID YOU KNOW?

Believe it or not, sea piracy can be a security concern for cruise ships. While there were almost 450 attacks on commercial shipping in 2003, until recently cruise ships have been relatively safe from this concern. However, pirates in two small boats carrying machine guns and a rocket-propelled grenade attempted to board the Seabourn Cruise Lines *Seabourn Spirit* in November 2005 off the coast of Somalia. Its captain was able to use a combination of speed, change of course to the open sea, and a long-range acoustic device (LRAD) that generates an ear-splitting noise in a directed beam toward the pirates. Additionally, crew members used high-pressure fire hoses to prevent pirates from boarding the ship.

Source: Ship used high-tech device to ward off pirates' attack. *USA Today*, November 9, 2005, page 12A.

At-Sea Illness Concerns

Hundreds or thousands of passengers confined to cruise ships can create opportunities for the transmission of illnesses. For example, numerous cruises have been shortened or terminated because of the Norwalk virus, which has flulike symptoms that last several days or longer. Careful attention to proper sanitation practices at port and during cruises is very important, as is the effective cleaning and sanitizing of the ships on which passengers have contracted diseases.

SUMMARY OF CHAPTER LEARNING OBJECTIVES

1. **Present a brief history of cruising.**
   Ships have long been used for commerce, warfare, exploration, and business travel. Only recently, however, have they been used by persons enjoying their leisure time. While the first scheduled trans-Atlantic passenger sailing was in 1818, it was not until the early 1900s that ocean travel became relatively common. In the late 1950s, commercial jet service provided a much faster alternative across the Atlantic, and it was not until the 1970s that leisure cruising became more popular. Today, megaships carrying 2,000 or more passengers are being built in anticipation of a still greater increase in the cruise industry.

2. **Explore typical reasons why people cruise.**
   Passengers take cruises to relax, for travel and education, for social and status reasons,

to be safe during their travels, and as a family tradition.

3. **Review basic features of modern cruise ships.**

Modern cruise ships are built for space, not speed, and have significant spaces allocated for passenger staterooms and for the crew's privacy. Additionally, and to remain competitive, public spaces are available for a wide range of purposes and activities to meet or exceed the passengers' interests during the cruise.

4. **Describe common ship- and land-based management positions in the cruise industry.**

Common shipboard management positions include those of captain, staff captain, chief engineer, and hotel manager. Common land-based management positions include those of vice-presidents of hotel operations, marketing and sales, finance, marine operations, human resources, and passenger services.

5. **Explain procedures used to sell cruise vacations.**

Most cruise vacations are booked by travel agents. The purchase of a cruise, especially for first-time cruisers, can be complicated, and numerous pricing alternatives make the decision more difficult.

6. **Note basic sources of revenue on cruise ships.**

Even though many services of cruise ships are all-inclusive, significant amounts of revenue can be generated from passengers through alcoholic beverage sales, photographs and videos, the ship's casino, merchandise with logos, beauty salons and spas, and shore excursions.

7. **Consider challenges confronting the cruise line industry.**

Challenges include increased competition (especially as larger-capacity cruise ships come on line), finding ways to increase incremental revenues, and at-sea security and illness concerns.

FEEDBACK FROM THE REAL WORLD

Our real-world advice comes from Mary Ann Ramsey, CTC, DS, President, Betty Maclean Travel, Inc., Naples, Florida.

Among many other industry honors, Mary Ann serves as a member of the board of trustees of the Institute of Certified Travel Agents and is a member of Travel + Leisure's travel agent advisory board. She has also served on the advisory boards of Seabourn Cruise Lines, Royal Viking Line, and Norwegian Cruise Lines. In 1999, Ramsey launched the Adventure Travel Company, which offers experiences for travelers from safaris to climbing Mt. Kilimanjaro.

Why are travel agencies the biggest generator of cruise sales?

Making the decision to take a cruise is a very big decision for many persons. Also, while they generally know what they want (a great time and pleasant memories at a reasonable price), many persons really don't know what is best for them because they do not know what is available. Also, many, especially first-time, cruisers have family and friends who have taken a cruise with the assistance of travel agencies; therefore, "if they used a travel agent, so should I!"

Purchasing a cruise is more complicated than, for example, buying an airline ticket. The numerous cruise lines offer different prices for different cabin types at different times of the year on cruises to different ports.

My agency deals primarily with upscale cruises to Europe, Tahiti, Africa, and similar non-Caribbean destinations. Travelers cannot receive all information required to make their decision simply by contacting the cruise line directly. Take, for example, documentation: our travel consultants work carefully with our clients to assure that their passports and visas are in order. Countries have different requirements regarding multientry (points and times), number of days in the country, the length of time that passports are valid after entry into the country, and related technical concerns that we can address as we provide individualized attention to our clients.

How do travel agents interact with the cruise lines as they sell cruises?

Believe it or not, very little of our contact with a cruise line is by computer. Instead, we use telephone lines to contact cruise companies, who, in turn, use fax services to send confirmation. My agency, like many others, belongs to a marketing organization (a consortia). The service we belong to is called "Virtuoso." We are members based on the agency's volume and type of travel; we have access to an excellent cruise line database. One service provided by this organization is a newspage that is updated throughout the day. It provides much information about all matters of interest to cruisers and potential cruisers. This is a great help to us, as we can then pass this information on to our clients.

Do discounts and agency rebates help to generate cruise business?

Basically, our marketing consortia (Virtuoso) negotiates rates with cruise lines that are utilized by its subscribers. We are able to pass on significant savings for group fares, special rates for other cruisers, exclusive shore excursions, and onboard credits (for example, a private onboard cocktail reception and use of the ship's spa). Our clients also have access to a Voyager's Club, which utilizes a travel agency representative (host) to help all cruisers onboard who are clients of travel agencies participating in the Virtuoso Consortia.

Rebates may be used by some travel agencies; we do not. In effect, a rebate is part of a travel agency's commission that is given back to a cruiser to lower the price. In my experience, we don't do well when we compete with other agencies by price. Some cruisers may give price the highest priority in their cruise decision; they will, then, shop travel agencies. By contrast, we emphasize service, and we want to establish a long-term relationship based on the service, including the information that we provide.

What types of positions are available in travel agencies specializing in cruise sales?

Agencies like mine have great opportunities. For example, a young person might begin after college as a sales assistant who does research and cruise package processing after a deal is made with a client. Those who do well will be promoted to travel consultant, have direct client contact, and do some package processing. Persons with 10 years of successful experience can become senior consultants, who primarily have contact with clients desiring our most complicated trips.

From the perspective of a travel agent, what do you see to be the future of the cruise industry?

I see a lot more competition between cruise lines seeking passengers and travel agencies seeking clients. The future is bright, however, because only a relatively small percentage of people have taken a cruise. This will change, and the base of first-time cruisers and their repeat-cruise counterparts will yield a steady business for those cruise lines and travel agencies who can find creative ways to increase their markets.

MASTERING YOUR KNOWLEDGE

Discuss the following questions.

1. How important is price to the typical cruise passenger? How do prospective passengers evaluate the alternative charges that, in total, make up the purchase price for the cruise?
2. What types of value-added services might you as an owner or manager of a travel agency provide to increase the amount of cruise business you do?
3. Pretend that you are considering taking a cruise or flying to a coastal city for a vacation. What types of costs would need to be considered with both alternatives to determine the lowest-cost alternative? What factors in addition to cost would influence your purchase decision?

4. What types of menu planning factors might differ for the foodservice operation on a cruise ship versus that offered by a high check average restaurant?

LEARN FROM THE INTERNET

1. Check out the websites for several cruise line companies:
   - Carnival Cruise Lines: www.carnival.com
   - Norwegian Cruise Lines: www.ncl.com
   - Royal Caribbean International: www.royalcaribbean.com

   What types of pricing structures do they offer and how do they sell alternative packages to prospective passengers? What types of onboard amenities do they publicize? How, if at all, do they suggest that a cruise experience on their ship is better than on their competitors' ships?

2. Check out the websites for still other cruise lines:
   - Galapagos Cruises Inc.: www.galapagos-inc.com
   - World Explorer Cruises: www.wecruise.com
   - Society Expeditions: www.pacificislandstravel.com

   What information do they provide about the geography of the cruises, the ports of call and pre- and/or postcruise packages relating to the educational and cultural aspects of these destinations?

KEY HOSPITALITY TERMS

The following terms were explained in this chapter. Review the definitions of any words with which you are unfamiliar. Begin to utilize them as you expand your vocabulary as a hospitality professional.

cruise ship
megaship
stateroom
embarkation
debarkation

concessionaire
yield management
bundled (charges)
travel agent

Casino Entertainment Management

Alan Keohane © Dorling Kindersley

Slot machines on gaming floor of New York Hotel and Casino, Las Vegas, Nevada

CHAPTER LEARNING OBJECTIVES

After studying this chapter you will be able to:

1. Present an overview of the gaming industry.
2. Discuss reasons why people visit casinos.
3. Explain the organization of a casino.
4. Review the revenue and support centers in a typical casino.
5. Briefly review social problems sometimes associated with gaming.
6. Discuss challenges confronting the casino entertainment industry.

This chapter was authored by Vincent H. Eade, MA, Professor/Founding Director of the UNLV International Gaming Institute, William F. Harrah College of Hotel Administration, University of Nevada, Las Vegas. Mr. Eade is a co-author with his brother Raymond of *Introduction to the Casino Entertainment Industry*, Prentice Hall, Inc., Upper Saddle River, NJ, 1997.

FEEDBACK FROM THE REAL WORLD

In this chapter, you will learn that the casino entertainment industry is very large and profitable and that it is experiencing unprecedented growth. However, does the fascination and appeal that attracts visitors in ever-increasing numbers also apply to those who work within it? More specifically:

- What types of positions within the industry are most attractive to graduates of postsecondary hospitality programs?
- How, if at all, do management positions in this industry differ from their counterparts in applicable positions in restaurants and hotels? How are they the same?

- How important are lodging and food and beverage services to the success of large casinos?
- What is a typical promotion or career advancement pattern for a talented person desiring a career in the casino entertainment industry?

As you read this chapter, think about the answers to these questions and then get feedback from the real world at the end of the chapter.

---

casino a business operation that offers table and card games along with (usually) slot operations and other games of skill or chance and amenities that are marketed to customers seeking gaming activities and entertainment; many casinos also offer food and beverage services and lodging accomodations for the convenience of their visitors

racino a race track that has added slot machines to increase revenues

gaming any activity that involves wagering (betting) something of value on a game or event with an unknown outcome

wager to pledge (promise) something as the result of an event for which the outcome is unknown; also called *bet*

OBJECTIVE 1
Present an overview of the gaming industry.

table games games of chance involving wagering between the casino and its customers

black jack a table game in which the winner is the person closest to 21 without exceeding that number; also called *twenty-one*

The **casino** entertainment industry has captured the imagination of the business world and the consumer. Until the late 1980s, gaming was restricted in the United States to Las Vegas and Atlantic City. However, since that time it has expanded rapidly across the country, surfacing on Native American tribal reservations, riverboats, dockside locations, and **racinos,** as well as in numerous cities in other countries. To put the size of the gaming industry in perspective, casinos retain more revenue annually than the total of all money spent at movie box offices and on books, attractions, and recorded music.

Our study of this chapter will introduce positions that are unique to casino organizations. The potential for visitor and employee theft of significant amounts of cash in very short periods of time requires the need for layers of control, and the positions to implement and manage these controls are not necessary in other hospitality organizations.

The casino entertainment industry is the "new kid on the block" relative to most other segments of the hospitality industry. It is growing quickly in size and, at the same time, evolving in sophistication. This chapter will provide an overview of the casino entertainment industry and help you to decide if a career within it might be right for you.

OVERVIEW OF THE GAMING INDUSTRY

The **gaming** industry is very broad and diverse, as outlined in the following:

Casinos

A large casino typically offers the following types of **wagering** activities:

- **Table games.** Table games involve wagering between the casino and its customers. Common examples of table games include **black jack** or twenty-one, **dice** or crap games, **roulette,** the **big six** (also called Wheel of Fortune or Money Wheel), **baccarat, mini-baccarat, pai-gow, pai-gow poker,** and other games in which wagers are placed on a table or table layout as an integral part of the game.

- **Card games.** Card games differ from table games. With card games, the casino does not wager against the players but, instead, offers games in which players wager against each other while a casino employee (dealer) deals the cards. The casino relies on a fixed percentage taken from each hand played as its revenue source for card games.
- *Slot machines and video games.* Slot machines use simulated or actual spinning reels activated by a handle pull or a button push with **payoffs** based on a computerized random-number generator program or the alignment of graphics or symbols on a reel (for example, "three cherries across"). Video games include video poker, keno, bingo, and lottery terminals.

The casino in the Las Vegas Hilton

- **Bingo.** Bingo is a game in which players match numbers on cards they have "purchased" with numbers drawn at random.
- **Keno.** Keno is a variation of bingo in which an electronic board or screen is used to display numbers 1 to 80. Twenty numbers are randomly selected, and players mark a keno ticket indicating which numbers they believe will be drawn. Keno is, then, similar to a lottery drawing. Casinos have a keno lounge with keno runners who circulate throughout the casino accepting wagers on each game. Most casinos now have keno slot machines.
- **Race** or **sports books.** Race books feature wagering on horse racing; sports books take action on professional or collegiate sporting events. Casinos establish a line on games or other wagering propositions and take a percentage on wagers and losing bets.

dice table games in which a player wins or loses based on dice rolls; also called *crap games*

roulette a table game in which a large wheel is spun by a dealer who simultaneously spins a small white ball around the inside top rim of the wheel; wagers are placed on a number or color upon which it is hoped the ball will fall

big six a carnival-style game in which a large, upright wheel is spun by a dealer and players wager on which number the wheel will stop; the higher the payout, the greater the odds against hitting the number

baccarat a high-stakes table game using playing cards in which the highest (best) hand is nine, and the winner is the player closest to nine. In casinos, this game is played in a formal, separate room; dealers wear tuxedos

mini-baccarat a lower-stakes table game similar to baccarat, except the player does not have a turn as the bank and there is one dealer; in casinos, this game is less formal: it is played on the main floor and dealers wear the usual casino uniform

pai-gow a game in which four cards or tiles are dealt to players, who must have two hands higher than the dealer's or bank's hand; casinos get a commission on winning hands

(Photo credit, rotated:) © Dorling Kindersley, Courtesy of the Las Vegas Hilton

Horse and Dog Track Racing and Racinos

Pari-mutuel wagering is the most common system. Many states have legalized off-track betting. Casinos typically feature video monitors televising races at multiple tracks, and they provide food and beverages for their patrons as they study data, place wagers, and watch races.

Lotteries

Government-sponsored lotteries involve matching numbers predrawn by purchasers with those later selected in a public drawing; they provide lucrative forms of tax revenues after making very large (sometimes multimillion dollar) payoffs to lottery winners.

Golden Nugget Casino, Fremont Street, Las Vegas, Nevada

Alan Keohane © Dorling Kindersley

RIVERBOAT, DOCKSIDE, AND NATIVE AMERICAN CASINOS

Historically, gaming in the United States was legalized only in Las Vegas, Nevada, and Atlantic City, New Jersey. This changed in 1989, when Iowa approved riverboat gaming. This form of casino gaming quickly won legislative approval in numerous other states. Riverboat casinos typically cruise on rivers or in harbors and offer table and card games, as well as slot operations. Dockside operations are better classified as barges that are moored to a dock and do not cruise on a waterway. The variety and number of permissible games vary according to the dockside vessel's size and state gaming regulations. Some gaming vessels charge an admission fee, and riverboats cruise for a predetermined number of hours.

Native American (Indian) tribal casino gaming began in the late 1980s out of economic need and unique legal circumstances. Historically, tribes were regarded (or regarded themselves) as sovereign nations living on reservations arranged through treaties with the U.S. government. Court decisions set the legal foundation for gaming by asserting that, if a state currently regulates a form of gambling, then tribes living within that state can engage in gambling. Tribes and states negotiate compacts that establish the terms and conditions of operating a casino (for example, the gaming taxes to be paid to the state). More than one-third of the nation's federally recognized tribes now sponsor some type of gambling. Legislation (the Indian Gaming Regulatory Act of 1988) helps to assure that tribes are the beneficiaries of gaming revenues.

pai-gow poker a combination of Chinese pai-gow and poker using 52 cards and a joker

card games games of chance in which customers (players) wager against each other while a casino employee (dealer) deals the cards

payoff (gaming) any wager or winnings paid to a player

bingo a game in which players match numbers on cards with randomly drawn numbers

keno numbers 1 to 80 are displayed on an electronic board or screen; players mark a keno ticket indicating which 20 numbers they think will be drawn; keno is similar to lottery drawings

race book or **sports book** a casino department that accepts wagers on horse races or professional and collegiate sporting events

OBJECTIVE 2
Discuss reasons why people visit casinos.

Charitable Games

Churches and religious and nonprofit organizations offer bingo games, raffles, and Vegas Night promotions to raise money.

Other Gaming Venues

These include slot and video operations, bingo parlors, bowling sweepstakes, and social games such as dominoes, backgammon, checkers, chess, darts, and numerous others.

WHY VISIT CASINOS?

There are a number of socioeconomic and psychological reasons why people visit casinos. Some are presented in Exhibit 1. Let's look at each of these factors in more detail:

- *Gaming.* Many people like to gamble, wager, or participate in games of chance or skill. For some, it means a chance to "strike it rich" or, at least, to win some extra spending money. Others see gaming as a chance to break the bank or test their skills when their ability is pitted against the casino.
- *Recreation and entertainment.* Persons with discretionary income often seek new and different ways to enjoy their money; casinos offer an attractive alternative. The environment offers an exciting form of entertainment and, for many, a mental escape from pressures of their work and/or personal lives. In addition to gaming alternatives, casinos frequently offer live entertainment in show rooms or lounges and numerous

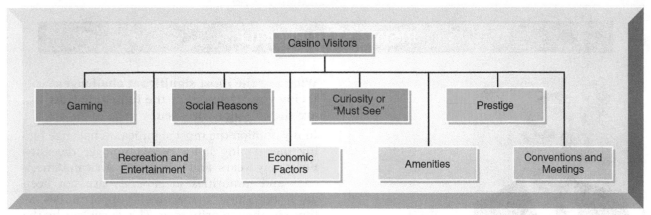

EXHIBIT 1
What Attracts Casino Visitors

restaurants (often including those affiliated with national chains). Other entertainment activities may include bowling, movie theaters, karaoke "sing-alongs," and shopping in retail outlets. Properties in applicable locations may incorporate water- or snow-related activities into their entertainment offerings. When traditional recreation, sporting, and entertainment amenities such as musical concerts, boxing matches, and golf are added to the potential experience, it is easy to understand the appeal of casinos to many visitors.

- *Social reasons.* Senior citizens and retirees more than any other group are drawn to casinos for the social interaction that occurs between customers and between customers and the property's employees. Civic organizations, clubs, and associations utilize casino meeting rooms for social gatherings.
- *Economic factors.* Since gaming is a vital source of revenues for hotels and casinos, these properties often offer excellent (low-priced) guestroom rates and value-priced buffets to attract visitors.
- *Curiosity or "must-see."* Today's mega-casinos have become "must-see" attractions for many persons. As casino gaming has progressed from being just legal to legitimate, more people want to see them.
- *Amenities.* Many people are drawn to the health spas, hair salons, beauty parlors, amusement centers, and theme attractions offered by casinos. Since these properties typically operate 24 hours a day, they serve as

pari-mutuel wagering
betting on horses in which odds based on the amount bet on each horse are established; winners share the total wagers placed in the pool among themselves based on the established odds

Slot machine players in action

PhotoEdit, Bill Bachmann photographer

RISING STAR PROFILE

Marcus W. Threats

My Advice: Be a Generalist!

Marcus has two associate of applied science degrees (in hotel administration and in casino management). He also earned a bachelors of science degree in hotel administration and a master in business administration. After graduation in 1987, he served for seven years as a naval officer and aviator in the U.S. Navy.

Marcus has worked in every major department in the gaming industry. He began as a bus boy at the age of 16 and worked his way up to the position of waiter. He has kitchen work experience as a dishwasher, kitchen runner, cook's helper, and fry cook and has also worked as a front-desk clerk to obtain hotel experience.

On the gaming side, Marcus has experience as a dealer, box supervisor, table-games supervisor, pit manager, and assistant casino shift manager. He gained his finance and accounting experience by working as a senior financial analyst and as a casino accounting manager.

What is the most unforgettable moment in your career?

The most unforgettable moment in my career was the last day I dealt dice at the Las Vegas Hilton. Dice dealers in those days split tips with the four dealers that made the team of the dice crew with whom you worked. That night, for the last two times I worked the stick position, the players never lost a bet. This allowed my crew to make more money than any of us had ever made in one night.

What are the most significant challenges facing your segment of the industry? How are they being addressed?

In my opinion the most significant challenge facing the gaming industry is employee diversity. For many years and still today African Americans and minorities in general have not been given the same management opportunities as those in the majority race. This is evident by the relatively few number of minorities working at the director level and above.

All the major gaming companies are working to address the issue of diversity. However, this is just the first step in a long journey. If the gaming industry is to mature as an industry and be recognized for its economic contributions to society, this industry must be willing to diversify its work force. This is important not only in entry-level positions, but also up to and including the executive level. I believe that it is just a matter of time before this maturity will occur.

What, if anything, would you do differently in your career?

I would change nothing in my career. I have been fortunate to have had some excellent mentors and instructors with whom I have maintained contact throughout my career. I continue to seek out these individuals and ask for their advice about my career.

What is your advice for young people considering a career in your industry segment?

My advice for a young person considering a career in the gaming industry is to get a college education along with work experience. The success of any person in the gaming industry lies in education, because the need to make educated business decisions will be crucial. Also, I recommend that young persons take the time to work in and learn about all the major areas of the industry, including hotel, food and beverage, and, finally, gaming. I believe that, in the future, it will be important to be a generalist. One will need to have a thorough knowledge about all the departments in the industry, rather than being a specialist with knowledge about only one area or department.

banking facilities to cash payroll and personal checks. Suites and public spaces may also serve as locations for weddings and parties.

- *Prestige.* Casinos attract gamblers by providing complimentary rooms, entertainment, food, beverages, gifts, and even airfare. This VIP (very important person) treatment provides status, and many recipients talk about the "comp" (complimentary) suites or "free" gourmet meals they receive.
- *Conventions, meetings, trade shows, and special events.* Casinos with public spaces book conventions, meetings, trade shows, or special events that draw attendees to the facility. While at these events, many people will visit the casino.

Not all casino visitors are attracted by all the factors noted in Exhibit 1. Many, however, are attracted by more than one factor. Each visitor, then, consciously and/or unconsciously is interested in attaining personal goals when he or she visits a casino. The extent to which these goals are met affects the quality of the casino experience.

ORGANIZATION OF CASINOS

Exhibit 2 shows a possible organization of a large casino property. While it is simplified (many additional positions are required), it does indicate how major responsibilities might be divided. Note, for example, that the general manager of the casino supervises directors of departments who are responsible for hotel operations, human resources, marketing, casino operations, finance, security, surveillance, food and beverage operations, and engineering and maintenance. With the exception of the director of casino operations, finance (who supervises the cage manager), and the director of surveillance (who has responsibility for control of significant amounts of currency assets), the responsibilities of the other casino directors are similar to those of their counterparts in other hospitality operations. (Some responsibilities of the director of security also differ. Detailed information about positions involving **casino cage** management, security, and surveillance will be presented in the next section of this chapter.)

Exhibit 2 also illustrates the management personnel who report to the director of casino operations. These individuals (the managers of customer development and VIP services, bingo, race and sports, slot operations, baccarat, table games, keno, and poker) occupy positions unique to their industry segment.

Let's look at one position, manager of table games, to see how career progression within this division might evolve. Exhibit 3 illustrates the chain of command for positions supervised by the manager of table games. Casinos typically develop detailed job descriptions that identify the tasks for each of these positions. Basic responsibilities for each include the following:

- *Manager, table games.* Responsible for the overall operation of the casino's table games and the personnel that staff them

casino cage the casino's banking center maintained by a cage manager; transactions with casino customers are conducted by casino cashiers at cage windows; the cage is responsible for the property's currency, coins, tokens, and gaming chips; casino pit clerks are an extension of the cage and work in the gaming pits on the casino floor; cage personnel prepare cash banks (for example, for restaurant cashiers) and bank deposits, cash checks for patrons, and place valuable items in safety deposit boxes; currency is also counted in a secure area of the cage

OBJECTIVE 3
Explain the organization of a casino.

Outdoor formal courtyard at Bellagio Resort Hotel in Las Vegas, Nevada

Russell MacMasters © Dorling Kindersley, Courtesy of the Spa Bellagio, Las Vegas

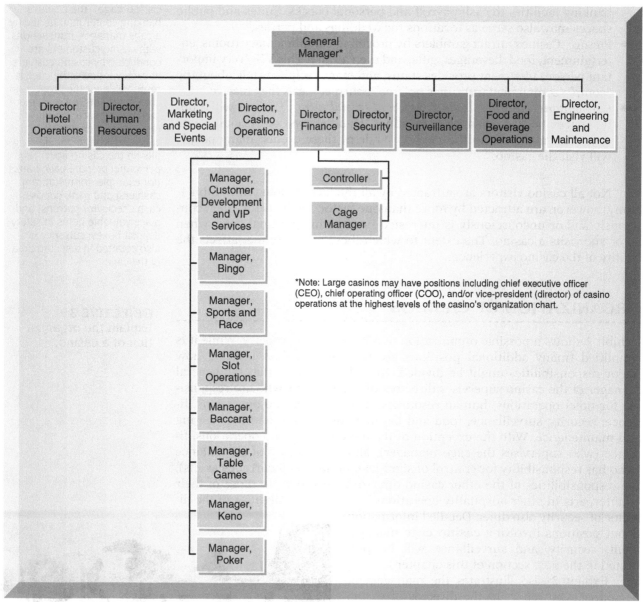

EXHIBIT 2
Organization Chart for Casino Operations

*Note: Large casinos may have positions including chief executive officer (CEO), chief operating officer (COO), and/or vice-president (director) of casino operations at the highest levels of the casino's organization chart.

- *Shift manager.* Responsible for the operation of table games and required personnel during a specific shift
- *Pit manager.* Responsible for the operation of table games and required personnel in a designated **pit** (specific tables in a designated location in the casino)
- *Floorperson.* Responsible for supervising an assigned group of tables within a pit
- *Dealer.* Responsible for the operation of a specific table game at one table within a pit
- **Boxperson.** Responsible for placing cash waged in a dice game into a drop slot in the dice table, placing waged chips in the rack, and protecting the integrity of the game

pit (casino table games) specific tables in a designated location in the casino

boxperson responsible for placing cash waged in a dice game into a drop slot in the dice table, placing waged chips in the rack, and protecting the integrity of the game

A similar chain of command exists for the other divisions within the casino operations department. Unseen in Exhibit 3 are other persons, including those in the surveillance and finance (casino cage) departments, whose very important work also affects positions in the games department. We will look at these positions more carefully in the next section.

REVENUE AND SUPPORT CENTERS

Revenue centers are, as the name implies, departments within the property that generate revenues. In a casino, there are gaming revenue centers (for example, table games and slots) and nongaming revenue centers (for example, lodging and restaurant sales). By contrast, **support centers** are nonrevenue-generating departments that are necessary to assist or support revenue centers. Exhibit 2 identified typical departments in a casino. Let's add a few more and sort them into revenue and support classifications.

Common revenue centers in a casino include the casino operations department, which, as you have learned, is responsible for the following:

Bingo	Table games
Race and sports books	Keno
Slots	Card games, including poker
Baccarat	

Other revenue centers include the hotel operations and the food and beverage operations departments. With the exception of these two departments, a casino's revenue centers are unique to this segment of the industry.

Support centers in a casino include the following:

Human resources
Marketing and sales
Finance (accounting and auditing)
Security
Surveillance
Engineering and maintenance

Some but not all of the functions performed by human resources, marketing and sales, and

Winning hand on a black jack table

Alan Keohane © Dorling Kindersley

EXHIBIT 3
Organization Chart: Focus on Manager of Table Games

engineering and maintenance personnel in hotels and other lodging properties are similar to those performed by their counterparts in casinos. However, much of the work undertaken by security and finance personnel and all the activities involving surveillance personnel are unique to casino operations. Let's look at these responsibilities.

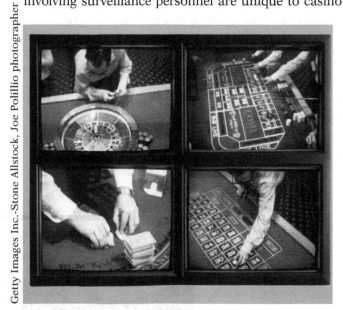

Surveillance scenes at a casino

A Close Look at the Security Department

Many of the responsibilities of a casino's security department are applicable to other hospitality operations. For example, security staff may escort employees to parking areas at night; assist local police authorities as they investigate criminal activities; maintain crowd control; ensure that all city, county, state, and federal codes and laws are complied with; and handle intoxicated or unruly guests. Other activities, however, are unique to casinos. These include the following:

- Escorting cash transfers from the casino floor to the casino cage
- Escorting guests who have won significant amounts of money to their car, airport, or other local destination
- Moving drop boxes from table pit games and transporting them to the casino cage
- Overseeing the slot drop done by a team of employees who remove coins from slot machines
- Guarding the casino cage and working to prevent robberies of and/or assaults on cage personnel
- Providing public relations assistance for the casino with its guests
- Assisting slot department personnel by witnessing the replenishment of slot booth bank rolls, hand-paying large jackpots won by slot players,

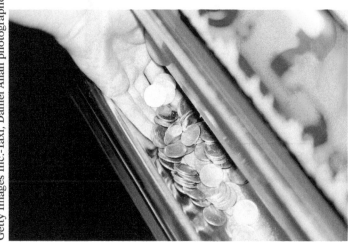

A slot machine pays a lucky player.

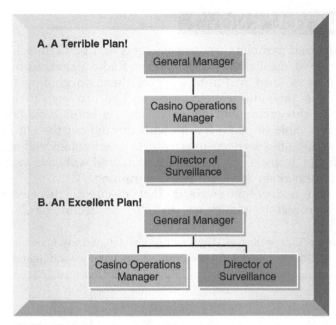

EXHIBIT 4
Effective Surveillance Is Critical

performing slot machine hopper fills (replacing coins in machines), and assisting with slot drops

- Assisting with credits and fills for table games (**credits** involve transporting gaming chips from a gaming table back to the casino cage; **fills** involve bringing gaming chips from the casino cage to fill the gaming tables' chip racks)

credits (casino gaming tables)   the security task of transporting gaming chips from tables to the casino cage

fills (casino gaming tables) the security task of transporting gaming chips from the casino cage to the tables

A Close Look at the Surveillance Department

A casino's surveillance department acts as a check and balance on the casino. As shown in Exhibit 4, it is critical that the director of surveillance report directly to the general manager. This reduces the potential for **collusion;** a separation of authority and power represents the foundation for sound and effective internal control procedures in a casino and in any other type of hospitality operation.

collusion   secret cooperation between two or more employees for the purpose of committing fraud

---

WHAT DOES THE SURVEILLANCE DEPARTMENT DO?

The primary function of a casino's surveillance department is detection of theft of company assets from gaming tables, slot machines, the casino cage, and all other revenue areas of the property.

Surveillance operations are done either with dedicated cameras permanently fixed on key revenue areas of the casino or by scanning cameras that randomly rotate and videotape less critical areas of the property. If a scam is detected, surveillance personnel contact the casino manager's office and call government regulators, who will then be available to arrest the cheater(s). (If casino floor supervisors believe that a problem is occurring in the gaming area, they will contact surveillance to request assistance in viewing the possible problem.)

Although it is impossible to catch every thief, especially with the high-tech devices now being used by scam artists, personnel casino surveillance departments historically uncover the major portion of scams. Certainly, the presence of cameras in the casino acts as a reminder to all visitors that surveillance personnel are on the watch!

DID YOU KNOW?

Chips that gamblers use to wage bets can be high-tech with radio frequency identification (RFID) inserts. Radio signals from the chips allow casinos to keep real-time track of them on gaming tables, to assess player points, and to help keep chips secure from theft or counterfeit. Use of this technology allows casinos to know their position on every gaming table in just a few seconds throughout the entire gaming floor. As well, pit bosses at casinos using this technology will no longer have to estimate drops at the end of each shift, and will have more time to focus on customer service and employee training.

To review one website that discusses this technology, go to www.progressivegaming.net and click on "technology."

Source: Tom Wilemon. High-tech chips let casinos keep track: radio signals thwart thieves. Retrieved February 7, 2006, from www.hotel-online.com

The first surveillance rooms in Las Vegas casinos featured an extensive network of catwalks over the casino. This enabled "eye-in-the-sky" personnel to visually view gaming areas through one-way smoked glass in the ceiling of the casino. Today's surveillance rooms use high-technology video cameras with zoom and wide-angle lenses, colored television monitors, computers capable of instantly reproducing photographs of suspected cheaters, and computer linkups to the slot tracking system so that surveillance employees can note cases of tampering. Videotape and digital recorders line the walls of the modern surveillance room, and this department maintains a video library of their observations, which can be used by casino department personnel for review purposes.

A Close Look at the Finance Department (Casino Cage)

The casino cage can rightfully be called the nerve center of the property. It has the responsibility for many vital functions.

- *Bank roll custodianship and accountability.* Bank roll requirements of a casino consist primarily of currency, coinage, and gaming chips (which must be accurately inventoried and closely monitored). One can imagine the extent of documentation and controls required of cage personnel as they account for millions of dollars on a daily basis.
- *Servicing the casino pits.* This involves providing table chip fills requested by a supervisor, receiving table chip credits authorized by a gaming supervisor, processing customer credit instruments (IOUs), and providing other help and information to casino supervisors.
- *Interaction with almost every revenue and nonrevenue department.* Casino cage personnel prepare cash banks and bank deposits, make customer payouts, and change customer's winning chips for currency and customer coins (for example, from slot winnings) to cash.

Exhibit 5 shows how a casino cage might be organized. The cage manager reports to the director of finance (or CFO or controller). He or she, in turn, supervises the work of the credit manager, who approves credit for casino customers, and the collections manager, who is responsible for collecting outstanding customer debts. (A basic principle of internal control is that

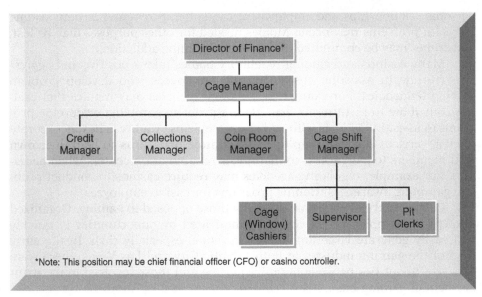

```
                    ┌─────────────────────┐
                    │ Director of Finance* │
                    └──────────┬──────────┘
                    ┌──────────┴──────────┐
                    │    Cage Manager     │
                    └──────────┬──────────┘
        ┌──────────────┬───────┴───────┬──────────────┐
   ┌─────────┐   ┌──────────┐   ┌───────────┐   ┌────────────┐
   │ Credit  │   │Collections│   │ Coin Room │   │ Cage Shift │
   │ Manager │   │ Manager  │   │  Manager  │   │  Manager   │
   └─────────┘   └──────────┘   └───────────┘   └─────┬──────┘
                                    ┌────────────┬────┴────┬───────────┐
                                ┌──────────┐ ┌──────────┐ ┌────────┐
                                │   Cage   │ │Supervisor│ │  Pit   │
                                │ (Window) │ │          │ │ Clerks │
                                │ Cashiers │ └──────────┘ └────────┘
                                └──────────┘
```

*Note: This position may be chief financial officer (CFO) or casino controller.

EXHIBIT 5
Organization of a Casino Cage

the individual who authorizes customer credit privileges should not be the same person who collects the debt. For this reason, then, these two positions are separated.)

Exhibit 5 also shows the coin room manager, who supervises the **slot drop** and count and is responsible for control of uncounted coinage during the drop. A team of employees circulates throughout the casino, removing coins from slot machines that have been won by the machine and have dropped or fallen into a bucket at the bottom of the machine. The team is known as the hard-count team (coins are hard and currency is soft; therefore, casinos have hard-count teams and soft-count teams). The hard-count team transports the coins to a hard-count room where the coins are counted by machines (actually they are weighed!) and wrapped for deposit purposes or for circulation back into the casino.

slot drop the collection of slot machine coins taken by casino personnel who transport the coins to the casino cage

The cage shift manager performs the duties and responsibilities of the cage manager in his or her absence. This includes the responsibility for the physical (custodial) control of all assets held in the cashier's cage during the assigned shift. The cage shift manager also supervises front-line cage personnel, including cashiers, supervisors, and **pit clerks** (who provide information helpful in generating **marker** transactions for a specified number of tables within the casino).

pit clerks a person reporting to the casino cage shift manager who provides information helpful in generating fill, credit, and marker transactions for a specified number of tables within the casino

marker similar to an IOU; casinos do a credit check on customers and extend credit by use of a marker based on their financial background and ability to pay; customers can sign these markers and use the money to gamble

GAMING AND SOCIETY

Some persons become addicted to gaming. When the need to gamble becomes a priority in one's life,

Coin bucket from Mirage Casino

© Dorling Kindersley

OBJECTIVE 5
Briefly review social problems sometimes associated with gaming.

personal relationships and employment can suffer. Stress and anxiety leading to health problems may occur. Monies needed for other purposes may be lost, and crimes may be committed to support the gaming addiction.

Many casinos and gaming regulatory bodies take a positive and aggressive attitude in assisting customers and employees who develop problem gaming tendencies. For example, regulatory agencies may require that casinos contribute to institutions that address problem gambling or develop programs to assist individuals with addiction problems. Many casinos incorporate referral services through **employee assistance programs** to help their own staff members to gain access to therapy or rehabilitation centers when necessary. For example, regulating agencies may require casinos to conduct problem gambling awareness training programs for casino employees.

employee assistance program a counseling and/or referral plan sponsored by an organization for its employees with personal problems

Concerns about crime are noted by those opposed to gaming. Organized crime, for example, has always been motivated by opportunities to quickly and easily generate large amounts of revenue, especially cash. In the early days of the gaming industry in both Atlantic City and Las Vegas, there were concerns about ties between organized crime and those involved in the management of gaming businesses.

Today, however, several things have changed. First, government regulations place significant controls on casinos. Also, the largest casino organizations are legitimate businesses in every sense, as are their counterparts in other segments of the hospitality industry. Most of the larger casino organizations are publicly traded and have stockholders. The integrity of owners and top-level managers provides another obstacle to infiltration by professional criminals.

There are also concerns about other types of crimes, sometimes called street crimes. Prostitution, crimes committed by persons to support their gambling habits, and crimes upon visitors to casinos are examples.

Elected officials and the voting public in general constantly evaluate the advantages of gaming, including a community's economic development and lowered unemployment rates, with the potential for criminal activity and social issues. These analyses include many of the same types of cost–benefit and decision-making processes that are applicable to numerous other issues within our society.

OBJECTIVE 6
Discuss challenges confronting the casino entertainment industry.

CHALLENGES! CHALLENGES!

Some challenges confronting casinos are similar to those of other segments of the hospitality industry; others are different. Let's look at both types.

Need to Attract and Retain a Qualified Work Force

Training needs to occur at three levels: skilled front-line employees, supervisory to mid-management personnel, and executives. Training venues include in-house programs, those offered by for-profit businesses such as dealer schools, and those provided by slot manufacturing companies (for technicians) and postsecondary educational facilities. It is likely that future casino managers and executives will have both postsecondary and graduate degrees. Also, a national certification program and exam for casino executives are likely.

Increased Government Regulation

Government is concerned that the industry be properly regulated. As an example, casinos must comply with federal laws designed to prevent money laundering. Recently, in the United States, a federally appointed committee conducted a lengthy study. It visited a number of gaming jurisdictions, assessed the impact

Spa Bellagio at Bellagio Resort Hotel in Las Vegas, Nevada

of gaming, and published its results and observations as part of the *Congressional Record*. There have also been legislative discussions about a wagering ban on collegiate athletic events.

Increased Efforts to Address Problem Gambling

Although problem gamblers represent a very small percentage of those involved in casino-style gambling, this is still a high-profile societal issue. Resistance to legalized gambling will likely continue, and those who research in this area will need to focus on solutions, as well as on the nature, causes, and extent of the problems.

Use of Technology

One of the greatest challenges confronting the future of gaming relates to technology. Gaming is already offered over the Internet. If legal issues involved in regulating computerized gaming are resolved, a whole new venue for gaming may emerge. Technological changes in slot machines have already been dramatic and, eventually, virtual reality will enhance the sight and sound experience to create the ultimate in technological slot play. Casino play-at-home may be the next frontier, with television sets used to display slot machines online from casinos. (While making gaming more accessible, this concept removes the excitement and live casino environment and would likely face legal challenges relating to underage gambling controls. However, it does point to the possibility of many different gambling opportunities both within and outside the traditional casino environment.)

Technology has also dramatically changed the slot industry. One of the most significant changes has been the conversion from slot machines that drop coins when a player cashes out to a coinless and reusable voucher or ticket system. This has resulted in the elimination of hopper fills (coins being placed in the machine hopper) and the need for a hard-count team and has yielded improved customer service. Technology will continue to drive the slot manufacturing industry based on customer need and demand.

The gaming leaders of tomorrow will need to pay close attention to customer expectations and how the use of technology can help exceed these expectations.

Increased Competition

An additional challenge relates to increased competition, which will cause many casinos to reinvent their operations and look for new ways to attract and retain new markets of customers.

More Nongaming Revenue

In recent years, the Las Vegas gaming industry has witnessed an interesting phenomenon: more money is being generated from nongaming revenue sources. Casinos have realized that guests are willing to spend money on items that, historically, were viewed as secondary sources of income. Today, Las Vegas casinos rely on the sale of food, wines, concerts, beverages at ultralounges (bars or nightclubs), shows and entertainment venues, bowling alleys, movie theaters, and special events to drive their bottomline. Much like Las Vegas, other gaming operators face the challenge of continuing to make their operations increasingly productive in a competitive environment and will need to examine ways to add new revenue streams to their businesses.

International Growth

Gaming has not only seen explosive growth in the United States in the past decade, but we have also witnessed the expansion of gaming globally. International gaming corporations have expanded or started casino operations in countries throughout the world. Gaming companies based in the United States have made business ventures into Macau and the Pacific rim. The members of the gaming industry are becoming fewer and more connected, and casino operators will face the challenge of global competition for customers.

SUMMARY OF CHAPTER LEARNING OBJECTIVES

1. **Present an overview of the gaming industry.**
Casinos are a significant part of the gaming industry. A large casino typically offers numerous types of wagering: table games, card games, slot machines and video games, bingo, keno, and race and sports books. Other venues for gaming include horse and dog track betting, lotteries, charitable games, and numerous other gaming venues, including slot and video operations, bingo parlors, bowling sweepstakes, and social games such as dominoes, backgammon, checkers, chess, and darts.

2. **Discuss reasons why people visit casinos.**
A number of socioeconomic and psychological reasons explain why people visit casinos. These include a desire to gamble, recreation and entertainment, social reasons, economic factors, curiosity (must-see), amenities, and prestige.

3. **Explain the organization of a casino.**
A casino is generally headed by a general manager. He or she directly supervises the work of department heads, including those for hotel operations, human resources, marketing, casino operations, finance, security, surveillance, food and beverage operations, and engineering and maintenance.

4. **Review the revenue and support centers in a typical casino.**
Revenue centers are departments within the property that generate revenues. These include gaming revenue centers in the casino operations department and nongaming revenue centers such as in hotel operations and food and beverage operations. Support centers are nonrevenue-generating departments that are necessary to assist or support revenue centers.

Common examples in casinos include human resources, marketing, finance (accounting and auditing), security, surveillance, and engineering and maintenance.

5. **Briefly review social problems sometimes associated with gaming.**

   Examples of social problems sometimes associated with gaming include addiction and concerns about organized crime and street crimes.

6. **Discuss challenges confronting the casino entertainment industry.**

   Challenges confronting the casino entertainment industry include the need to attract and retain a qualified work force, the likelihood of increased governmental regulation, and the need to more proactively address problem gaming concerns. Other challenges relate to the use of technology, which may make gaming more accessible offsite and can be used to further improve casino equipment and machines, and increased competition, which may cause casinos to reinvent their operations. Generation of significant revenue streams from nongaming sources and fast-paced international growth in gaming are additional issues confronting today's decision makers in this segment.

FEEDBACK FROM THE REAL WORLD

Our real-world advice comes from the chapter's author, Vincent H. Eade, MA, Professor/Founding Director of the UNLV International Gaming Institute, William F. Harrah College of Hotel Administration, University of Nevada, Las Vegas.

Vince joined the UNLV faculty in 1986. He came to Las Vegas in 1975 to work for the Aladdin Hotel, where he was the assistant general manager and the rooms division manager until 1980. Thereafter, he worked as the corporate director of labor relations for the North Las Vegas Casino Corporation (the Silverbird, the Silver Nugget, and Silver City Casinos). He also served as the Aladdin's director of personnel and labor relations.

What types of positions within the industry are most attractive to graduates of postsecondary hospitality programs?

Graduates seeking a career in the casino entertainment industry often begin in entry-level management positions, in pit operations, and in the slot department, such as a slot floor person. Other graduates pursue careers as casino analysts or in casino marketing. Graduates are also frequently employed in nongaming departments in a hotel–casino in human resources, food and beverage, and the rooms division. Still other graduates work in the gaming industry, but not directly in a casino (for example, in sales positions for slot manufacturing companies or as game trainers for companies that develop new games or gaming devices). Other graduates work in the government regulatory sector.

How, if at all, do management positions in this industry differ from their counterparts in applicable positions in restaurants and hotels? How are they the same?

Let's first address how positions are the same. The casino segment, like the hotel and restaurant segments, is part of the hospitality industry. All segments are in the people or customer service business. Managers in the hospitality industry must understand customer service strategies,

(continued)

whether they work in a casino, hotel, restaurant, club, or other segment. Furthermore, as is the case with any other hospitality segment, the business cannot operate successfully without excellent employees. Managers must have strong human resources management skills, understand employee motivational strategies, including team building, and demonstrate strong coaching, mentoring, and leadership abilities.

The casino industry does have some unique features, challenges, and situations that confront its managers. For example, most casinos operate 24 hours a day, 7 days a week, and are fast-paced businesses. Managing in this environment requires the ability to work nontraditional shifts and to handle heavy volumes of customers (many of whom wager large sums of money). The products (table games and slots, for example) offered in a casino are unique, and managers must understand how the games operate, including the mathematics and game performance expectations. Rooms division managers in a hotel–casino may have to alter their thinking when it comes to selling some rooms. For instance, the top suites in a hotel–casino may not be for sale to the general public but, rather, are put on reserve to be "comped" for top casino customers.

How important are lodging and food and beverage services to the success of large casinos?

Lodging and food and beverage services are vitally important to the success of a casino for several reasons. At one time, casinos virtually gave away rooms, food, and beverages, believing this loss of revenue could be made up by the casino. Today, casino managers want to generate a profit in as many areas as possible or hope, at least, to reduce losses in other areas. Lodging, food, and beverage have become important nongaming revenue centers for casinos. Additionally, these operations serve as a marketing tool for casinos. Guests staying in a casino with lodging accommodations and food and beverage operations can plan extended stays and can enjoy the convenience of meals on-property if they choose to do so. Finally, these amenities add to the entertainment experience people can enjoy at a casino.

What is a typical promotion or career advancement pattern for a talented person desiring a career in the casino entertainment industry?

A person starting a career in pit or table game operations should have an extensive understanding of table game operations and customer relations. Some would argue that they must also have dealer experience. Thereafter, a typical promotion path would be to a floor person, pit manager, director of table games, assistant shift manager (or shift manager), and, finally, casino manager. Those pursuing a career in slots would likely start as a floor person, then progress to shift manager, and eventually to director of slot operations.

Once a student is 21 years old, it would be advantageous to do an internship and/or to secure a part-time job at a casino. This experience will help students understand the various components of the business and provide insights into potential career paths.

MASTERING YOUR KNOWLEDGE

Discuss the following questions.

1. What challenges might confront an experienced hotel manager who assumed that position in a hotel operations department of a casino? Conversely, what challenges will likely confront the experienced hotel operations manager in a casino organization who accepted a top management position in another segment of the lodging industry?
2. What challenges might confront an experienced food and beverage director who moved into the food and beverage department of a casino? Conversely, what challenges will likely confront the experienced food and beverage director in a casino organization who accepted a top management position in another segment of the foodservice industry?
3. What are examples of ways that casinos use two or more persons to control (manage) cash revenues in efforts to reduce theft?

LEARN FROM THE INTERNET

1. Check out the websites of several casinos that are not operated by Native Americans:
   - Resorts Atlantic City: www.resortsac.com
   - Bellagio Hotel & Casino: www.bellagio.com
   - MGM Grand–Las Vegas: www.mgmgrand.com
   - The Venetian Resort: www.venetian.com

   What attractions in addition to gaming do they make available for visitors?

2. Check out the websites of the following casinos and review the information provided about responsible gaming awareness:
   - Greektown Casino: www.greektowncasino.com
   - Mirage Hotel and Casino: www.themirage.com

   - Treasure Island Hotel & Casino: www.treasureisland.com
   - Trump Plaza: www.trumpplaza.com

3. Check out the websites for several Native American casinos:
   - Foxwoods Resort and Casino: www.foxwoods.com
   - Pechanga Resorts & Casino: www.pechanga.com
   - Soaring Eagle Casino & Resort: www.soaringeaglecasino.com

   How is the information provided in these websites similar to that offered by very large casino organizations? How is it different?

KEY HOSPITALITY TERMS

The following terms were explained in this chapter. Review the definitions of any words with which you are unfamiliar. Begin to utilize them as you expand your vocabulary as a hospitality professional.

casino
racino
gaming
wager
table games
black jack or twenty-one
dice
roulette
big six
baccarat
mini-baccarat
pai-gow
pai-gow poker
card games
payoff (gaming)
bingo

keno
race book or sports book
pari-mutuel wagering
casino cage
pit (casino table games)
boxperson
revenue centers
support centers
credits (casino gaming tables)
fills (casino gaming tables)
collusion
slot drop
pit clerks
marker
employee assistance program

Professional Meeting Management

Allyn & Bacon, John Coletti photographer

Meetings are an aspect of business that cannot be avoided.

CHAPTER LEARNING OBJECTIVES

After studying this chapter you will be able to:

1. Identify three types of meeting planners.
2. Describe basic responsibilities of meeting planners as a meeting is planned.
3. Explain basic procedures for meeting attendee registration.
4. Review basic information about housing meeting attendees.
5. Describe basic responsibilities of meeting planners as the meeting evolves.
6. Describe basic responsibilities of meeting planners as a meeting is concluded.
7. Discuss special aspects of a conference center education coordinator.

This chapter was authored by Curtis Love, PhD, Associate Professor, Department of Tourism and Convention Administration, William F. Harrah College of Hotel Administration, University of Nevada, Las Vegas.

FEEDBACK FROM THE REAL WORLD

A professional meeting planner has a very big job: to plan all the details of a meeting in such a way that it is successful within the financial boundaries established for it. One of the most important factors that will determine a meeting's financial success relates to the meeting site. The meeting planner is a professional, but so is the marketing and sales representative with whom the meeting planner must negotiate on behalf of the meeting's sponsor.

How would you answer the following questions:

- What are some of the most important tactics that a meeting planner can utilize during the negotiation process with representatives of the prospective meeting site to minimize costs without compromising the meeting's objectives?

- On what items is a hotel or other meeting site representative most likely to negotiate? Least likely?
- What are common mistakes that meeting planners make while planning a meeting?
- What are the most frequent problems that occur as attendees preregister for a meeting; what tactics can a professional meeting planner use to address these potential problems?
- What are the most important tasks that a meeting planner should do immediately after a meeting is concluded?

As you read this chapter, think about answers to these questions and then get feedback from the real world at the end of the chapter.

Meeting management is an integral part of the hospitality industry because meetings represent a very big business. They require sleeping rooms for those who travel long distances and food and beverage services for those attending them. In addition, the significant time and expenses incurred by attendees require that the meetings be professionally planned and managed to maximize their effectiveness. In this chapter, we will explore what meeting planners do in corporations and associations with sufficient meeting activities to require this position and in companies owned by entrepreneurs who plan and manage meetings for their clients.

OBJECTIVE 1
Identify three types of meeting planners.

meeting planner   a specialist who plans, manages, and follows up on all details of meetings and/or conventions

TYPES OF MEETING PLANNERS

There are three basic types of **meeting planners;** those who work for

- Corporations
- Associations
- Individual clients (independent planners)

Let's look at each of these types of meeting planners.

Corporate Meeting Planners

Corporate meeting planners are employed by a single company and may be involved in planning numerous meetings for personnel in different locations in different company divisions at the same time. Large organizations may employ many meeting planners, whose work is directed by a corporate meetings director (or similar title).

MEETINGS: ROI IS A MUST!

Business meetings are held for a purpose, and they must be worth more than they cost! It is relatively easy to determine a meeting's cost: attendee travel-related expenses and compensation while attending the meeting, site costs, speakers' fees, and numerous other charges can be calculated. Meeting budgets must be carefully planned to assure that these costs are managed. However, what is the worth of information presented at meetings? How can the value of the meeting to attendees be quantified? How can planners assure that there is an acceptable **return on investment (ROI)** so that meeting costs justify the expenses? These are questions that persons funding, planning, and attending meetings must increasingly answer.

Attendees at corporate meetings are generally required to attend; their travel, lodging, and related expenses are typically paid by the organization. Therefore, one challenge confronted by other types of meeting planners, promoting and estimating attendance, is less of a challenge. However, since corporate meetings typically involve persons who have attended previous meetings, planners are challenged to assure that sessions are creatively planned to maintain their interest.

return on investment (ROI) the measure of managerial efficiency that correlates profitability with the investment made to generate the profit

Association Meeting Planners

Thousands of business or trade and professional **associations** exist to provide education, lobbying, group purchase, and/or other services for members who share common professional, hobby, or other interests. Many of these associations have regional or national meetings and/or **conventions** or **trade shows.** In small associations, the planning may be the responsibility of the executive director (typically a compensated administrator). This official may retain the meeting planning task within the organization or may utilize an independent meeting planner to assist. Typically, volunteer members of executive boards, committees, and other influential members of associations provide input to meeting goals and determine the topics to be discussed. In larger associations, specialized meeting planners who are employees of the organization are utilized.

Association members decide if they wish to attend these meetings and, if so, they must pay their own expenses (or solicit funds from their employers, if applicable). The association meeting planner's task is to encourage attendance; this is a challenge in times when prospective attendees want to assure that return on investment concerns will be met.

association an organization with volunteer leadership (and usually a paid staff) that serves persons with a common interest or activity

convention a meeting of association members or those working within a profession

trade show an industry-specific event that allows suppliers to an industry to interact with, educate, and sell to individuals and businesses that are part of the industry; also called *exhibition*

Independent Meeting Planners

Independent meeting planners are in business to help customers such as small corporations, associations, and others who cannot afford or who do not need a full-time meeting planner. Independent planners may be entrepreneurs operating a one- or several-person business to larger organizations specializing in offering meeting planning services to numerous smaller businesses and associations.

The tasks of independent meeting planners are twofold. They must, first, generate clients and, second, assist clients with their meeting planning needs.

Many meetings are informal.

Getty Images, Inc.-Photodisc, EyeWire Collection

People like to attend meetings because of their direct benefits and also because many persons enjoy travel to and from the sessions and the opportunity to discover the community or area in which the meeting is held. While teleconferencing has a niche in the meetings industry, hotels, conference centers, and other locations will continue to be preferred sites for the conduct of meetings.

WHY DO PEOPLE ATTEND MEETINGS?

Meetings need to have well-thought-out objectives, and these objectives must drive the planning and conduct of the meeting. Meetings are held for numerous reasons, including the following:

Sales meetings. To introduce new products and services, to motivate salespersons, and to reward effective performers.

Stockholder meetings. To inform investors about the financial status of the business and to discuss problems, plans, and other matters of interest.

Management meetings. Managers and administrators at different organizational levels and/or in separate locations meet to develop plans, address problems, and discuss business concerns and opportunities.

Board of directors meetings. Top-level officials of associations and businesses meet to discuss the present and to plan for the future of their organizations.

Association conventions and trade shows. Professional associations may have an annual meeting that can attract thousands or more attendees to hear speakers and to participate in discussion sessions; booths manned by suppliers to the industry may be available to enable attendees to learn more about the products and services offered by the vendors.

Professional development meetings. Postsecondary educational institutions, for-profit training organizations, and others offer meetings that address ad hoc topics; these programs are marketed to a general and, often, very large group of potentially interested attendees.

Motivational meetings. Numerous professional motivational speakers offer programs ranging from several hours to several days, which are marketed to organizations and/or to individual attendees.

TECHNOLOGY AND MEETING MANAGEMENT

Modern technology enables the use of satellite and Internet-based conferences to minimize travel to common meeting sites. With this plan, meeting attendees can participate in **teleconferencing.** Sophisticated systems allow real-time, interactive conversations and discussions between participants. However, technology has not reduced the need for or benefits to employees in the same or different organizations in widespread locations to convene in traditional meetings for discussions about common issues.

RESPONSIBILITIES OF MEETING PLANNERS

OBJECTIVE 2
Describe basic responsibilities of meeting planners as a meeting is planned.

Persons who plan meetings must be creative, well organized, and able to manage, seemingly, a million and one details at the same time. The ability to effectively communicate is a necessary trait, as is the ability to negotiate for the best use of the resources available to the organization for which the meeting is intended. As Exhibit 1 illustrates, the work of a meeting planner can be divided into three components:

teleconferencing the conduct of meetings by using audio and visual communication technology to link persons in different locations

- Planning the meeting before it begins
- Managing the meeting as it evolves
- Following up after the meeting

SuperStock, Inc.

Planning the Meeting

The process of planning begins by defining the meeting's objectives. Effective meeting objectives focus on the attendees. What exactly is the purpose of the meeting? What will we accomplish if the meeting is ideal? Who should attend the meeting, and what is in it for them? How can we make our meeting more desirable than a competitor's event?

Videoconferencing provides another meeting alternative.

A common method of writing effective meeting objectives is to use the **SMART** approach. Each letter of the SMART approach reminds the planner of critical components of a well-written objective:

SMART the tactic of writing objectives that are **s**pecific, **m**easurable, **a**chievable, **r**elevant, and **t**ime focused

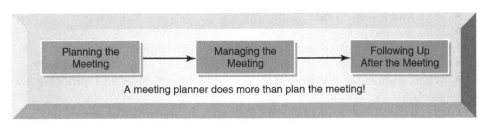

A meeting planner does more than plan the meeting!

EXHIBIT 1
A Meeting Planner's Activities

Specific. Only one major concept is covered in each objective.

Measurable. Must be able to quantify or measure whether the objective has been attained.

Achievable. Is it possible to accomplish the objective?

Relevant. Is the objective important to the organization's overall goals?

Time. By when should the objective be completed?

Meeting objectives should typically include cost factors (if applicable) and indicate who is responsible for achieving the objective.

The site-selection process can begin after meeting objectives are developed because they guide the planner in decisions about physical location, type of facility, transportation options, and many other meeting components. Site selection may occur days, weeks, months, or even years before the event. For major conventions, a city is usually selected three to five years in advance. Small corporate meetings are usually planned less than six months in advance. Factors such as location of attendees, costs, accessibility (transportation), type of meeting facility, and meeting space requirements are critical to the site-selection process.

After meeting objectives and the basic location are determined, a **request for proposal (RFP)** is written to describe all major needs of the meeting. It will typically contain information such as the following:

- Meeting name
- Meeting start and end dates
- Key contact information
- Expected attendance
- Number and type of sleeping rooms required
- Number and size of meeting and exhibition space (if any) required
- Food and beverage requirements
- Acceptable rates for rooms, meeting space, and food and beverage
- Expectations of comps (free services)
- Cutoff date for the submission of RFPs

The RFP is circulated to hotel properties and convention facilities that may be interested in submitting a bid. If a meeting facility decides to submit a proposal, representatives of its sales department review meeting specifications and create a response.

The ultimate goal for the property submitting the bid is to balance what the planner wants and can afford with the revenues needed by the property. Many factors must be considered. If low room rates are important to the planner, then perhaps a guarantee of providing all food and beverage during the meeting will balance out reduced room rates. Conversely, if the group does not want the facility to provide food and beverage, then additional charges for guest-room or meeting space rental will likely be assessed.

After the planner has reviewed the RFPs returned, negotiations between the planner and the prospective meeting site sales representative can begin.

The meeting planner's budget will be at the heart of the negotiation process. It will address questions such as these:

- How much will it cost?
- Who will pay?
- How much will attendees be charged for registration?
- What food and beverage events are planned and what will be served?
- What additional revenues are available to produce and promote the meeting?

The three basic steps for planning the meeting's budget are previewed in Exhibit 2. Let's look at each of these three steps more closely.

request for proposal (RFP) a formal document that incorporates the organization's needs expressed in the form of detailed specification requirements; the objective of the RFP is to define the required services so clearly that prospective bidders can develop costs and other estimates used in their proposal responses

RISING STAR PROFILE

Julie Price

Managing Meeting Details Has Its Rewards!

Julie's first hospitality position was as a food server at a restaurant in her home town while she was in high school. During college, she worked at the snack shop at the student activity center, as a front-desk attendant at a residence hall, and as a food server at a Bennigan's restaurant. During the summer after her sophomore year, she completed an internship with the Michigan Municipal League (the state's association of cities and villages), which, in hindsight, was very significant to her career. Julie received an undergraduate degree with a major in integrative public relations and a minor in broadcast cinematic arts.

She remained in contact with supervisors from her internship at the Michigan Municipal League after her internship. She desired a position in event planning and, as fate would have it, that organization was searching for someone with these responsibilities.

As the education coordinator, Julie coordinated about 80 training programs annually for city officials throughout the state. Site visits at hotels and conference facilities are needed and after the space is secured, the education coordinator is responsible for all logistics, including food and beverage, audiovisual, and special arrangements. It is also important to promote the training programs to increase attendance and to plan large events that may have as many as 1,200 attendees. For one of these (the Michigan Municipal League's state convention), she served as the media relations representative and wrote news releases, distributed press tips, and interacted with the news media.

Julie has an unforgettable moment: "Seeing everything come together with nearly 700 attendees at our annual convention; everything ran smoothly!"

Julie is well aware of the most significant challenges confronting the meetings industry: budget cuts and resulting drops in attendance. "Local governments run on very strict budgets and so does our association. We have to be practical. We cannot plan elaborate meetings and events, and I must constantly address prices."

Julie has some great advice for young persons considering a career in the meetings industry: "Attention to detail is a must, as is effective communication and negotiation skills. Always make sure to read the fine lines of contracts, and carefully negotiate with a facility before you sign any documents.

"Know that you are not going to make a lot of money right after graduation. However, positions like mine are a lot of fun and very rewarding. You don't have to sit behind your desk all day. You are always meeting people and planning things. This industry is amazing. There are so many 'perks,' and you make so many connections."

Step 1: *Establish Financial Goals* Financial goals should incorporate the SMART process. They may be established by the meeting planner, association management or corporate mandate, or the account (client) of the independent meeting planner. Financial goals are very important to develop and continually consider because they establish the financial expectations of the meeting. Some events may be not for profit (for example, an awards ceremony to honor top achievers in a company). Most association meetings, by contrast, rely heavily on conventions to produce operating revenues. A third economic goal can be to break even: revenue collected from all activities should cover the expenses.

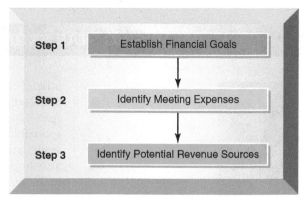

Step 1	Establish Financial Goals
Step 2	Identify Meeting Expenses
Step 3	Identify Potential Revenue Sources

EXHIBIT 2
How Is the Budget for the Meeting Planned?

Step 2: *Identify Meeting Expenses* Expenses vary according to the meeting's objectives and will be affected by location, season, type of facility, services selected, and other factors. Examples of costs include the following:

Registration materials
Speakers' travel expenses and fees
Signs, posters, and banners
Gratuities and gifts
Printing and photocopying
Room rental
Decorations and flowers
Shipping and freight charges
Complimentary registrations
Temporary staff
Food and beverage functions
Promotion
Multimedia equipment
Staff travel and expenses
Insurance
Supplies
Labor charges

Step 3: *Identify Potential Revenue Sources* How are meetings funded? Corporations include meeting costs in their operating budgets. Corporate planners must work within the constraints of the budget. Associations must be more creative in finding money to plan and implement an event. If the registration fee is too high, people won't attend. If it is too low, the association itself may not achieve revenue expectations. Association planners often look to funding sources, in addition to registration fees, such as these:

- Corporate or allied association funding
- Private funding
- Exhibitor fees (if trade show)
- Sponsorships (for example, of a speaker and/or a luncheon)
- Selling logo merchandise

Getty Images, Inc.-Image Bank,
Larry Dale Gordon photographer

Meetings can occur in a hotel conference room.

CLOSE LOOK AT THE MEETING PLANNING TEAM

Some members of the meeting planning team make decisions; others may be needed to implement the decisions. Decision makers are typically executives within the organization who approve the meeting and its budget, supervise the meeting planning team, and have responsibility for all legal, financial, and policy matters.

Meeting planners negotiate and recommend contracts, solicit bids, and hire and supervise suppliers. They also prepare drafts to monitor budget revenues and expenses, establish a planning schedule, recommend and implement policies and procedures, manage the on-site meeting as it evolves, and prepare follow-up documents and reports.

A wide variety of technical staff may be necessary depending on the size and type of meeting. These include specialists to:

Develop program topics and select speakers

Design copies for marketing and promotional pieces

Develop accounting and record-keeping systems for the meeting

Coordinate press relations

Assist with meeting technology needs

Review contracts and agreements

Prepare training materials and conduct sessions

Assess insurance coverage and risk management issues

- Advertising fees (banners or ads in the convention program, for example)
- Local, state, and national government assistance
- Renting membership address lists for marketing purposes
- Establishing official partnerships with other companies to promote products
- Contributions in cash or in kind (services or products)

Special Concerns: The Meeting Program

The program for the meeting involves all its scheduled activities, including presentations, food and beverage-related functions, trade show hours, non-meeting recreational alternatives, and **unscheduled time.** As with all other aspects of meeting planning, the objectives of the meeting drive its program of events. Meeting planners often help to select topics, presentation formats, and speakers that will most appeal to the meeting attendees.

Times for meeting schedules are important. How many days should the meeting last? How many hours per day should be allocated? How much time is needed for each program component and speaker? Since meetings may be planned years in advance, you can see that the meeting planner's scheduling concerns range from years to minutes.

unscheduled time time during a meeting when no events or activities are planned; this represents the attendees' personal time

OBJECTIVE 3
Explain basic procedures for meeting attendee registration.

MEETING REGISTRATION PROCEDURES

Registration is the process of gathering all necessary information and fees required for an individual to attend a meeting. It may begin several weeks or months before the event and continue to the last day of the meeting. Discounts are often provided to attendees who register in advance. (This can help planners to determine if attendance will reach anticipated levels. If not,

registration the process of gathering all necessary information and fees required for an individual attending a meeting

This political convention attracts thousands of delegates and is structured around hundreds of small and large meetings.

Pearson Education/PH College, S. M. Wakefield photographer

marketing efforts can be increased and efforts to negotiate within the hotel or meeting facility to reduce costs may be undertaken.)

Data collected on the registration form may include name, title, occupation, address, e-mail, phone, fax, membership category, desired workshop sessions, social functions, and more. Some organizations inquire about company size, attendee's supervisory or financial responsibilities, and the extent of their purchase decision making. Registration data are valuable and can be used before, during, and after the meeting.

Prior to the meeting, the data can be given or sold to exhibitors or advertisers so that they can promote their company, products, and services before the meeting date. During the meeting, registration data can be used as a promotional tool to gain media attention for the organization, sponsors, and exhibitors. It can also help the local **Convention and Visitors Bureau (CVB)** to justify the costs of marketing and soliciting groups to visit the area. After the meeting, registration data can be used to update association membership records and solicit new members or it can be sold to interested parties. Most importantly, it can be used to help the planner with the logistics and promotion of the next meeting.

Convention and Visitors Bureau (CVB) organizations, generally funded by taxes levied on overnight hotel guests and/or from membership fees paid by members; their purpose is to increase the number of visitors to the areas they represent

---

FOCUS ON MEETING ATTENDEES

Meeting planners must know and remember many things. When considering specific sessions, they must consider these factors:

Attention span. Most meeting attendees cannot concentrate on a topic for an extended amount of time. Short, fast-paced sessions generally work best.

Attendee retention. People typically remember more when they have participated in a presentation, rather than when they have just listened to it. How can this concern be addressed during meetings?

Use of visuals. Technology can be used to help presentations come to life.

Meeting environment. Table arrangements, comfort of chairs, lighting, room temperature and ventilation, and a wide range of other details applicable to the meeting space can have a dramatic impact on a meeting's success.

These details must be anticipated, planned for, and addressed during the meeting to help to assure that it is successful.

Preregistration is the process of registering attendees in advance of a meeting and provides information about who will be attending the meeting. For example, it can help the meeting planner to determine room capacities for educational sessions and can inform speakers about the estimated number of people that may attend a session. Whether paper based or electronic, and regardless of whether it is completed in advance or at the meeting site, the prospective attendee must typically complete a registration process.

The registration area is the first experience an attendee has with a meeting or convention. A slow or complicated registration process can set the tone for the entire meeting. Therefore, the registration area should be heavily staffed the first day and should remain open throughout the event. The check-in process for large groups is often expedited by sending necessary material to

Press conferences are a type of meeting. AP/Wide World Photos

preregistered attendees prior to the event. These attendees will then only need to show identification and registration confirmation to receive meeting materials.

Registration is often **outsourced** by the meeting planner for large events. Some hotels or convention centers work with temporary agencies that provide staff to perform the registration activities. Some registration management companies also handle housing.

preregistration the process of registering attendees in advance of a meeting

outsource to employ a person or organization to perform activities that would otherwise need to be done in-house (within an organization)

BASIC HOUSING PROCEDURES

When attendee housing is needed, four basic methods are typically utilized:

OBJECTIVE 4
Review basic information about housing meeting attendees.

- Attendees arrange for their own room. The meeting sponsor makes no prior arrangements about price or availability.
- A group rate is negotiated by the planner, and attendees respond directly to the reservations department of their preferred hotel.
- The meeting sponsor handles all housing. Attendees book rooms through the meeting sponsor, who provides the hotel with a rooming list of confirmed guests.
- A third-party housing bureau (outsourced company) handles all arrangements either for a fee or paid by the CVB.

The first method is easiest for the planner. However, if rooms are not **blocked,** there will assuredly be a premium for renting meeting space and other services, because the hotel will have no assurance about the largest amount of potential revenue (guest-room rental) it may receive.

block guest rooms reserved for members of a specific group

The last three options require that the meeting planner establish a rate for the attendees that reflects prior negotiations with the sales department about the total value of the meeting to the property. As with food and beverage events, the planner must estimate how many people will rent a guest room. If the planner blocks 100 rooms and only 75 attendees rent a room, the planner may be responsible for part or all of the cost of the unrented rooms. This is referred to as the **attrition rate.**

Having attendees call or reserve rooms online directly with the hotels is a good option. They will benefit by the negotiated room rate, and the hotel can handle the reservation processing directly. The meeting planner will be only minimally involved. When larger meetings require multiple properties,

attrition rate the number of guest rooms in a block of rooms that are not rented

planners often provide a range of hotel prices to accommodate the budgets of all attendees.

Outsourcing the housing process to a third-party vendor or CVB is most common with medium- and large-sized meetings. Housing for a city-wide meeting is best left to professionals who have the most current technology and are well equipped to handle thousands of housing requests. Reservations through a housing service can be made by mail, phone, fax, and Internet.

MANAGING THE MEETING

OBJECTIVE 5
Describe basic responsibilities of meeting planners as the meeting evolves.

A meeting will not be successful if it is not properly planned. However, a properly planned meeting cannot be successful unless it is also properly managed as it evolves.

The meeting planner typically arrives at the meeting site one or more days early to confirm that all arrangements have been made and to plan last-minute details. Materials must be shipped to the meeting site, unpacked, and organized, and the meeting's headquarters, media, and perhaps other offices must be set up.

All particulars of the meeting should have been planned and be on paper in the **meeting specification guide.** Information should include the following:

meeting specification guide
a book (binder) containing all information and details applicable to a meeting, including agenda and schedule, contracts, purchase orders for products and services, and applicable communications

master account the folio established by the lodging property that allows certain preapproved charges made by or on behalf of a meeting sponsor to be charged to the meeting sponsor, rather than being the responsibility of the individual incurring the charge

- *Meeting overview.* General information including:
  Group profile
  Names and responsibilities of meeting planners
  Number of guest rooms in a block with rates
  Details about the **master account** (including persons authorized to charge and types of allowable charges)
  Information about complimentary products and services
  Dates and times of all events and sessions
- *Detailed instructions.* Specific information about interacting with personnel in each area of the hotel including:
  Procedures for auditing and signing hotel bills
  Receiving equipment sent to the meeting site
  Lodging contacts and scheuled hours on-site
- *Meeting services contacts.* Information is needed for all vendors and suppliers who will be providing products and services for the meeting including:
  Audiovisual services
  Floral arrangements
  Convention Bureau staff
  Entertainment
  Photographers
  Office equipment rentals
  Exposition (exhibit) services
- *Event requirements.* Details of all events that are part of the meeting including:
  Banquet event orders (BEOs), which detail all requirements for a food and beverage function
  Audiovisual, room setup, and other details about each meeting room for each meeting session
  Details such as delivery times, quantity, price, and locations

banquet event order (BEO)
a form used by the sales, catering, and food production areas to detail all requirements for a banquet; information provided by the banquet client is summarized on the form, and it becomes the basis for the formal contract between the client and the hotel

Getty Images Inc.-Image Bank, Britt Erlanson photographer

Technology helps with meeting presentations.

for receipt for all items purchased from all contracted service organizations

During the meeting, the meeting planner will likely be busy from very early in the morning until very late at night coordinating activities, managing details, and expediting promised services that might be behind schedule or overlooked by providers.

Other details that may require the meeting planner's attention during the meeting include these:

Much of a meeting manager's work involves negotiating on the telephone.

- Assessing on-site attendance is necessary to gather information for future meetings. If, for example, only a specified percentage of attendees participate in general, breakout, or trade show sessions, this is must-know information for future meetings.
- Managing **guarantees.** Information about food and beverage functions is necessary when the event's sponsor may be charged for meals in excess of the guarantee. For example, the meeting planner will want to know if an event with a guarantee of 1,000 diners was actually attended by 1,025 diners because of the additional charges involved.
- Supervising on-site staging (for example, of general meeting breakout sessions and trade show setup)
- Interacting with key organizational representatives to assess perceptions about the meeting and whether any immediate corrective action(s) may be necessary
- Helping to assure that messages and information between on-site meeting planners are coordinated and efficient
- Assuring that signage is placed when and where planned
- Providing special treatment for very important persons (VIPs), including speakers
- Providing for last-minute script changes, if necessary, for speakers

guarantee a contractual agreement about the number of meals to be provided at a banquet event; typically, a final guarantee must be made several days in advance of the event, at which time the entity contracting with the hotel agrees to pay for the larger of the actual number of guests served or the number of guests guaranteed

precon (preconference) session a session attended by meeting planners and applicable hotel personnel to review details and make final decisions about an upcoming meeting

DON'T FORGET THE PRECON MEETING

A **precon (preconference) session** should be held at least one day before the meeting to enable planners and organization representatives and property staff to assure that all the groups' expectations, needs, and special requirements can be met. Members of the hotel's management team (general manager, sales manager, convention services managers, and department heads or their representatives) should attend. Details about the meeting planner's expectations for each event and the hotel's representatives' responsibilities are discussed. Often a separate meeting is held with food and beverage department personnel regarding specifics of food and beverage functions. In addition to precon sessions, additional daily meetings are often held when a large meeting is being managed and/or when on-site problems occur.

- Adjusting the environment; heating, ventilating, air conditioning (HVAC), smoking, housekeeping, noise, and lighting issues (among others) may need to be addressed
- Coordinating the movement of large numbers of people between general sessions and breakout or other meeting spaces
- Managing on-site data collection from attendees; attendees' evaluations of sessions and attendance registration forms at sessions for certification and/or other purposes may need to be collected
- Troubleshooting; problems (or potential problems) always occur as meetings evolve, which meeting planners must address in a way that makes these issues unnoticeable to attendees

FOLLOWING UP AFTER THE MEETING

OBJECTIVE 6
Describe basic responsibilities of meeting planners as a meeting is concluded.

The meeting isn't over until it's over! As attendees return to their homes, the meeting planner still has work to do:

- Auditing and approving master accounts
- Tipping: While some tips are paid by attendees (such as for a la carte dining service and bellpersons) and while there are likely automatic food and beverage **service charges,** tips may also be paid to others providing services for the meetings. Tips (or gifts that can be shared) are often given to housekeepers, security and shipping personnel, audiovisual technicians, and front-desk staff members, along with sales managers and convention service managers.
- Auditing all other invoices presented for payment
- Summarizing and evaluating attendees' meeting evaluations
- Conducting a **postcon (postconference) meeting** with hotel staff

service charge a mandatory amount added to a guest's bill for services performed by a staff member of the hospitality organization

postcon (postconference) meeting a session attended by meeting planners and applicable meeting site personnel to evaluate a meeting that has concluded

The meeting planner should create a written document to record all key events to help plan the next meeting. The postcon serves as a report card to tell what went right and wrong during the meeting. Attendees typically include the planning staff, a sales department representative, the food and beverage director, the audiovisual manager, and accounting staff. Discrepancies in billing, service failures, and problems and praises are addressed.

FOCUS ON CONFERENCE CENTER EDUCATION COORDINATORS

OBJECTIVE 7
Discuss special aspects of a conference center education coordinator.

We have just previewed important tasks that are part of a meeting planner's job. Recall that one important responsibility is to negotiate with and select a property location for the meeting. By contrast, **conference center education coordinators** have a role that is the opposite: to attract meetings to his or her employer (a conference center). They do this through marketing and sales activities to attract meetings and by assisting meeting sponsors and planners with housing, food and beverage services, meeting activities, management, and all other activities that are the responsibility of a sales and marketing staff member in the hotel. This role is similar to someone in a property's marketing and sales department with one big difference: the conference center education coordinator typically works with the meeting planner to define educational needs, select topics, and identify prospective speakers. In the case of nonorganizational-specific conferences, they also

conference center education coordinator the person performing the work of a meeting planner who represents a potential meeting site (conference center) and works with meeting sponsors and planners to plan on-site activities, including educational programs

---

ALL ABOUT CONVENTION AND VISITORS BUREAUS (CVBs)

Convention and Visitors Bureaus are located in many areas and can have a dramatic influence on attracting meetings to their areas. Hotels, restaurants, and area recreational sites typically fund CVBs. In some areas, tax revenues may be used for financial support. CVBs undertake advertising and promotional campaigns to attract groups to business meetings and conventions and individual travelers to the area. CVB personnel may help meeting planners with activities such as these:

Manning registration and information booths

Providing brochures and inexpensive souvenirs (novelties) to be used with other promotional information

Coordinating housing between several hotels when large meetings require guest rooms in other than the primary meeting hotel

Providing ongoing services for meeting planners as programs are planned and convened

---

use a much broader marketing approach to reach a widely diverse group of potential attendees.

What Does a Conference Planner Do?

Many universities have continuing education or professional development conference centers that generate significant revenues. They employ professional education coordinators who serve as account executives working to meet the specific educational needs of several assigned clients. An important

---

HURRICANE KATRINA AND THE MEETINGS BUSINESS

Hurricane Katrina struck New Orleans and the Gulf Coast in Fall 2005 and showcased just how fragile tourism and the meetings industry can be. Following the disaster, hundreds of meetings and conventions had to be canceled or postponed. This, in turn, led to hundreds of millions of dollars of lost revenues to New Orleans and the region. It affected meeting facilities, industry suppliers, gaming venues, hospitality industry employees, local restaurants, retails stores, and every other component of the hospitality industry. It also created innumerable challenges for many planners who had to cancel or postpone their events or reschedule them to another location. The New Orleans Metropolitan Convention and Visitor's Bureau did a fantastic job of informing the meeting planning community about the clean-up efforts and the rebuilding of the convention infrastructure. It posted informative streaming videos on its website on a regular basis (www.neworleanscvb.com) and created a marketing campaign, Make Way for the Rebirth, to promote New Orleans. The first major group to meet in New Orleans was the American Library Association, which brought 18,000 members to the city in June 2006. The event was an overwhelming success, and it proved that New Orleans was coming back strong.

Damian Dovarganes, AP/Wide World Photos

open-enrollment program
an educational program developed by a continuing education and professional development conference center on a generic topic that is marketed to attendees from different organizations

Airport hotels frequently have meeting rooms to accommodate persons flying to a central site for a several-hour meeting.

responsibility is to learn the educational needs, goals, and objectives of their clients so that they can customize a specific topic to better meet the unique needs of the client.

Education coordinators generally work on three types of programs:

- **Open-enrollment programs.** Designed to present a generic topic to attendees from different organizations; these programs may be widely marketed to attract attendees from broad national and international locations.
- Generic topics for a single organization
- Customized programs for a specific organization

Planners in executive education centers typically have access to academic and industry experts with the knowledge and presentation skills to yield very high quality programs. They also utilize extensive networks to assist in locating special presenters for special topics.

BOOKING OUTSIDE THE BLOCK AND ROOM BLOCK PIRATES

An unfortunate consequence of online travel sites is that attendees can often book a room at a lower cost in the same hotel in which the meeting planner has established a room block. This is called "booking outside the block." When negotiating a contract, a smart planner will include protection that prohibits the hotel from selling rooms during the conference dates to the general public for less than the agreed on conference rate. If this is not possible, then the planner should include a clause that credits (includes) rooms used by meeting attendees who are not part of the block to the overall room pickup for the event.

Room block pirates are another problem. These are companies that target meeting attendees with reduced rates for rooms either at the headquarters hotel or, perhaps, another nearby property. They often rent association membership lists from the parent organization and then promote their services under the pretense of being connected to the group. Although this is highly unethical, it is not illegal. The best way for a meeting planner to protect the room block (and the attendees) is to alert members prior to the housing process about fraudulent companies trying to attract them with lower rates or alternative locations. Remind attendees that, if the negotiated room block is not met, the group will still pay for any unused rooms. This, in turn, will have a negative impact on the event's financial success and could lead to higher registration rates in the future. Again, protecting the meeting with specific contractual clauses is essential.

SUMMARY OF CHAPTER LEARNING OBJECTIVES

1. **Identify three types of meeting planners.**
   There are three basic types of meeting planners: those who work for corporations, associations, and individual clients (independent planners).

2. **Describe basic responsibilities of meeting planners as a meeting is planned.**
   The meeting planner begins by defining the meeting objectives using the SMART (specific, measurable, achievable, relevant, and time-focused) approach. Site selection must consider, first, the geographic location and then the hotel, conference center, or other site within that location for the meeting. A request for proposal describing the major needs of the meeting is circulated to potential meeting sites, and proposal responses are analyzed upon return. Then the negotiation process begins and, upon successful completion, a meeting budget can be finalized. Another important concern relates to the schedule for the meeting program.

3. **Explain basic procedures for meeting attendee registration.**
   Registration involves gathering the information and fees required for an individual to attend a meeting. A wide range of information can be collected that is helpful before, during, and after the session. Many meetings allow attendees to preregister and, for big conferences, the registration and preregistration tasks are outsourced.

4. **Review basic information about housing meeting attendees.**
   Four basic methods can be used for housing: attendees can arrange for their own room,

attendees can respond directly to their preferred hotel, the meeting sponsor can handle housing needs, or a third-party housing bureau can be utilized.

5. **Describe basic responsibilities of meeting planners as the meeting evolves.**
   During the meeting, the meeting planner will be busy with many tasks. The meeting specification guide lists numerous details to help avoid surprises during the session. A preconference session is held before the meeting begins so that meeting representatives and those from the host site can undertake detailed planning. A wide range of other activities is necessary and should be done in a way that is not noticeable to attendees.

6. **Describe basic responsibilities of meeting planners as a meeting is concluded.**
   After the meeting is completed, the meeting planner must audit master accounts and other invoices, tip necessary personnel, summarize and evaluate attendees' meeting evaluations, and conduct a postconference meeting with hotel staff.

7. **Discuss special aspects of a conference center education coordinator.**
   The meeting activities of conference center education coordinators are similar to those of a meeting planner. However, there are at least two differences: they have an additional role to attract meetings to their conference center and, in the case of university-sponsored centers, conference planners are involved in helping meeting planners to plan educational sessions and select potential speakers.

MASTERING YOUR KNOWLEDGE

Discuss the following questions.

1. What are examples of communication and negotiating skills that effective meeting planners must be able to utilize?
2. What are ways in which the work of meeting planners for corporations, associations, and individual clients is the same? Different?
3. What types of questions must be answered by small associations or companies as they consider the use of an independent planner for an upcoming meeting?
4. If you were a meeting planner, what types of concerns would be important to you when

evaluating alternative meeting sites within a specific city?

5. What are examples of topics you as a meeting planner would address in a precon meeting? A postcon meeting?
6. What are examples of surprises that may occur as a meeting evolves that must be effectively managed by a meeting planner?
7. You are an association meeting planner. Preregistration for an upcoming conference is lower than expected. What are some tactics you can use to address this challenge?

FEEDBACK FROM THE REAL WORLD

Our real-world advice comes from the author of this chapter, Curtis Love.

Curtis Love is an associate professor in the Department of Tourism and Convention Administration at the William F. Harrah College of Hotel Administration, University of Nevada, Las Vegas. Love's teaching and research concentrations are in the areas of meeting planning and exposition management. Prior to joining the faculty at UNLV, he was the vice-president of education for the Professional Convention Management Association. He has presented numerous workshops for industry associations, including the International Association of Exposition Management, Professional Convention Management Association, Association for Convention Operations Management, International Special Events Society, Meeting Professionals International, and Canadian Society of Association Executives. He specializes in assisting organizations in the development and implementation of evaluation instruments to measure customer service and satisfaction with educational programming and in collecting and analyzing association membership data.

What are some of the most important tactics that a meeting planner can utilize during the negotiation process with representatives of the prospective meeting site to minimize costs without compromising the meeting's objectives?

A key negotiation tool is for the meeting planner to fully comprehend the overall economic value of the meeting from the facility's perspective. Hotels and other meeting facility personnel look at the combined economic impact of a group before they submit a bid for the business. How many and what type of sleeping rooms will be used? How many food and beverage functions will take place? What menu selections and decor will be needed? Will recreational facilities such as spa and golf courses be utilized? In a gaming facility, is the group likely to gamble or use other entertainment venues? Providing a detailed history of past meetings to the facility greatly enhances one's bargaining power.

Being flexible with meeting dates can also be economically beneficial for meeting planners. Most hotels have peak seasons and off-seasons. Holding a meeting during a hotel's off-season can yield comparable levels of facilities and service at reduced prices. Likewise, facilities in major resort cities like Orlando and Las Vegas will negotiate lower rates for meetings held Monday through Thursday, because this leaves peak days (Friday, Saturday, and Sunday) open for the leisure market, which will pay higher room rates.

On what items is a hotel or other meeting site representative most likely to negotiate? Least likely?

Room and meeting space rates are typically the most flexible due to supply and demand. Rates at a four-star property during the off-season can be extremely affordable. If enough sleeping rooms are reserved, meeting space may be provided free. Amenities such as admissions to spa and recreational facilities may also be highly negotiable. Fixed costs such as food and beverage are less flexible. Food costs can vary dramatically due to the availability and seasonality of menu selections. Typically, hotels will only guarantee pricing a few months prior to the actual event.

What are common mistakes that meeting planners make while planning a meeting?

Failing to keep the host facility informed about changes in housing, session locations, meeting room sets, audiovisual needs, security, and other facility concerns can be problematic. The facility needs adequate time to communicate changes to the service personnel responsible for implementing the meeting. Planners also must keep detailed written records of all communication with facility staff. Without proper documentation, it is easy to forget "who has been told what." It also serves as a record should there be problems down the road.

Not anticipating emergency situations can also be a big problem. Transportation strikes, adverse weather conditions, security threats, political protests, and other unexpected situations can have a devastating impact on a meeting. Detailed written emergency plans should be made well in advance of the meeting and should be communicated to all staff.

Keeping the big picture of a meeting in mind can also be troublesome. A meeting planner working to produce a major convention with a large trade show and many ancillary events can easily lose sight of the overall goal of the meeting. If the planner focuses only on his or her own part of the convention, such as arranging educational sessions, and does not comprehend the trade show component, scheduling and communication problems can (and likely will!) arise.

What are the most frequent problems that occur as attendees preregister for a meeting? What tactics can a professional meeting planner use to address these potential problems?

Preregistration is very important, especially for the association planner. Many decisions are based on preregistration numbers. This information helps the planner to adjust room blocks, catering guarantees, educational sessions, room sets, and many other key components.

A planner always looks to the past when examining preregistration numbers. All things equal, how do the preregistration numbers compare with last year at the same point? (If numbers are down, then perhaps more promotion is needed to encourage prospective attendees to sign up.) Multiple methods of registration must be made available. For example, if only Internet-based registration is available, those without computer access may be excluded. Registration should be made available by every means possible: mail, fax, phone, and Internet. Using a professional registration service generally alleviates most potential problems.

What are the most important tasks a meeting planner should do immediately after a meeting is concluded?

An after-conference (postcon) meeting with the facility's staff is advisable for any meeting of substantive size and complexity. It may be the planner's last time to sit face to face with the convention service manager and other key facility staff to review what went right or wrong. It's much easier to address concerns while they are fresh on the planner's mind. On return to the office, any bills due should be reviewed promptly for payment. (One doesn't want to get the reputation of being a slow-paying customer.) Other duties include writing thank you notes or letters of recognition to those who made your meeting a success. Making notes to help to plan the next meeting is also important.

LEARN FROM THE INTERNET

1. Check out the websites for the following associations:
   - International Association of Healthcare Central Service Materiel Management: www.iahcsmm.org
   - International Carwash Association: www.carcarecentral.com
   - American Marketing Association: www.marketingpower.com

   Literally tens of thousands of associations are part of the meetings market. If you want, select several about which you are familiar or want

   to learn more and obtain information about their educational and/or trade show sessions.

   What kind of information do they provide to help market upcoming conferences, conventions, or trade shows?

2. Check out the following websites for several hotel and conference centers:
   - New York Marriott Marquis: www.nymarriottmarquis.com
   - Opryland Hotel: www.gaylordhotels.com
   - Sheraton Waikiki Beach Resort: www.sheraton-waikiki.com

Also, check out websites for hotels in your area.

What type of information is provided to sell meeting planners on the use of their facilities?

3. Check out the websites for the Convention and Visitors Bureaus in your community and other communities close to you. How do these organizations attempt to encourage meeting planners to offer meetings within their areas?

4. Check out the websites for independent meeting planners including:

- Conference & Logistic Consultants, Inc.: www.gomeeting.com

- Meeting Expectations, Inc.: www.meetingexpectations.com
- Meeting Solutions, Inc.: www.meetingsolutions.net
- Premier Meetings: www.premiermeetings.com
- Professional Meeting Planners: www.pmpmeeting.com

What advantages do they cite for using their organization?

KEY HOSPITALITY TERMS

The following terms were explained in this chapter. Review the definitions of any words with which you are unfamiliar. Begin to utilize them as you expand your vocabulary as a hospitality professional.

meeting planner
return on investment (ROI)
association
convention
trade show
teleconferencing
SMART
request for proposal (RFP)
unscheduled time
registration
Convention and Visitors Bureau (CVB)
preregistration

outsource
block
attrition rate
meeting specification guide
master account
banquet event order (BEO)
guarantee
precon (preconference) session
service charge
postcon (postconference) meeting
conference center education coordinator
open-enrollment program

Special Events Management

From Chapter 30 of *Discovering Hospitality and Tourism: The World's Greatest Industry*, Second Edition, Jack D. Ninemeier, Joe Perdue. Copyright © 2008 by Pearson Education, Inc. Published by Pearson Prentice Hall. All rights reserved.

Special Events Management

Spectators line up for admittance to an Olympic event.

PhotoEdit, Robert Ginn photographer

CHAPTER LEARNING OBJECTIVES

After studying this chapter you will be able to:

1. Define the term *special events management*.
2. Provide a brief history of special events.
3. Describe the type of markets in which special events are conducted.
4. Explain recent trends in the special events industry.
5. Review a flow chart of the activities required to plan a special event.
6. Review some major responsibilities that are part of positions within the special events industry.
7. Discuss significant challenges confronting the special events industry.

This chapter was authored by Kathy Nelson, PhD, CSEP, CMP, Assistant Professor, Tourism and Convention Department, William F. Harrah College of Hotel Administration, University of Nevada, Las Vegas.

FEEDBACK FROM THE REAL WORLD

Large events such as the International Olympics attract tens of thousands of athletes, coaches, trainers, and members of the news media and hundreds of thousands of spectators. How do officials plan for the food and lodging needs of these people? More specifically:

- How far in advance of a large, world-class event such as the International Olympics does planning for its foodservices begin?
- What are some logistics about the volume of foodservices that are offered?

- What are the most critical aspects of planning the event?
- How important is teamwork in the planning process, and what function does each team member assume?

As you read this chapter, think about answers to these questions and then get feedback from the real world at the end of the chapter.

Special events management is an exciting and growing industry. It attracts persons who possess creative talents and organizational skills. Special events professionals enjoy a work environment in which no two days are the same. They create and customize events that provide their clients with entertaining, unique, and memorable experiences. Events also have the ability to reflect and mold our society. **Hallmark events** (those that are sustainable and revivable), such as the International Olympics, the World Cup, and, most recently, the 9/11 remembrance ceremonies, are important milestones in shaping the culture of the United States and the world.

hallmark events special events that are repeated because they are significant, sustainable, and revivable

OBJECTIVE 1
Define the term *special events management.*

WHAT IS SPECIAL EVENTS MANAGEMENT?

Special events management is the profession that involves public assembly for reasons of celebration, entertainment, and education (among other purposes). Special events management includes several activities: event research, design, planning, coordination, and evaluation.

Special events management is a multidisciplinary profession. The elements of most events are basically the same: entertainment, decorations, lighting, sound, special effects, catering, and often transportation. Employment in special events management transcends many hospitality positions in hotels, food and beverage, tourism, and the meetings and conventions industries.

special events management the profession that plans and manages public assemblies for reasons of celebration, entertainment, and education (among other purposes)

OBJECTIVE 2
Provide a brief history of special events.

SPECIAL EVENTS: A HISTORICAL REVIEW

As long as there have been groups of people, special events have celebrated human triumphs and milestones. Events celebrate past, present, and future lives and all the accomplishments (wonderful, terrible, and bittersweet) that accent life's journey. The special events management profession originated within the discipline of **public relations** when specialists became necessary to manage the activities (**special events**) that creative organizations use to obtain publicity and to build corporate images.

The term *special event* represents an extraordinary moment in our lives. Robert Jani (one of Walt Disney's imagineers) is credited with first using the term in 1955. He proposed the creation of a nightly parade in Disneyland (the

public relations activities designed to build good relations with a company's numerous constituencies by use of tactics such as press releases, product publicity, corporate communications, and public service

special event an activity, program, or occasion that represents a memorable experience that requires an unusual degree of planning and creativity

177

Main Street Electric Parade) to solve the problem about how to keep visitors in the park after 5:00 P.M. When a reporter asked, "What do you call that program?" he replied, "A special event." By that, he meant something that someone experiences that is different from a normal day of living.

EVENT MARKETS

OBJECTIVE 3
Describe the type of markets in which special events are conducted.

cause-related events those undertaken for reasons of charity (private or public relief for persons in need)

life-cycle events activities that celebrate or recognize significant milestones in one's life

Many event planners classify events by markets. The most commonly considered are noted in Exhibit 1. Event markets include those sponsored by associations, corporations, and casino hotels. Other events are **cause related.** Retail and sporting events, fairs, festivals, parades, and social and tourism events are also part of the event market, and we will look at each in this section. Corporations typically spend the most money on events, but the social market is the largest because it encompasses **life-cycle events** such as birthdays, bar or bat mitzvahs, weddings, anniversaries, and funerals.

Association Events

Associations sponsor innumerable events of all types, including award presentations, political rallies, community service, installation of officers and leaders, training programs, conventions, exhibitions, and seminars.

Corporate Events

Corporate events are sponsored to achieve specific goals, including celebratory events such as product introductions, customer appreciation, grand openings, and incentive programs.

Casino and Hotel Events

Special events are a significant part of a casino's marketing activities today. In addition to corporate events that occur at casinos, such as grand openings and numerous types of celebrations, special events attract and reward casino players. For example, boxing matches and rock concerts attract the highest level of VIP players, and high-roller parties are often utilized as a customer-appreciation tool.

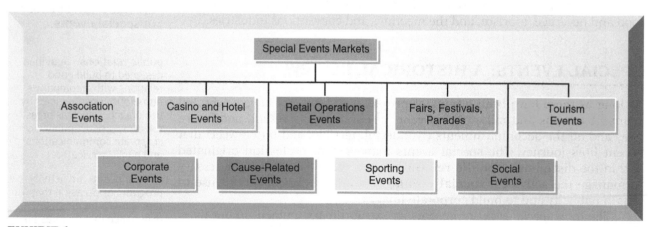

EXHIBIT 1
The Special Event Markets

SPECIAL EVENTS OCCUR EVERY DAY IN CASINOS

Slot clubs and tournaments increase casino revenue during slow periods, build customer loyalty, and develop a customer database. Slot tournaments are a perfect example of how the casino uses special events as a marketing tool. Players are encouraged to join slot clubs and are given a membership card. When they do so, this card tracks each member's play (number of hours and dollars spent playing the slots). It also has a built-in reward system so that customers can earn points toward meals, shows, and hotel rooms and receive the appropriate level of VIP treatment.

Casino club members are often invited to participate in monthly slot tournaments that are highly themed and feature a high-ticket prize at the tournament's end. These events have become highly competitive between casino properties and rely on the next creative theme to attract new and retain existing players in the tournaments. An awards banquet, including themed entertainment, food, and beverages, frequently concludes these special events.

Cause-Related Events

Many **not-for-profit organizations** raise a huge portion of their annual budgets from fund-raising events. As inducements to participate, part of the fees paid by those attending may be tax deductible as a charitable contribution.

not-for-profit organizations
a group of persons working for reasons other than to make profit from their efforts; many nonprofit organizations have charitable objectives

Retail Operations Events

The main purpose of retail event promotions is to introduce and sell merchandise. During the 1960s and 1970s, retailers could attract thousands of consumers to their stores with one-day events that included the appearance of soap opera stars and athletes. Today, retailers design long-range promotional events using an integrated approach to attract consumers on a steady basis. Consider the Sony Metreon Complex in San Francisco. Shoppers can enjoy the maximum of entertainment and events with 15 movie screens, an IMAX theater, eight restaurants, and numerous stores and attractions that would rival many amusement parks.

Sporting Events

Sporting events bring lots of visitors and therefore lots of money into a community. A few of the top sporting events each year are the National Collegiate Athletics Association's (NCAA) Men's Final Four Basketball Tournament, Junior Olympic Games, and the ESPN Summer X Games. Sporting events are a perfect platform for corporate sponsorship. No other single event in America is more attractive to corporate America than the annual Super Bowl football game. In 1999, Las Vegas attracted 250,000 visitors to the Super Bowl who spent millions of dollars while visiting the area.

Stephen Whitehorn © Dorling Kindersley

Crowds gather at the Edinburgh festival in Scotland.

SUE SHIFRIN-CASSIDY: KIDSCHARITIES.ORG

KidsCharities.org grew from an idea in early 1999 during the Kosovo crisis. Songwriter Sue Shifrin-Cassidy and her husband (world-renowned entertainer David Cassidy) wrote the song "Message to the World" to benefit WarChild USA's efforts for Kosovo refugees. The song, produced by a multiaward winner (Narda Michael Walden), became bigger than life with featured artists including Rosie O'Donnel, Wyclef Jean, Sam Moore, David Cassidy, and many more.

From that effort and the joy of helping others, Sue founded KidsCharities.org, the first worldwide website benefiting the world's children. KidsCharities.org donates 100 percent of its online donations to children's charities, including Juvenile Diabetes Foundation, Special Olympics Nevada, City of Hope, Planet Hope, Reggie Jackson's Mr. October Foundation for Kids, and others.

Fairs, Festivals, and Parades

These events provide many opportunities to bring communities together to celebrate various cultures and interests through performances, arts, crafts, and socializing, while, at the same time, boosting tourism dollars. For example, the Kentucky Derby Festival (horse race) attracts 1.5 million visitors to Louisville, and the Rose Bowl parade (prior to the annual football game) attracts 1 million visitors for that one-day event in Pasadena (Los Angeles). Whether people attend a Pumpkin Festival in Circleville, Ohio, or the Cannes Film Festival in France, chances are they will come away exhausted, entertained, and gastronomically satisfied.

Social Events

The social (life-cycle) market continues to grow as health conditions improve and people live longer. Once, celebrating a fiftieth wedding anniversary was rare; today it is almost commonplace. Celebratory events that recognize the passage of time are usually ritualistic in nature.

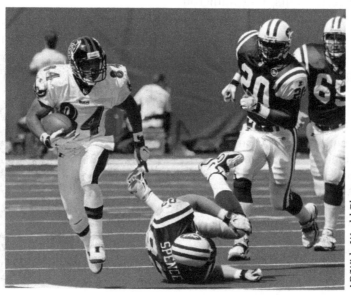

Many special activities are scheduled around important sporting events.

AP/Wide World Photos

IT'S ONLY MONEY!

Life-cycle events are important to clients. Today, some weddings are upscale and themed events that last for days. In 2001, an award-winning wedding was produced at a Las Vegas casino resort property. It utilized 32 florists and a 4,000 work-hour setup crew to carefully attend to the bridal couple's every wish at a cost that exceeded $1 million!

Tourism Events

Communities that do not have the facilities to offer large events can still utilize tourism events to attract visitors. Redevelopment projects are reviving the downtown areas of many U.S. cities. With this redevelopment comes the opportunity for creating tourism events. As an example, consider Cleveland, Ohio, which has been named one of North America's 10 most improved cities. Cleveland's entertainment district, called the Flats, lines the Cuyahoga River and has transformed old industrial sites into party meccas. In 1994, the city unveiled its $450 million Gateway Sports Complex, which includes both Jacobs Field (home of the Cleveland Indians baseball team) and Gund Arena (home of the Cleveland Cavaliers basketball team). The Cleveland Browns' new football stadium and the Rock and Roll Hall of Fame and Museum have helped Cleveland earn a spot on *Travel & Leisure's* top 10 vacation destinations.

Here are two additional examples. Fort Worth, Texas, transformed its downtown stores into Sundance Square with entertainment attractions, modern shopping areas, restaurants, and museums. Chattanooga, Tennessee, centered its downtown redevelopment around the $45 million Tennessee Aquarium. New hotels, museums, modern shopping, theaters, and other attractions provide the setting for numerous tourism events.

OBJECTIVE 4
Explain recent trends in the special events industry.

sponsorship money, goods, and/or services rendered by an organization in exchange for a return, including public relations, advertising, and/or charitable tax benefits

TRENDS IN THE SPECIAL EVENTS INDUSTRY

One of the biggest trends in the event industry today is the merging of corporate and public events. This is accomplished through many forms of **sponsorship.** Money, goods, and/or services are provided by an organization in exchange for public relations, advertising, and/or charitable tax benefits. In times when there is dwindling public funding for the arts, for example, corporate sponsorship of museums is rising rapidly. In addition to the arts, corporate sponsorship plays an increasingly important role in numerous public events, including festivals and holiday celebrations.

The arrangement between Saber of America and Philadelphia's Franklin Institute Science Museum illustrates the new forms of sponsorship. When the museum's traveling science show rolls into schools, it travels in a fleet of four Saber Legacy station wagons donated by the auto maker. A second example: The Houston

Parades are highlights of many events.

PhotoEdit, Mary Kate Denny photographer

Wedding ceremonies are an important market for event planners.

Livestock Show and Rodeo has 41 sponsors. Each pays between $60,000 and $1 million to sponsor an event, ranging from a milking parlor to the playing of the national anthem.[1]

Another trend in the special events industry is a renewed interest in professionalism. The nation's current economic uncertainty, rapid technological advances, and increased competition, among other factors, have prompted event professionals to differentiate themselves by professional credentials and practices. Certification designations are more important today than they have even been in the special events industry. In many cases, they distinguish a certified event professional as being the "best of the best!"

Since the events of September 11, 2001, it is increasingly common to produce events perceived to be more meaningful, as opposed to events that are just celebratory or that can be seen as financially wasteful. This trend toward cause-related events, rather than those with incentive and reward purposes, will likely remain popular.

As is true in other segments of the hospitality industry, risk management concerns are a hot topic at industry-related education and professional development conferences. In the wake of the horrific fire that killed 99 club goers and injured nearly 200 more in West Warwick, Rhode Island, in 2003

Safeco Field is named after its corporate sponsor, Safeco Corporation, a property and casualty insurance company.

---

[1]K.D. Washington and R.K. Miller, *The 2003 Entertainment Media and Advertising Market Research Handbook*, Richard K. Miller and Associates, Inc., 2003.

MEET YIFAT OREN, CERTIFIED SPECIAL EVENT PROFESSIONAL (CSEP)

Yifat Oren

Yifat Oren began her career in the special events industry in the early 1990s as the publisher of *Wedding Celebrations,* a complete guide for special events. As a result of that successful venture, Yifat noticed the need for a knowledgeable, stylish, and visionary individual to ease the stress associated with the planning and production of a successful event. She launched Yifat Oren & Associates Special Events, a complete event planning company that specializes in exquisite social gatherings. With the technical knowledge attained through extensive experience, Yifat combines flair for art and style to provide the most discerning clientele with incomparable experiences.

Yifat believes, "Each wedding day is a complex blend of family, emotion, social occasion, religious ceremony, passion, and coincidental elements. The challenge is to see the event through the bridal couple's eyes, to reflect their personal style, to get to know them and to deliver what their wedding dreams are made of."

With a growing and hip celebrity clientele, Yifat Oren & Associates has been touted as one of the most up and coming event planners in Los Angeles. The strategy: take events to the next level by personalizing them to each specific client with details from the moment the first guest arrives. The goal is to consistently create imaginative styles and trends. Her organization will tailor every aspect of an event to the whims and wishes of the most discriminating clients.

(which occurred just four days after 21 people were killed in a stampede at a Chicago nightclub), event professionals are now very serious about risk management; they recognize that it is everyone's responsibility, but that these concerns begin at the time of event planning.

A CLOSE LOOK AT EVENT PLANNING

The work of an event planner is in many ways similar to that of a meeting planner. Exhibit 2 is a flow chart that identifies major steps in planning a special event. When reviewing this figure, note that the event's purpose and

High-society receptions require significant special event planning.

Index Stock Imagery, Inc., Spencer Grant photographer

CHECK IT OUT!

Special Events Magazine offers the opportunity to view an extensive number of activities and information about many topics of importance to special event planners. Want to learn about hotel events, catering, or risk management concerns in special events planning? Just enter these or other topics of interest in the website's "Search This Site" box at www.specialevents.com.

OBJECTIVE 5
Review a flow chart of the activities required to plan a special event.

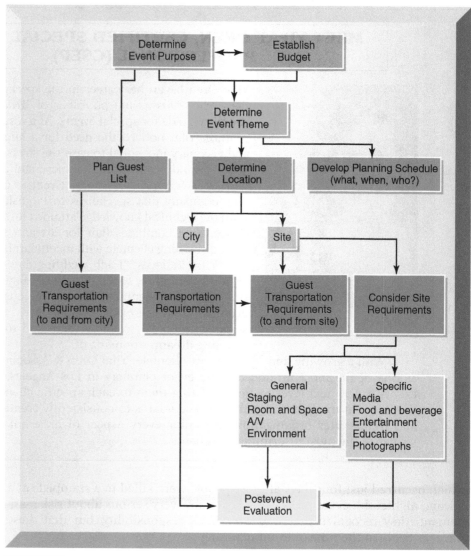

EXHIBIT 2
Steps in Planning a Special Event

budget are typically considered before its theme and the guest list. The theme, then, may drive the event's location and its planning schedule. Details, including transportation requirements (to move guests to and from and within the event's location) and numerous general and specific details relating to the conduct of the event at a specific site, are required. Postevent evaluation is a must, especially if events are repeated. Then all parties will learn about planning procedures that should be continued (because they work!) or that may need modification (because they were ineffective!).

The phrase "attention to details" is an appropriate way to describe the work of special event planners. This is especially important as one considers that planners frequently are working on several special events at the same time.

OBJECTIVE 6
Review some major responsibilities that are part of positions within the special events industry.

SPECIAL EVENTS MANAGEMENT POSITIONS

The International Special Events Society (ISES) categorizes members into event disciplines. This classification (see Exhibit 3) suggests some of the specialized positions within the industry.

EXHIBIT 3
Common Positions Within
the Special Events Industry

Position	Examples of Position Titles and Responsibilities
Events planners (coordinators)	Persons in this position serve as event planner, coordinator, meeting planner, wedding consultant, fund raiser, exposition service manager, and other entities.
Special events managers	This individual should have a minimum of three years experience in the special events industry as an event coordinator, designer, production manager, or technical director.
Special events producers	Individual special events producers have a minimum of five years experience in the industry. They have produced or had a major role in producing at least 10 events.
Design, decor, or graphic arts specialists	Floral designers and floral and plant suppliers; set, prop, and display designers; lighting designers; balloon artists; graphic and advertising artists; flags and banners producers; suppliers of decorative materials, invitations, and calligraphy; and persons with similar responsibilities.
Technical service and products specialists	Audiovisual services; sound and staging; lighting; photography and video; computers and software; event staffing and security; special effects; fireworks and pyrotechnics; generator rental; other positions.
Hardware rental and construction personnel	Equipment rental; party hire; tenting; staging; set and props construction; stadium and seating; temporary structures; catering equipment; apparel (formal and costumes); linen rental; restroom; trailers and other positions.
Entertainers	Theme or amusement parks; booking agencies; musicians; vocalists, disk jockeys, magicians, sporting event and concert promoters or managers; specialty acts; performing artists; casino and carnival entertainment and equipment; amusement and interactive games; virtual reality; ticketing services; professional speakers; novelties and caricature artists and other entities that provide or produce entertainment.
Food service and product personnel	Catering (on- and/or off-site); ice sculptures; bakery and wedding cakes; food staffing and other positions.
Venue (location) managers	Hotel and specialty venues; bleachers, skyboxes, and other venues.
Travel and transportation personnel	Destination management services; incentive travel companies; valet parking services; ground operators; ground transportation (bus, van, and limousine) services; tours, charters, and other positions.
Event public relations and marketing specialists	Advertising agencies; media companies; public relations firms; marketing companies; awards and promotional products companies; accounting and financial services; speakers' bureau; publications and media; insurance; professional support services and other positions.

CHALLENGES! CHALLENGES!

As is true with all segments of the hospitality industry, the special events segment is confronted by several challenges.

Bar mitzvah celebrations are a large part of the special events market.

Risk Management Concerns

Risk management remains a challenge even though the awareness of its importance has already been raised throughout the industry. Surprisingly, this topic has not received serious attention until recently, in part because event managers tend to be very creative by nature. Educational conferences, professional literature, and other venues for advancing the profession have focused more on the new and different creative aspects of event planning, rather than on the nuts and bolts of basic planning principles. After September 11, 2001, however, this all changed.

There also is the human tendency to want to shift blame to someone else. Consider, for example, the tragic fire in Rhode Island referenced previously. Accusations were made about the band whose pyrotechnics ignited the blaze, the owners of the establishment, the company that supplied the foam used as soundproofing material, the fire marshall who gave the club a seal of

Fireworks are part of Fourth of July celebrations in many cities in the United States, including New York City.

approval, the town of West Warwick, and the state of Rhode Island. In the future, event planners will more consistently and adequately address risk management concerns to assure that they are doing their part to provide a safe environment for event guests.

Raising the Level of Professionalism

Historically, the special events industry has comprised small entrepreneurial businesses who learned the business from experience, rather than through formal education and professional development. Experience is absolutely critical to the success of an event planner; however, so is more formalized training. The primary professional association for the International Special Events Society (ISES) has developed an effective certification program that is driven by excellent professional development programs in increasingly successful efforts to raise the standard of excellence in the industry.

Marketing Issues

The goals and objectives for many events have shifted to cause-related events. This poses marketing challenges for event companies who need to reinvent themselves. Also, the events industry rises and falls in concert with the economy. Consider, for example, the September 11, 2001, tragedy. Special events companies lost all or most of the business on their books after that event, and it was more than a year before planning for new events began.

PROFILE OF A SPECIAL EVENTS COMPANY

Most businesses providing special events services are independently owned and provide opportunities for creative persons to identify and serve the special events needs of selected markets. Here's an example.

VP Events, Inc., is a full-service event, design, and production company. The firm was founded in 1994 as Vintage Productions, specializing in vintage weddings and so-

Mary Litzsinger

cial events. Since that time, the company has evolved into an award-winning design and production firm specializing in a broad range of entertainment, corporate, and social events. Clients look to VP Events, Inc., for something different and unique that allows them to emphasize their individual expressions. While the firm has enjoyed notoriety for its specialty, unique wedding design and other off-premise events, the true focus is on elegance, style, and individuality.

President and owner Mary N. Litzsinger, CSEP, has a bachelor's degree in marketing. She received the designation CSEP (Certified Special Events Professional) in 2001 from the International Special Events Society. She has served on the faculty of the UCLA Extension Program, where she encouraged students to join the special events planning industry. For the

(continued)

Karey Williams

past 15 years, she has developed and produced events, fundraising opportunities, public relations, and corporate branding programs for local, regional, and national organizations.

Karey Williams graduated from the University of Southern California and serves as event and marketing manager. She has been a full-time event and marketing manager for over four years. Her first major wedding received high reviews and earned a featured spot in a national publication. She brings a background in the cosmetics and fashion industry to the firm. Karey uses her knowledge and experience to help clients with their specific needs related to dress design and hair and makeup consultations. In addition to working with social clients of VP Events, Inc., Karey develops opportunities for the firm in corporate, sports, and fund-raising events

SUMMARY OF CHAPTER LEARNING OBJECTIVES

1. **Define the term *special events management*.**
   Special events management is the profession that plans and controls public assemblies gathered for the reasons of celebration, entertainment, and education (among other purposes). Activities integral to the process include those related to event research, design, planning, coordination, and evaluation.

2. **Provide a brief history of special events.**
   Celebration of special events has been part of human history. The special events management profession originated within the discipline of public relations when specialists became necessary to manage activities that creative organizations used to obtain publicity and to build corporate images. The term *special events* was coined by Robert Jani (a Walt Disney imagineer) in 1955 when he used it to described the Main Street Electric Parade in Disneyland.

3. **Describe the type of markets in which special events are conducted.**
   Special events markets are those sponsored by associations; corporations; casinos and hotels; cause-related and retail organizations; sporting events; fairs, festivals, and parades; and social and tourism-related activities.

4. **Explain recent trends in the special events industry.**
   Recent trends include sponsorship (the merging of corporate and public events) and an increased interest in professionalism within the special events industry.

5. **Review a flow chart of the activities required to plan a special event.**
   The purpose of the event and its budget are initially established. Then the guest list and transportation requirements can be considered. At the same time, the event's theme may determine its location (which will also affect transportation). When the event site is known, general and specific event planning activities can begin. A postevent evaluation should be undertaken at its conclusion.

6. **Review some major responsibilities that are part of positions within the special events industry.**
   Numerous positions within the special events industry involve their coordination, management, and production. Design, decor, graphic arts, and technical service and products specialists may also be needed. Related positions include hardware rental, construction personnel, entertainment, foodservices, location management, travel and transportation, and event public relations and marketing specialists.

7. **Discuss significant challenges confronting the special events industry.**
   Challenges confronting the special events industry include concerns about risk management, raising the level of professionalism within the industry, and marketing concerns relating to the need for event companies to reinvent in a new age or in a weak economy.

MASTERING YOUR KNOWLEDGE

Discuss the following questions.

1. How does the work of a special events planner (coordinator) or manager differ from that of a meeting planner? How is it similar?
2. How might nonprofit corporations and government organizations seek corporate sponsorships for, respectively, member or public events?
3. What types of features would attract you to a special event in another community? If you were responsible for marketing the event in that community, what tactics might you utilize?
4. Pretend that you are a special events planner who has been retained by a regional shopping center to plan an event celebrating a major addition. How could you utilize the steps noted in Figure 2 to plan the event? Develop an example.

FEEDBACK FROM THE REAL WORLD

Our real-world advice comes from Marc Bruno, Regional Vice-President, ARAMARK Business Services, Philadelphia, Pennsylvania

How far in advance of a large, world-class event such as the International Olympics does planning for its foodservices begin?

The International Olympic Committee (IOC) is responsible for overseeing the Olympic process and selecting the host cities for each Summer and Winter Olympics, which are held every four years. Approximately 10 to 12 years prior to each Olympic Games, cities from around the world begin to compete for the votes of the various IOC delegate members to become the host city. Only one city per country can be selected (for example, the United States Olympic Committee selected New York City as the city to compete for the U.S. location for the 2012 Summer Olympics). Seven years prior to the Games, the voting to determine the host city occurs and election results are announced. The successful hosts of the Summer and Winter Games now known are Summer, 2008, Beijing; and Winter 2010, Vancouver.

Once the city is announced, a local Organizing Committee is formed and begins planning for hosting the Olympics. It focuses on five major areas:

Athletic competition   Transportation
Security   Foodservices
Housing

Typically, the local organizing committee (for example, the Athens Olympic Committee was called ATHOC) will outsource the foodservices to one or more companies. The three primary areas are these:

- The Olympic Village, where the athletes, coaches, officials, and staff reside for approximately 30 days
- The venues (competition sites)
- Corporate hospitality

ARAMARK has been involved in previous Olympic Games in some or all of these three areas and is usually the largest provider of foodservices. For example, ARAMARK has served as the foodservices manager for 13 games in which it managed the foodservice needs for the Olympic Village.

Planning for each Olympic Games takes approximately 2 years, usually with a core group of 5 to 10 people. As the Games approach, the group expands to hundreds of managers and thousands of employees.

(continued)

Here are the major Olympic activities and international sporting events that ARAMARK has managed:

Summer Olympic Games

1968	Mexico City
1976	Montreal
1984	Los Angeles
1988	Seoul
1992	Barcelona
1996	Atlanta
2000	Sydney
2004	Athens

Winter Olympic Games

1980	Lake Placid
1984	Sarajevo
1988	Calgary
1994	Lillehammer
1998	Nagano

Major International Sporting Events

1970	Caribbean Games—Panama City, Panama
1971	Pan American Games—Cali, Colombia
1974	Caribbean Games–Santa Domingo, Dominican Republic
1979	Pan American Games–San Juan, Puerto Rico
1981	Bolivarian Games–Barquisimeto, Venezuela
1983	Pan American Games–Caracas, Venezuela
1984	Olympic Torch Run–9,000 Miles USA
1987	Pan American Games–Indianapolis, Indiana
1990	Goodwill Games–Seattle, Washington
1994	12th Asian Games–Hiroshima, Japan
1998	Commonwealth Games–Kuala Lumpur, Malaysia
1998	13th Asian Games–Bangkok, Thailand
1999	Pan American Games–Winnipeg, Canada
2002	FIFA World Cup–Korea and Japan

When we are involved with Olympics in countries outside North America, we partner with a local company that brings extensive knowledge of the local customs, service levels, purchasing and distribution systems, and human resource contacts.

What were some logistics about the volume of foodservices offered?

As a case study, let's consider the 2004 Summer Olympic Games in Athens, Greece. The 2004 Olympic Village in Athens was the largest Olympic Village in history. It hosted 23,800 athletes, coaches, officials, and Games personnel. The Parolympic Village hosted 12,250 additional persons. The ARAMARK/Daskalantonakis Group serviced the dining and catering needs for both villages 24 hours a day for approximately 60 days during the summer of 2004. Over 2 million meals were served to Olympic athletes, coaches, and officials during this time. In addition, we managed the construction of temporary dining and kitchen facilities to service these dining outlets. The athletes' main village was the world's largest temporary dining facility ever, housing over 6,000 seats and capable of serving over 80,000 meals a day. In addition, we operated a staff dining and retail casual dining facility capable of feeding an additional 20,000 meals per day. We utilized approximately 2,500 employees and purchased well over $10 million in food for the month-long event.

What were the most critical aspects in planning the event?

The most critical aspects in planning were as follows:

- *Human resources.* Recruiting, hiring, accrediting, training, and servicing temporary employees and chefs for the approximate 30-day period.
- *Culinary.* Planning a menu for over 15,000 athletes from around the world, each with their own preferences and food needs during training and competition. The menu is huge, and we brought in chefs from around the world to assist in the production of such mammoth quantities and varieties of food items.

- *Technology.* Assuring that all the proper systems were working and in place and that there was a backup plan in case it failed for some reason is critical. Technology can make the planning process much easier if it works well.
- *Finance.* Making sure that budgets and expenditures were correct and that tracking of all costs was complete.
- *Construction.* Designing and operating in temporary facilities that need to be precisely planned and constructed without delays.
- *Operations.* There were many moving parts when operations got underway, and systems, processes, and people needed to be in harmony or major chaos could have occured.
- *Food safety.* Serving so many meals and utilizing products from around the globe was a challenge. We ensured that the food was handled and prepared safely from the farm to the plate and along every step of the way.
- *Communication.* Proper communications among all departments and shifts and to the customers was critical. This is especially true when one considers that we dealt with athletes from 197 different nations, with their different languages.

How important was teamwork in the planning process and what function did each team member assume?

Teamwork was of the utmost importance. It was critical that all departments and functions be in harmony with each other before and during planning and execution. Everyone's individual responsibilities were very important, but they became much greater when combined with the interdependence of the other necessary functions during the actual operations. The core team focused on many issues initially, and then we separated the issues and let each team focus solely on its area. The project was so incredibly huge (it was like having a Super Bowl going on 24 hours a day for 30 days straight!) that it helped to have individuals oversee the following departments:

Operations	Purchasing
Culinary	Information technology
Human resources	Design and construction
Recruiting	Warehousing and logistics
Training	Finance
Accommodations	Food safety and sanitation
Transportation	

LEARN FROM THE INTERNET

1. Check out the websites for the following special event planners:
   - Action Events: (www.actionevents.com)
   - Bravo Productions: (www.bravoevents-online.com)
   - Summit Events: (www.seonthenet.com)
   - Corinthian Events: (www.corinthianevents.com)

What are some features that make them very competitive with others? What features make them less attractive? What types of information about their past experiences are provided? How might this information be of interest to you if you were responsible for a similar event? What are examples of information provided that might help you as an event sponsor to evaluate whether these organizations would be helpful to you?

KEY HOSPITALITY TERMS

The following terms were explained in this chapter. Review the definitions of any words with which you are unfamiliar. Begin to utilize them as you expand your vocabulary as a hospitality professional.

hallmark events

special events management

public relations

special event

cause-related events

life-cycle events

not-for-profit organization

sponsorship

Index